DISCOVER SOUTH AMERICA

Reader's Digest

PUBLISHED BY THE READER'S DIGEST ASSOCIATION LIMITED

LONDON   NEW YORK   SYDNEY   MONTREAL

DISCOVER SOUTH AMERICA

Translated and edited by Toucan Books Limited, London
for Reader's Digest, London

Translated and adapted from the French
by Richard Walker, Robin Hosie, Alex Martin and John Man

For Reader's Digest
Series Editor: Christine Noble
Editorial Assistant: Caroline Boucher
Production Controller: Byron Johnson

Reader's Digest General Books
Editorial Director: Cortina Butler
Art Director: Nick Clark

First English language edition Copyright © 2001
The Reader's Digest Association Limited
11 Westferry Circus, Canary Wharf, London E14 4HE
www.readersdigest.co.uk

We are committed to both the quality of our products and
the service we provide to our customers. We value your
comments, so please feel free to contact us on 08705 113366,
or via our website at www.readersdigest.co.uk
If you have any comments about the content of our books,
you can contact us at gbeditorial@readersdigest.co.uk

ISBN 0 276 42512 X

Discover the World: SOUTH AMERICA
was created and produced by ML Éditions, Paris
for Selection Reader's Digest S.A., Paris, and first published
in 2000 as *Regards sur le Monde: L'AMÉRIQUE DU SUD*

©2000 Selection Reader's Digest, S.A.
212 boulevard Saint-Germain, 75007, Paris

CONTENTS

INTRODUCING
SOUTH
AMERICA

Ever since the Spaniards assaulted it in the
16th century, South America was linked
with the myth of Eldorado. The legendary city of
gold was never found, but the reality of South
America today surpasses the myth. The region runs
the gamut from the exotic to the familiar.
Amazonian Indians and Andean farmers whose
ways reach back millennia contrast with
westernised, urban cultures mere centuries old.
In this land of extremes – of teeming rain forests
and deserts of lunar sterility, of beauty and brutality
– nothing seems to come in moderation.

Images of a continent

Seen from space, this land of extremes is a triangle, the bulk of which – 84 per cent – lies in the tropics, straddling the equator. Stretching from Venezuela in the north, it runs for 4500 miles (7200 km) down to Tierra del Fuego, broadening to a width of 3100 miles (5000 km) between Recife in Brazil and Guayaquil on the Pacific coast. On this solid base, the apex thrusts south along the great spinal column of the Andes into the Antarctic Ocean.

Running along the Pacific façade from 11 degrees north to 55 south, the Andes is the longest mountain range on Earth. The Spaniards called it the cordillera – the 'little rope' – to describe its unique double-ridge structure, and the term has stuck. It forms the continent's meridian, creating a spectrum of climates, ecologies and cultures. It was this cordillera that nourished South America's first civilisations. Here, on the so-called Altiplano – the 'high plain' basin between the two parallel Andean ranges – the Inca Empire arose, and here the Spaniards founded three capitals – Bogotá, Quito and La Paz. In all three, new visitors are often left panting for breath, for they lie above the 8200 ft (2500 m) level, higher than any other capital city except Lhasa, in Tibet.

To the east of this bastion, plains stretch out, running to the primeval highlands of Brazil, Guyana and Patagonia. These flat lands have extremes of their own: vast areas, few people, huge sluggish rivers meandering to the Atlantic seaboard, dominated by the world's second longest river, the Amazon. And, to cap the catalogue of extremes, these sparsely populated lowlands lead to some of the most densely packed areas on earth, the mega-cities of the Brazilian coast: Recife, Salvador, Rio de Janeiro and São Paulo.

River deep, mountain high *The Andes, stretching down the western coast, and the vast Amazon basin are clearly visible in this satellite photograph of South America.*

The plains – whether grasslands like the Venezuelan llanos and Argentinian pampas, or the rain forests of the Amazon and Orinoco – were for millennia the domains of hunter-gatherers before the arrival of European colonists. While Andean peoples like the Quechua and Aymara retained their ancient ways, the lowlands were opened for exploitation. Spanish and Portuguese colonists shipped in slaves by the million to work their ports and plantations (slavery in Brazil was ended only in the late 19th century). Finally, for over a century, immigrant Europeans flooded into the empty grasslands of Argentina, Uruguay and the Brazilian south.

In the last century, immigrants came from all over the world. Japanese (in Brazil) and Chinese (on the Pacific coast) joined the European and African populations, all contributing to the racial melting pot responsible for the new, independent nations emerging from three centuries of Spanish and Portuguese rule. Despite their differences, all the new nations had one thing in common: their roots lay in an assault on indigenous peoples which at best dispossessed the victims, sometimes enslaved them and in extreme cases led to genocide.

In the early 19th century, South America's greatest revolutionary, Simon Bolivar, had hoped for unity. Today, his hopes remain mere dreams. Everywhere, the appealing façades of the great cities overlie appalling contrasts: rich and poor, urban and rural, educated and illiterate. Some differences were imposed by geography and race, others by the random course of history and economic development. The result is a continuing struggle for wealth, for influence, for survival. The continent's two largest nations, Argentina and Brazil, wield huge influence as a result of their size and economic potential. At the other end of the scale, the Andean nations of Peru, Ecuador, Columbia and Bolivia seem trapped in a vicious circle of poverty and violence. Inequality, it seems, has become as much a defining trait of South America as its astonishing diversity.

Continental divide *Heaving, fire-breathing and as dangerous as they look, the Andes are by far the longest mountain chain in the world, stretching 5500 miles (8900 km) from the Caribbean to Cape Horn, and second only to the Himalayas in height – the highest peak is Aconcagua, in Argentina, at 22 834 ft (6960 m).*

Not one rampart but several coiling cordilleras (ranges), the Andes are studded with live volcanoes and breached only by treacherously high and narrow passes. The name may derive from Antisuyo, one of the four quarters of the Inca Empire, or it may come from anta, a pre-Inca word meaning copper-coloured – though in fact

the mountains are of every hue from tropical green to glacial white. In southern Peru near the source of the River Amazon (above), the Andes form a system of two cordilleras whose 20 000 ft (6000 m) peaks frame a wide tract called the Altiplano (high plain), where conditions are strikingly similar to those in Tibet.

Fatal attraction As well as being the loftiest peak in the Andes, Aconcagua is also the highest mountain in the entire Southern Hemisphere. The summit was first conquered by a Swiss mountaineer, Matthias Zurbriggen, in 1897 – beating by months a successful attempt by the British explorer William Martin (later Lord) Conway. However, it was 1954, a year after the conquest of Everest, before the treacherous south face (below) was successfully climbed – by a French expedition. At the foot of these ramparts is the Cementerio de los Andinistas, a graveyard for climbers who die on the mountain.

Glacial legacy Man-made salt pans near Cuzco, Peru, eerily mimic the cultivated terraces of the mountain slopes. Natural salt deposits are also found throughout the high Andes; these are the evaporated residue of lakes formed by the melt of the last Ice Age. The Salar de Uyuni in Bolivia covers more than 4000 sq miles (10 500 km²), making it the largest salt pan in the world. At 11 995 ft (3656 m), it is also the highest.

Landscape of departing souls   There is a saying in Venezuela that a dying person has 'reached the páramo'. The páramo (left) is one of innumerable Andean eco-niches – and a dank and eerie one at 12 000 ft (3600 m) – high above the coffee plantations of the foothills. Here grows the surreal frailejón (tall friar) or Espeletia, a giant herb which can grow to 20 ft (6 m) and live for 200 years. The secret is its trunk of layered dead leaves, which form a weather seal. When the frailejón flowers, in October, these high moors resound to the throb of hummingbirds, attracted to its flowers.

Hardy stock   Relatives of the camel, llamas and alpacas (below) possess similar tolerance of extreme conditions – and the same habit of spitting when irritated! Domesticated since ancient times, they may have originated by crossbreeding from their wild cousins, the guanaco and vicuña.

World of water The first Spaniards to venture into this mysterious place emerged with tales of women warriors like the Amazons of Greek mythology – 'tall and white, with long braided hair...'. And so, in their honour, it was named Amazon. At over 4000 miles (6400 km) long and fed by more than 1000 tributaries, the Amazon is the mightiest river on earth. It accounts for a fifth of the world's readily available fresh water and drains an area almost the size of Australia or the continental United States. It is so deep that ocean liners can reach Iquitos, 2300 miles (3700 km) inland and, most famously, it bisects the world's largest tropical forest. Seen from the air, a tufted green carpet unrolls, broken only by occasional glints of reflected sunlight, which upon closer approach becomes an emerald forest shot through with snaking bodies of water. If you could drop down through the dense foliage, you would enter the enveloping damp of a twilight world of strangling lianas and giant bamboos, ferns and creepers, mosses and lichens, mysterious squawks, chirps and buzzing, pungent scents of lily and orchid, and musty decay: Amazonia!

Backwater highway Until the 20th century, rivers were South America's highways – the only means of accessing the interior. This is still true of the continent's densely forested north-east corner, where the Marowijne (Maroni) forms the border between Dutch-speaking Surinam and French Guiana. In its time, the river has provided a path for expeditions in quest of Eldorado, the mythical kingdom of gold, and for prisoners escaping the notorious French penal colony at its mouth. Today, it still serves riverbank communities of Noir Marrons, descendants of escaped slaves, and gold-mining operations far upstream. Some of the world's finest surviving tropical rain forests are in this region – once squabbled over by Spanish, English, French and Dutch, yet penetrated by none. The virgin forests are sanctuary to many creatures endangered elsewhere, such as rare parakeets, giant anteaters and the jaguar. The dark rivers teem with turtles, caimans, piranhas, tucunares and peacock bass.

Empty frontier The vast campos cerrados (scrub grasslands) of the Mato Grosso plateau, to the south of Amazonia, were virtually inaccessible until the latter part of the 20th century, when the Brazilian government opened up the interior. A new inland capital, Brasília, was constructed, followed by a massive road-building programme. But the plans were not properly thought out and emphasis reverted to large-scale fazenda agribusiness at the expense of small-scale farming. Brazil is not alone in this problem. South America has been called the 'hollow continent' because of the extent to which populations are concentrated in the coastal cities, ringed with shantytowns.

Southern prairie When people think of Argentina they imagine the pampa, ridden by romantic gauchos. This vast prairie is a powerful source of argentinidad, nostalgic nationalism, while it remains the foundation of the economic wealth of the nation. Pampa means 'flat surface' in the Quechua tongue. From the capital Buenos Aires, it stretches from the Andes to Paraguay and Patagonia, 600 miles (1000 km) in every direction. Except for the deep, loamy soil, little of its original nature survived after the 19th-century 'pacification' of the plains Indians and the importation of British livestock breeds, alfalfa and other non-indigenous grasses and plants. Wheat long ago replaced cattle as the main product, but much national pride is still invested in the quality of pampa beef.

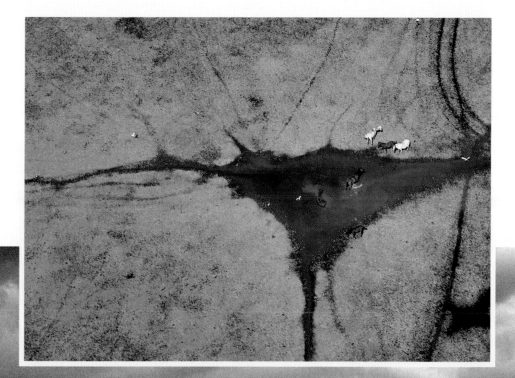

Tropical plains The Llanos, the torrid central plains of Venezuela, reach from the Orinoco Delta to the Andes. Parched in the dry season and flooded in the wet, this is the land of the legendary llanero, the hard-bitten, hard-riding tropical cowboy of the hatos (ranches). 'The Llanos are terrifying, but this fear does not chill the heart – it is hot like the great wind of its sunburnt immensity, the fever from its swamps,' wrote Venezuela's novelist-president Rómulo Gallegos in his epic Doña Bárbara.

Resident patrol The Emperor penguin is alone (apart from a few humans) in wintering in Antarctica. More than 40 sea-bird species breed here in summer, attracted by the nutrient-rich waters and freedom from predators. The Emperor (Aptenodytes forsteri) is the largest penguin, standing almost 4 ft (1.2 m).

Fire on ice The volcanic plume rising from Mount Erebus, 11 700 ft (3800 m), adds a surreal touch to the desolate surroundings of the Ross Ice Shelf. It is one of two known active volcanoes in Antarctica.

Frozen assets Argentina lays claim to a large wedge of the frozen continent, and so does Chile. In 1961 the signing of an international treaty suspended all territorial claims in the interest of scientific cooperation.

A brief history

The arrival of Stone Age hunter-gatherers in South America marked the end of one epic journey and the beginning of a new one, just as astonishing. Their remote ancestors, the true discoverers of the New World, had crossed the land bridge that linked Siberia to Alaska during the last Ice Age. Some authorities believe that this migration happened some 30 000 years ago, but linguists point to the development of about 2000 South American languages (450 of them still spoken today) and argue that it would take 40 000 years for such diversity to come about. What is clear is that succeeding generations spread across North America, and eventually some groups trickled across the Isthmus of Panama. There, they found another virgin continent to explore. By about 15 000 BC, the hunter-gatherers had reached the Peruvian Andes,

They left their traces

The walls of a cave in Patagonia were decorated 11 000 years ago with the outlines of hands. At Lauricocha and Toquepala in the central Andes, other prehistoric artists painted animal images on cave walls, while on the Patagonian coast near the Strait of Magellan the vigorous cave art is reminiscent of Lascaux, the famous site in France.

Prehistoric hands   An example of graffiti that has become art: hands stencilled by prehistoric humans on a cave wall near Perito Moreno, Patagonia.

The doomed land

Tierra del Fuego (Land of Fire) was named after the fires lit along its shores by the Ona hunters and fishers. They are now extinct – wiped out by disease and by 19th-century bounty hunters, paid to clear the land for sheep.

Huddling for warmth   An 18th-century engraving of Fuegans sheltering in a hut.

where archaeologists have dated the butchered and fossilised remains of their prey. Within 6000 years, beckoned by the prospect of new horizons and prey, bands of prehistoric hunters had reached Tierra del Fuego, at the continent's southern tip.

From hunters to farmers

The Ice Age ended 10 000 years ago and, under the combined impact of hunting and climatic change, mastodons and other giant mammals passed into extinction. With their prey dying out, the hunters turned to cultivating – maize, manioc and potatoes – and to raising flocks. The north-western corner of the continent set the pace for social progress. The Valdivian culture that developed on the coast of Ecuador around 3500 BC produced sophisticated weaving and pottery. Finds from the area include 'Venuses' – figurines that may have played a role in fertility cults. Later, on the same stretch of coast, the goldsmiths of La Tolita developed rare skills and

worked in platinum 1000 years ahead of Europe. But it was in the mountains of north-eastern Peru that development was at its most dynamic.

The gods of Chavín

Chavín de Huántar was more than a city: it was a civilisation. Its massive ruins contain images of a fanged god, among pyramid temples that hold a labyrinth of galleries and passageways. Clearly, its planners had outstanding organisational skills. For 1000 years, the half-human, half-animal gods of Chavín held sway. Then, in about 200 BC, this first civilisation of the Andes collapsed. The ruins of fortresses and other evidence of warfare tell of a brutal end.

The next dominant group were the energetic and bloodthirsty Moche, named after the site of their great flat-topped pyramid of sun-dried brick near Trujillo on Peru's northern coast. As well as pyramids they built temples, aqueducts and irrigation canals up to 75 miles (120 km) long. The empire of the Moche lasted from around 100 BC to AD 700, and their pottery preserves a record of their life as cultivators, artisans, builders, traders and warriors.

Around the same time the puzzling Nazca people also left their mark farther south. There has been speculation that the large-scale geometrical and animal-based patterns they etched into the ground across miles of stony desert may have formed an astronomical calendar. But the marks fall into shape only when seen from the sky – a viewpoint the

Golden girl   Gold was the first metal worked in South America. This mask from Ecuador's La Tolita culture dates from c.2000 BC.

Nazcans did not have. The Nazcans also made pottery unlike anything else found in Peru – multicoloured, highly polished and often moulded into human shapes.

Nazca bird   Imaginative, brightly painted pot from Nazca. Such flights of fancy add to the mystery that surrounds the culture.

The people of the arid Paracas peninsula, some 125 miles (200 km) from Nazca, produced resin-painted pottery. What little else is known about them arises from the fact that the dry air mummified their dead and preserved the intricately woven fabrics in which the bodies were wrapped.

Gateway of the Sun

More lasting and more influential was a religious cult that arose on a plateau near Lake Titicaca, between Bolivia and Peru.

Pre-Columbian sites and cultures

Moche ear-plugs   Moche nobles in ancient Peru spared no expense in personal decoration.

The new religion, centred on the city of Tiahuanaco, near the southern end of the lake, was devoted to the worship of the creator god Viracocha. The ruins of Tiahuanaco are still compelling today, after more than 1000 years. Imposing buildings such as the Gateway of the Sun and the Temple of Kalasasaya were built of massive blocks of stone, assembled without mortar. Tiahuanaco flourished from AD 500-1000, spreading its culture through eastern Bolivia, northern Chile and Peru. It even influenced Huari, a new kind of aggressive city-state whose power was to reach from the highlands down to the coast.

Around the year 1000, the Huari Empire broke up, and within 200 years a new empire emerged – that of the Chimú,

Built to last   Remains of a palace reception room in Chanchan, Peru, one of many cities conquered by the Incas. Originally covered in plaster, and brightly painted, the ruins are now a silent testimony to the skill of the Chimú.

The Lords of Sipan

The discovery near the village of Sipan, in northern Peru, of the 1700-year-old tomb of a Moche lord marked a major advance in efforts to understand South America's ancient past. Since the initial find, in 1987, further burial chambers have been opened, revealing treasures that include gold face masks with eyes of silver, lapis lazuli or emeralds.

Aristocrat at rest A Moche lord lies buried in all his finery, with soldiers and servants to attend him in the afterlife.

descendants of the Moche. Expanding on the engineering skills of their ancestors, the Chimú laid out canals that made deserts fertile. Their dominion stretched north for 600 miles (960 km) from where Lima now stands, and their capital, Chanchan, was the largest adobe (sun-dried brick) city on earth, covering some 8 sq miles (20 km²).

Mighty as they were, the Chimú were no match for a ferocious new military machine from the high Andes – the Incas. Chanchan fell to the all-conquering Incas in about 1470, and, true to their policy of learning from their foes, the victors immediately marched into captivity the best artisans among the city's 50 000 inhabitants.

Empire of the Sun

From an unpromising start in the bleak mountains of Peru, the Incas created the most extensive and best-organised empire of ancient America. At its peak, under Huayna Capac (1493-1525), it stretched for 2500 miles (4000 km) from Quito in Ecuador to

*Doomed Inca
The Emperor Atahualpa.*

Sacrifices to the sun

At times of national peril, such as a plague or famine, or the start of a new reign, the Incas resorted to human sacrifice. Because the victim had to be without blemish, children were preferred – usually boys and girls of ten, chosen for their comeliness. They were well treated and fed beforehand, so as not to enter the presence of the creator god hungry or weeping. In normal times, a llama or a guinea pig was a sufficient offering.

Imperial ramparts *The fortress of Sacsahuamán overlooks Cuzco. Its unmortared stone blocks, weighing up to 125 tons, fit together perfectly.*

the centre of what is now Chile. It had more than 80 subject peoples, and a population estimated at 6-12 million. The founder of the Incas' greatness, Emperor Pachacuti (c.1440-71), was a brilliant leader, and much of their success was due to his policy of absorbing conquered tribes into Inca society. They had to use the Inca language, *quechua*, and to worship the main Inca god, the Sun. The emperor, the Sapa Inca, was himself a living god – the son of the Sun, and so far above his subjects that only his sister was allowed to be his principal wife. All land belonged to the state but was divided in practice into one-third for the Inca and high officials, one-third for the priests and one-third for peasants. In a land where money was unknown, taxes were due in the form of labour. In return, the peasants were looked after when times were hard. Officials dispensed justice and exacted tribute, keeping records on coloured and knotted cords called *quipus*, for the Incas had no writing.

Nor did they have the wheel. But Cuzco, their capital, kept in touch with the provinces through a road system built in difficult mountain terrain. Relay-running messengers could cover up to 150 miles (240 km) in a day. The Incas had no sentimentality about children. The sons of high officials were hardened for battle by being sent on 9 day survival courses without food, sandals or weapons. The most beautiful girls were selected at the age of ten to be trained for the emperor's court or to become Virgins of the Sun in the temples, dedicated to life-long chastity.

Onslaught of the Conquistadores

In September 1532, the Spaniard Francisco Pizarro struck out with 62 horsemen and 104 foot soldiers from his base on the coast of Peru to topple an empire. They were far from being the first Europeans since Christopher Columbus's voyages of discovery to covet the legendary wealth of the New World. So frenzied was the scramble to lay hands on the gold and silver that in 1494, under the Treaty of Tordesillas, the Pope had given his approval to a line on

Moment of conquest
Francisco Pizarro (inset) and his men seize the Inca Atahualpa in a scene fancifully imagined by an artist in faraway Spain.

Moment of generosity
At the beginning of the conquest the Spaniards and local people exchanged gifts of animals, plants and produce such as potatoes, maize, tomatoes and chocolate.

Bound for the New World A golden setting sun beckons ships westwards from Lisbon.

the map that divided the new lands between Spain and Portugal. Effectively, Brazil went to Portugal and the rest to Spain. Dozens of bold adventurers applied for royal warrants to win new realms. Amerigo Vespucci, after whom the Americas are named, explored the coast of Venezuela. Pedro Alvares Cabral took possession of Brazil. Ferdinand Magellan sailed from the Atlantic to the Pacific, through the strait that now bears his name. In 1519-21, Hernán Cortés, with 600 men, plundered the Aztec Empire in Mexico.

Pizarro, a veteran conquistador, was inspired by what Cortés had achieved in Mexico. As he and his men pushed into

Voyage down the Amazon

In February 1541, 200 Spaniards and 4000 Indians under the command of Pizarro's brother, Gonzalo, set out in search of the fabled Eldorado, the 'Land of Gold'. They floundered in the rain forests, and Gonzalo sent his lieutenant, Francisco de Orellana, to look for forage. When he failed to return Gonzalo turned back, but Orellana had reached a great river. Floating with the current, his party reached the mouth of the Amazon nine months later. They were attacked on the journey by long-haired Indians, whom Orellana mistook for Amazons, the female warriors of Greek mythology.

Calendar of Conquest

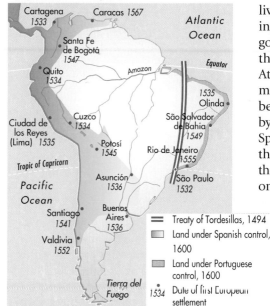

Cartagena 1533	Caracas 1567
	Atlantic Ocean
Santa Fe de Bogotá 1547	
Quito 1534	Equator
	Amazon
	1535 Olinda
Cuzco 1534	São Salvador de Bahia 1549
Ciudad de los Reyes (Lima) 1535	
Potosí 1545	Rio de Janeiro 1555
Tropic of Capricorn	
Asunción 1536	São Paulo 1532
Pacific Ocean	
Santiago 1541	Buenos Aires 1536
Valdivia 1552	
Tierra del Fuego	

— Treaty of Tordesillas, 1494
☐ Land under Spanish control, 1600
☐ Land under Portuguese control, 1600
1534 Date of first European settlement

the heart of the Inca Empire they were met at Cajamarca on November 15, 1532, by Atahualpa and an army of 30 000 men. The emperor, carried on a golden litter and protected by 80 nobles, was handed a Bible, but flung it contemptuously to the ground. At this, Pizarro gave the signal to attack. The Incas had never seen horses; never encountered cannons or harquebuses. Their slings, spears and clubs were no match for the Spanish firepower and they were slaughtered. Their living god was captured, and despite paying a mighty ransom – a room filled with gold and silver – he was later executed by the garotte. A year to the day after Atahuallpa's capture, the Spaniards were masters of Cuzco. The Inca Empire had been weakened by a dynastic civil war and by an outbreak of smallpox. Moreover, the Spaniards seemed to fulfil an Inca legend that the light-skinned Viracocha, a god they had inherited from the Moche, would one day return to claim his kingdom.

End of an empire

To consolidate Spanish power, expeditions went out in every direction. To the north, New Granada (now Colombia) was acquired after the subjugation of the Chibcha tribes.

Funeral rites Sketch by an Indian, depicting life and death in Peru.

The conquistadores met the fiercest resistance from the tribes to the south, where Pedro de Valdivia was killed by Indians during his conquest of Chile. In Peru, the Incas carried on a hopeless struggle. Manco Capac laid siege to Cuzco and fought a guerrilla war from his jungle strongpoint, but was killed by treachery. Tupac Amaru, last of the rebel Incas, was captured and executed in 1572. The Inca Empire had been destroyed even faster than it had arisen.

The years of ordeal

In the year 1545, at Potosí, in what is now Bolivia, an Indian shepherd, chasing a stray llama up a mountainside, grabbed a shrub and discovered silver at its roots. The mountain was one enormous pile of silver-bearing ore. It was soon to become a living hell for some 65 000 Indian slaves, mining the precious ore for their Spanish

Founder of cities Pedro de Valdivia, conqueror of Chile and founder of several cities including Santiago and the port of Valdivia.

The defender Bartolomé de Las Casas (1474-1566), the priest who became a champion of the Indians.

masters. Tens of thousands of them died in their first year, and the rest had to chew coca leaves to stave off the cold and hunger. Having won an empire, the Spaniards fully intended to profit from it. Indians were there to be robbed of their treasures, converted to Christianity and set to work.

A system called *encomienda*, or trusteeship, was meant to provide some protection for the Indians and even pay them for their labour, but it soon degenerated into tyranny. On the island of Santo Domingo, Indians who refused to work were killed. Some Spaniards spoke out against such cruelty. Bartolomé de Las Casas, a priest and author of *The Destruction of the Indians*, secured an audience with the King of Spain, who enacted laws forbidding the enslavement of Indians. The colonists ignored them, and when the king's viceroy in Peru tried to enforce the laws he was shot dead by Pizarro's brother, Gonzalo. Even priests joined in the outcry against

the new laws, for not all were as compassionate as Las Casas. But the Catholic Church also established schools for the Indians, promoted the study of their languages and founded universities that gave places to exceptional Indian students.

In 1556, when Philip II came to the throne of Spain, he tried to ease the lot of the Indians. The word 'conquistador' was banned from official documents and the *encomienda* system of forced labour, already weakened by the attacks of Las Casas, began to decline in Peru. It remained in full vigour, though, in other Spanish colonies, and the colonists still made enormous fortunes. Indians were tortured to force them to reveal any hidden treasure. If the Indians under Portuguese rule were less

vigorously exploited, this was largely because Portugal was too small to produce large numbers of colonists: Brazil was rich in land rather than gold, and Indians were thought not to have the stamina for work in the sugar-cane fields.

The Negro slave trade

Blacks from Africa were better able to perform the hard labour of cane-cutting, and they had built up a measure of immunity to diseases such as measles, smallpox and tuberculosis, to which the Indian populations were particularly vulnerable. The Portuguese imported Negro slaves from West Africa to work in the cane fields, and in the mills where the cut cane was refined.

Slave labour Under the sometimes drowsy eyes of guards armed with whips, Negro slaves pan for precious stones.

The journey, in the stench-filled holds of slave ships, was horrific enough – it was not unusual for one-third of the human cargo to die on the way – and what awaited at the other end was nearly as bad. Slaves who mutinied or ran away did so at the

Vice-royalties and Captaincies-general at the end of the 18th century

Jesuit missions

Most Spaniards were feared and hated by the Indians, but one group was admired and in some regions even loved – the Jesuits. Their missions among the Guaraní Indians of Paraguay were models of efficiency and justice, where Indians lived in Christian communities, with schools, colleges and well-tended fields. They were constantly menaced, however, by merciless *bandeirantes* from São Paulo in Brazil, who raided fortified mission stations and carried captives off to slavery. At one stage, the Jesuits armed their Indians to fight off attacks. Despite all threats, the Guaraní population grew: by the middle of the 17th century it numbered 100 000. But when the Jesuits were expelled by Spain, in 1767, the missions collapsed, for the Jesuit Fathers had failed to teach the Indians to survive.

The Jesuits in Paraguay

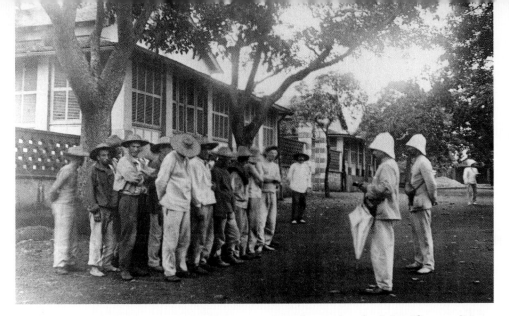

Prison island *Roll-call in a penal colony off the coast of French Guiana. Political prisoners, as well as hardened criminals, were condemned to hard labour in such places. The most notorious, on Devil's Island, was founded in 1852.*

risk of death. By 1650 there were already 380 000 blacks in South America – almost equalling the whites. By 1829, Brazil alone had nearly 2 million. Their labour supported a feudal lifestyle for the slave-owner, in his *Casa Grande*, or 'Big House'. Interbreeding between whites, blacks and Indians produced a society in which, until modern times, social status was largely determined by skin colour.

The 'second discovery'

During the 18th century, intellectuals in Europe 'discovered' South America all over again. Its forests were seen as havens for the 'Noble Savage', a creature with a natural moral code. Scientific expeditions were sent out, like those of the German explorer Alexander von Humboldt and the Frenchmen La Condamine and Aimé-Jacques-Alexandre Bonpland. But it was in the following century that the continent made its greatest contribution to science. In the 1830s the naturalist Charles Darwin studied its flora and fauna, making observations that became the basis for his theory of evolution.

Tensions in the New World

As the 18th century drew to an end, the Spanish and Portuguese possessions in South America were seething with unrest. At the top of the ladder, holding all the real power in the government, Church and army, were men who had been sent out from the Iberian Peninsula. Next were the creoles, of Iberian descent but born in the New World. They took pride in the conquistador blood that ran in their veins, and resented being edged into second place by newcomers from the other side of the Atlantic. Rich creoles studied in Europe, where they were exposed to liberal ideas and to the notion of the Rights of Man, and were inspired by the American Revolution. Fear of the 'people of colour' united both communities.

Measuring the earth: the triumphs of La Condamine

In 1735 the Academy of Sciences in Paris sent an expedition to South America to determine whether the circumference of the earth is greater at the Poles or at the equator. Appointed to lead it was the mathematician and naturalist Charles-Marie de la Condamine (1701-74). His task was to measure, on the equator, an arc of the meridian (an imaginary circle on the surface of the earth, passing through both Poles). He also took the opportunity of making the first scientific exploration of Amazonia, during which he discovered, for Europe and the world, the rubber tree – called by the Indians *cau-chu*, the 'tree that weeps'.

Man of Amazonia *Bust of La Condamine, scientist and explorer.*

Scrambling for the spoils

Other nations in Europe, especially Protestant nations, did not accept the Pope's right to divide the New World between Spain and Portugal. The French, though Catholic, attempted to set up a colony in Brazil in 1555, and the Dutch tried in 1624 and again 30 years later. These attempts failed, but the Dutch and the French finally gained footholds in what are now the Guianas. Sir Walter Raleigh explored the region in 1595, on a quest for the legendary Eldorado. Britain took possession of what is now the independent nation of Guyana in 1796, and the Dutch held Dutch Guiana until, in 1975, it became the new nation of Surinam.

Eldorado *Map made c.1600 by Sir Walter Raleigh (1552-1618).*

Voyages of scientific exploration in the 18th and 19th centuries

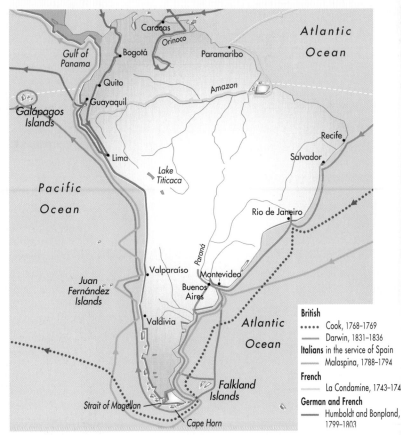

Caracas
Orinoco
Gulf of Panama
Bogotá
Paramaribo
Atlantic Ocean
Quito
Amazon
Guayaquil
Galápagos Islands
Lima
Recife
Salvador
Lake Titicaca
Pacific Ocean
Rio de Janeiro
Paraná
Valparaíso
Montevideo
Juan Fernández Islands
Buenos Aires
Valdivia
Atlantic Ocean
Falkland Islands
Strait of Magellan
Cape Horn

British
····· Cook, 1768–1769
—— Darwin, 1831–1836
Italians in the service of Spain
—— Malaspina, 1788–1794
French
—— La Condamine, 1743–174
German and French
—— Humboldt and Bonpland, 1799–1803

23

Victory in Peru *Bolívar's General Sucre (left) strikes a hero's pose after the Battle of Ayacucho (1824), which drove the royalists out of Peru.*

Triumph in Chile *Argentinian General San Martin (right), victorious at the battle of Chacabuco, Chile (1817), after an epic march with his army over the Andes.*

Far more numerous than the creoles, and far lower down the social scale, were the mestizos and the mulattos. The first group were the offspring of Whites and Indians, and the second were part White, part Black. Below both were the Indians, whose numbers had grown to around 8 million. When they erupted out of their misery in bloody rebellion, they were just as bloodily suppressed – as happened when a Spanish-educated Indian leader who took the name of the Inca emperor Tupac Amaru was defeated and brutally executed in 1781. At the bottom of the social ladder were some 5 million black slaves.

The road to independence

The eruption of ideas released by the French Revolution caused a swell that travelled across the Atlantic to South America, where the creoles found the notions of Liberty, Equality and Fraternity appealing, so long as they did not go too far and infect the 'men of colour'. Francisco de Miranda, who rose to the rank of general in the French Revolutionary army, returned to his native Venezuela and proclaimed a republic there in 1806, but won little support. When Napoleon invaded Spain in 1808, deposed King Ferdinand VII and placed his own brother, Joseph, on the throne, royal authority in the colonies was fatally weakened. In cities from Caracas to Buenos Aires, revolutionary *juntas* spoke out against the monarch who had been imposed upon them. A liberal constitution proclaimed in Spain in 1812 raised hopes in the colonies – hopes that evaporated when it became clear that it was not liberal enough to allow trade with foreign nations.

Miranda made a second attempt to create a republic in Venezuela, this time alongside Simón Bolívar. Their army was defeated, in 1812, by royalists, aided by mulattos and mestizos, who hated the creoles. Miranda was imprisoned in Spain, but Bolívar escaped. Meanwhile, the tide of war turned against the French in Spain, and Ferdinand, restored to the throne, sent 10 000 troops to South America, led by General Morillo.

The torch of freedom was extinguished in most of South America. But Bolívar hit back with a series of victories. From 1821 to 1826 he drove the Spaniards out of Venezuela, Colombia, Ecuador and Peru. What Bolívar did in the north, José de San Martin did in the south. He liberated Argentina in 1816 then took his army over the Andes to support a revolt led in Chile by Bernardo O'Higgins. The British sailor Lord Cochrane led the Chilean navy in an attack on the Spaniards in Peru. San Martin played his part in its liberation and for a time was Protector of Peru, but he and Bolívar quarrelled.

Brazil's history over this period was less bloody. In 1808 the Portuguese royal family fled to Rio de Janeiro under a British naval escort, to escape Napoleon's advance. The Portuguese Empire was governed from Rio until 1821, when the king returned to Lisbon, leaving behind his son, Pedro, as regent. In 1822, Pedro was proclaimed constitutional emperor of Brazil.

Bolívar, the Liberator whose dream was dashed

Simón Bolívar (1783-1830), born in Caracas, Venezuela, was an admirer of the French Revolution and of Napoleon. He led so many South American countries to freedom from Spain that he was named 'The Liberator' – even though he once said : 'I prefer the title of Citizen to the title of Liberator.' His vision was to unite all Spanish-speaking South Americans in one country, but he failed, and abandoned power in 1830. He died the same year.

Bolívar *Portrait by the Cubist Fernand Léger.*

Life at the bottom *Mulattos, black slaves and other 'men of colour' led wretched lives at the bottom of the social pyramid in colonial South America.*

The bitter harvest

South America emerged exhausted after nearly 15 years of war. Freedom brought a bitter harvest, for the victors quarrelled over the spoils. Bolívar's dreams of forging a single nation were soon shattered. By the time of his death in 1830 the makeshift republic of Greater Colombia had broken up, with Ecuador and Venezuela going their own ways. Nor was disunity the only problem. The road to progress for the new countries was full of hazards: war, civil war, tyranny, corruption, poverty and bloody revolt. In a costly saga of land-grabbing, nation fought nation. Bolivia was the heaviest loser in terms of territory: at independence, in 1825, it was almost twice its present size. Bloodiest of the wars was that of 1865-70, when Paraguay was left in ruins after taking on Brazil, Argentina and Uruguay. Chile won territory, securing the nitrates and copper of the Atacama region in the War of the Pacific (1879-83) against Bolivia and Peru.

The day of the caudillo

The typical national leader in unstable times was the *caudillo*, a ruthless dictator, usually with a military background. One of the earliest was, curiously perhaps, a doctor of theology – Gaspar Francia, El Supremo of Paraguay. To protect his country from the surrounding anarchy, he closed borders and banned foreign trade. Critics of his policies were hanged.

In Argentina, the barbaric Facundo Quiroga, 'Tiger of the Pampas', was murdered on the orders of the even more ferocious Juan Manuel de Rosas. Adored by his gaucho followers, Rosas kept his opponents in festering jails, from which the main exit was execution, usually after torture. In Bolivia, the drunkard Mariano Melgarejo, the 'Scourge of God', came to power by the simple but effective method of shooting the president in his palace. One of the last of the breed was Juan Vicente Gómez, of Venezuela – known as 'The Barbarian', though not to his face.

Brazil's escape

Brazil escaped the privations of *caudillo* rule, thanks to the wisdom of its emperor, Dom Pedro II. Only 14 when he came to the throne, he upheld the constitution and answered his critics with toleration rather than terror. The country still had serious problems, including the enormous gap between the illiterate peasants and those who owned the resources, including slaves, that produced wealth in the form of sugar, rubber, coffee and cotton. The Royal Navy tried to suppress the

Map labels:
- Carabobo 1821
- VENEZUELA 1830 (Bolívar)
- THE GUYANAS
- Atlantic Ocean
- Boyacá 1819
- COLOMBIA 1819 (Bolívar)
- ECUADOR 1830 (Sucre)
- Pinchicha 1822
- Equator
- Amazon
- PERU 1824 (Sucre)
- BRAZIL Empire 1822 (Pierre I)
- Ayacucho 1824
- BOLIVIA 1825 (Sucre)
- Pacific Ocean
- Antofagasta
- PARAGUAY 1811
- ARGENTINA 1816 (San Martín Belgrano)
- Atlantic Ocean
- Chacabuco 1817
- Maipú 1817
- Mendoza 1818
- URUGUAY 1828
- CHILE 1818 (O'Higgins San Martín)

Legend:
- ✕ Decisive battle
- (Bolívar) Liberator
- 1819 Date of independence
- ▭ Republic of Greater Colombia founded 1819, dissolved 1830
- Territories:
  - Spanish
  - Portuguese
  - English
  - French
  - Dutch

The *caudillos*: heirs of the Indian chieftains?

A *caudillo* was a charismatic leader who rose to power by force of personality as well as force of arms. He ruled paternalistically, punishing transgressors but looking after his own. Many historians see the *caudillos* as inheriting a tradition established long before the Spaniards arrived – the Indian tradition of authoritarian rule by chieftains.

War for a desert Chilean forces attempt a landing under bombardment at Pisuaga, Peru, during the War of the Pacific (1879-83). Chile defeated Peru and Bolivia and emerged with a rich prize – the northern Atacama Desert, beneath which lay copper ore and vast deposits of nitrates.

Strong man Juan Vicente Gómez, President of Venezuela 1908-35.

slave trade, largely for humanitarian reasons, but also because Brazilian sugar was serious competition for sugar growers in Britain's West Indian colonies. The abolition of slavery in Brazil, in 1888, caused such a storm of protest that the emperor abdicated, making way for a republic to be declared the following year.

'One-crop' countries

Like Brazil, many South American countries were over-dependent on a narrow range of products. Chile had nitrates and copper; Argentina and Uruguay relied heavily on grain and beef; Bolivia at one stage had little to offer other than tin; Venezuela, in the 20th century, had oil. Economically, they were in a weak position: a downturn in world markets could ruin their export trade overnight and drive them into debt. When world demand for a commodity was high, however, there were boom times – at least for the rich. Chile was in this position before the First World War, when nitrates were in high demand as fertilisers and for use in explosives. But the war created a demand for man-made substitutes and Chile's nitrate boom was over.

Marching to defeat   Bolivian troops march out from La Paz to fight the Paraguayans in the Chaco War (1932-5). Paraguay won, and took most of the Chaco region, but at a terrible cost – the loss of 35 000 of its men.

Coffee harvest   Preparing coffee for the market. Top: Gathering the crop and measuring it into bushels. Centre: Washing the coffee beans. Bottom: Spreading the beans to dry in the sun.

With a near-insatiable demand for rubber tyres from the fast-growing motor industry, Brazil profited for a time from having a world monopoly of rubber. But an Englishman named Henry Wickham smuggled rubber seeds out of Brazil in 1876, and by 1912 the Far East was producing rubber in commercial quantities. Brazil's rubber boom was over.

Lack of capital for investment was yet another problem facing the continent. South America had to look abroad for the money to build such basics as roads and railways. The railways of Argentina, for example, were built largely with British capital. Exports suffered badly during the Great Depression of the 1930s, leaving South America unable to pay for overseas goods. Many nations decided to industrialise and make their own. This accelerated a process that was already well under way in Brazil and Argentina – encouraging a flow of immigrants from Europe. They came in their thousands, especially from Italy and Spain. The rapid growth of industry led to an equally rapid growth of cities, their populations swollen by peasants looking for a better chance in life. Millions ended up living in disease-ridden *barrios*, with no sewers or electricity, where children picked over rubbish tips for scraps.

The military men take over

Poverty bred unrest and rebellion, and politics throughout most of South America settled into a pattern: military dictatorships, skilled in the arts of suppression,

Coffee to burn During the Depression of the 1930s, Brazil ran out of buyers for its coffee. This train gang is using surplus beans as fuel for their locomotive.

punctuated by brief periods of civilian rule. Ecuador had 14 presidents in 14 years, only one of them not from the army. After a military coup in 1930, Argentina was controlled by the army, even when there was a civilian president. Roberto Ortiz was ousted in 1943 for being too liberal and for favouring the Allies against the Nazis in the Second World War. One of the officers who toppled him, Juan Perón, became president in 1946. Helped by Eva Duarte, who became his wife, he wooed the industrial workers and their unions. Perón's free-spending programmes nearly bankrupted the country and he was ousted in 1955.

In Colombia, riots that followed the assassination of the Leftist president Gaitán in 1948 were the start of years of terror and

L'Estado Novo

Getúlio Vargas declared a 'New State' in Brazil in 1937 and won the title 'Father of the poor'. But he was a great admirer of European dictators such as Mussolini in Italy and Salazar in Portugal, and ran a near-Fascist regime.

Getúlio Vargas (1883–1954) was president of Brazil from 1934 to 1945, and again from 1950 to 1954.

banditry, in which 200 000 died. Revenues from oil paid for land reform in Venezuela, but it, too, suffered from dictatorship. The regime of Perez Jiménez (1948-58) was so unpopular that it was overthrown by an angry mob. Bolivia suffered military coups after losing more than 50 000 of its men in the Chaco War against Paraguay (1932-5). Chile was one country where the military kept out of politics – until the 1970s.

In Paraguay, General Alfredo Stroessner's regime made the country a natural bolt-hole for Nazi war criminals. He was deposed by an army coup in 1989. Brazil suffered severely in the Great Depression. Coffee prices fell so low that it was cheaper to burn beans in the fields than take them to market. Getúlio Vargas attacked the coffee barons and set up a dictatorship that

Boy soldiers It was hardly possible to be too young to fight in Colombia's civil war of 1902.

Evita, the woman behind Perón

One of the reasons why Juan Perón was wildly popular with Argentina's working classes was his wife, Evita, a former actress born to a poor family. The more glamorous her lifestyle, the more she was adored by the poor – her 'shirtless ones'. Her death from cancer at the age of 33 sent the nation into mourning, and was a heavy blow to Perón's political career.

Face of the times Eva Perón adorned the covers of magazines for nearly a decade.

he called *L'Estado Novo*, the New State. In 1954 he committed suicide rather than submit to a coup.

His successor, Juscelino Kubitschek, built a futuristic new capital, Brasília, deep in the interior. It was impressive, but the government had to print money to pay for it, making the country's chronic inflation even worse. Instability and urban terrorism marked the 1960s and most of the 1970s in Brazil, until the police defeated the terrorists through a ruthless vigilante-style 'shoot to kill' policy.

Impact of the Cold War

Early in the 19th century, US president James Monroe announced the 'Monroe Doctrine', warning the European powers not to interfere in American affairs, and in particular not to establish any further colonies in South America. The 20th-century Cold War version of that doctrine was

the firm conviction that communism should be kept out of North America's 'backyard'. The doctrine was breached when Fidel Castro led a revolution in Cuba and set up a communist state. President John F. Kennedy backed up his success in the 'Missile Crisis' that followed by setting up, in 1961, the Alliance for Progress, which offered financial aid to South American countries opposing communism. But aid could be withheld from countries seen to be hostile to the USA – as happened to Peru when its government became involved in a dispute with the International Petroleum Company, a subsidiary of the US giant Standard Oil. The contrast between the poverty of the masses and the wealth of the few was a fertile breeding ground for communism – as Castro well knew. In Bolivia his charismatic lieutenant Che Guevara was shot dead by police while trying to spread the revolution.

Tanks in the streets *On September 11, 1973, tanks rumbled onto the streets of Santiago in a coup d'état directed by General Augusto Pinochet. President Salvador Allende was killed during the shelling of the presidential palace.*

The oil price shock

For most countries in South America, the oil crisis of 1973 was as jarring an economic shock as the Depression of the 1930s. Desperate for cheap energy to power their new industries and to move their goods along newly built highways, they saw oil prices increase fourfold. For Brazil, this was a disaster mitigated only by a rise in world coffee prices in the late 1970s. Inflation soared to 5000 per cent and terrorism was suppressed only when the military took over, in 1979. Free elections were restored ten years later.

The 'Dirty War'

In Argentina, Perón was re-elected in 1973, but died the next year, leaving an unstable country that once again fell under military rule. In Argentina's 'Dirty War' 20 000 suspected opponents of the regime simply disappeared, after being dragged to torture cells. The army commander, General Galtieri, sent troops to invade the Falkland Islands in 1982, to divert attention from

Judging the junta *Judges appointed by Argentina's new democratic government hear the case, in September 1985, against the country's discredited and overthrown junta.*

troubles at home, but humiliating defeat forced him out of office. Carlos Menem, a Perónista, was elected president in 1989 and again in 1995 and began the task of restoring a near-bankrupt economy.

Until the 1970s, Chile was the one South American country with a settled tradition of democracy. This changed after Salvador Allende, the first open Marxist anywhere in the world to come to power in free elections, began breaking up big estates and nationalising banks. With inflation soaring, General Augusto Pinochet led an army coup in which Allende was killed. The junta suppressed labour unions, but democratic elections were restored in 1989.

Boom in Venezuela

Venezuela benefited from the 1973 oil crisis. The boom, which fuelled inflation, lasted for ten years before oil prices fell. President Andrés Pérez introduced austerity measures in a bid to control inflation, but they provoked riots in which 300 died. After Pérez was suspended on charges of embezzlement in 1993, the country entered a period of military control. In Peru, power alternated between juntas and civilian rule. But whoever was in charge, the country's wealth stayed in the hands of the '40 families'. The gap between rich and

War for the Falklands

Argentina has long claimed the islands it calls the Malvinas, which lie some 400 miles (600 km) off its southern coast. Britain calls them the Falklands, and its inhabitants are British subjects. In April 1982, to restore the waning popularity of his junta, Argentina's General Galtieri sent an invasion force to the Falklands. At first, this move was acclaimed in Buenos Aires (above), but the jubilation did not last long. Britain's prime minister, Margaret Thatcher, sent a task force to the islands and the war was over in ten weeks. The Argentinian nation mourned its dead and blamed Galtieri for the humiliation of defeat. The price paid by the junta was to be thrown out of office.

Young workers protest *In Bolivia, the 1980s were a decade of crisis. Galloping inflation and a steep fall in the price of tin hit the poor hardest. Workers of all trades and all ages, including some who were barely in their teens, came out on strike to claim better pay and conditions.*

poor spawned terrorism: a Maoist guerrilla group, the Shining Path, waged a merciless campaign that was reduced in intensity only after the capture of its leader, Abimael Guzmán, in 1992.

Terrorism was by no means confined to Peru. Uruguay, South America's first welfare state, could not afford its swollen bureaucracy and plunged into financial crisis. The Tupamaro urban guerrillas, named after the 18th-century Peruvian rebel Tupac Amaru, counted members of the middle and upper classes in their ranks. The government fought terror with terror and by 1978 the Tupamaros had been wiped out.

The Indian problem

Indians make up the majority of the population in Bolivia, Peru and Ecuador, and a sizable minority in Colombia. Bitterly resentful at losing their ancestral lands, for years they knew no other way of protesting than through rebellion. There was an Indian insurrection in Ecuador as late as the 1980s. In Bolivia, though, the Guarani

One city, two nations Caracas, capital of Venezuela, where a shantytown nation of the poor, swollen by migration from the countryside, has grown up alongside the luxurious skyscraper apartments of the rich.

Indians have opened peaceful negotiations with the government to win back their rights. But in Amazonia, where logging interests and land developers are destroying huge swathes of rain forest, Indian rights have been brushed aside.

Towards tomorrow

The future for South America is at best uncertain. The population is increasing, and Argentina is the only country in the continent capable of consistently growing enough food to feed itself – yet Argentina suffered bankruptcy in 2002, forcing many people to fall back on a barter economy. Finances elsewhere are not fully stable. Ecuador adopted the US dollar in 2000 due to the massive depreciation of the sucre, and Venezuela, under President Chavez, is threatened with a crippled economy. Social inequalities and the *barrios* remain, illiteracy is still widespread, and criminal drug cartels have stepped up the level of violence. But the outlook is not entirely bleak. Democracy has been restored in many countries and efforts are being made to breathe life into a South American free trade area – the Mercosur – comprising some 240 million consumers.

THE PLACE

AND ITS

PEOPLE

S outh America's identity is elusive, escaping whenever you think you have grasped it. It seems close as you shiver in the thin, biting air of the Andes, or stare at the face of a peasant whose way of life predates Columbus. Then something disturbs the impression – a Baroque church apparently transported from Andalusia, or a Chilean fjord with wooden houses that would seem at home in Norway. In this kaleidoscopic continent of a dozen independent countries, imported and indigenous images shift and intermingle and idiosyncracies abound.

CHAPTER 1

NATURAL WONDERS

A paradise on Earth – that phrase often came to Old World travellers as they explored the New. Thoughts of Eden arise easily when one is faced with the grandeur of the Iguaçu Falls or the early morning purity of an Andean peak patrolled by circling condors. South America's unique landscapes and life forms inspire awe and wonder, but this is a vulnerable land, and nowhere more so than in the Amazon basin. It scarcely seems credible that a forest three-quarters the size of the USA could vanish. But chainsaws have already removed more than 10 per cent of it. The rest could go in less than a lifetime. No wonder the rain forest has become a symbol for conservationists fighting to preserve this earthly paradise.

Lakes and beech forests near San Carlos de Bariloche, in Argentina.

Lost worlds of Venezuela's Gran Sabana

Spirit world   *Swirling clouds are an appropriate shroud for Auyán-tepui, 8460 ft (2580 m). The name means 'hell mountain'. According to Indian lore, its summit is the abode of malevolent spirits.*

No popular fantasy has contributed more to the exotic allure of South America than Sir Arthur Conan Doyle's tale of a remote and inaccessible plateau where prehistoric monsters still roamed. That 'Lost World' really exists – if not with dinosaurs.

Spanish conquistadores in quest of gold in the 16th century got no nearer than the swamps of the Orinoco River, at which point their feet rotted off. A dogged British botanist, Everard Im Thurn, did rather better in 1884. Pushing up the Orinoco, he struck deep into the interior of the continent and came upon a region of enormous blocks of red sandstone, called mesas, whose tops disappeared into the clouds.

Above the clouds

Thurn managed to scale one of the mesas and a descriptive lecture he delivered in London was enough to stir the imagination of Sir Arthur Conan Doyle, the celebrated author. The result was the fantasy classic, *The Lost World*, published in 1912. The world in question is that of the Gran Sabana, a surreal landscape chopped up and worn down over a period of 1.8 billion years. Geologists explain that it is part of a formation known as the Guiana Shield, one of the original building blocks of the South American continent. The local Pémon Indians call these monolithic mountains *tepuis*, and are respectful of the powerful spirits that inhabit them. Appearing like fortresses from some age of giants, the rock-walled *tepui* typically rises 5000 ft (1500 m) to a plateau summit with jagged edges, which in the rainy season spout the highest waterfalls in the world.

These summits truly are lost worlds – eerie, dank, primordial, and isolated for so many millions of years that each has evolved life forms of its own. The largest, atop Auyán-tepui, covers 280 sq miles (700 km^2). The loftiest, Roraima, straddles the borders of Venezuela, Brazil and Guyana at an altitude of 9094 ft (2772 m). This is where Thurn climbed in 1884. The cloud world of Roraima has been likened to a Salvador Dali dreamscape, or a dinosaur

Uncertain future   More than a hundred sheer-sided tepuis *rise out of the forests along Venezuela's southern border. Remnants of a continental landmass that existed 1.8 billion years ago, their peace may soon be disturbed by development.*

graveyard. Dank mists swirl over a landscape eroded into grotesque shapes and blackened by aeons of algae. Dark canyons and menacing sinkholes make exploration dangerous.

The plant-life of Roraima is appropriately macabre. In the competition for sparse nutrients, many species have turned carnivorous, attracting and trapping insects with an array of seductive scents, sticky tentacles, trap doors and drowning vats in which to suck up the juices of their small visitors. The lost world is indeed inhabited by strange life-forms, but they belong to the realm of plants.

Tension in Tepui-land

Most *tepuis* are sheer-sided and too difficult to climb. Many have yet to be explored, even by helicopter. However, Roraima is more accessible, and is beginning to show signs of despoliation. There is also concern over what the future holds for the entire mineral-rich Guiana Shield, holding as it does an unbroken expanse of rain forest that stretches from Venezuela across Guyana, Surinam and French Guiana. Virtually inaccessible until the 1970s, when a dirt track was cut through to the Brazilian border and a large part of the area was proclaimed a national park, the Gran Sabana is now a popular tourist attraction that is accessible by road, and is also on the daytripper flight path.

In the lowlands, the rivers that rise in the Gran Sabana have been dammed to provide power for steel and aluminium smelting plants, while through the national park a high-voltage electricity line marches towards Brazil. In 1999, the Pémon attempted to sabotage the line, which they feared as a spur to development.

Thousands of illicit gold-miners have added to the threat facing the region, uprooting trees and poisoning rivers with mercury. A territorial dispute with Guyana and tensions on the border with Brazil lend a strategic dimension to the problems of a region once ruled by the harpy eagle and the jaguar.

Taking the tourist flight to Angel Falls

Pilots manoeuvre their jets like feathers floating on the air currents as they dip into Diablo Canyon to give passengers the thrill of closely inspecting the world's highest falls. Then they execute their exit by sharply banking over a spinning horizon of moss-green jungle, coiling rivers and towering *tepuis*. Promoted in tourist brochures as 'The Angel's Leap', the falls are in fact named after a mere mortal – American gold prospector and stunt pilot James Angel, who found the falls in 1935 and crash-landed near their summit. Seen from below, the water seems to descend the rust-red rock face in slow motion. From about halfway, it dissolves into a swirling, smoky spray that finally bursts onto black rocks at the base of the falls.

Forest cataract   At 3212 ft (979 m), Angel Falls incorporate the longest clear drop (2648 ft/807 m) in the world.

Forest lagoon   Seven waterfalls and beaches of pink sand make Canaima Lagoon, downstream from Angel Falls, a tourist attraction.

Iguaçu: the ultimate spectacle

Brazil and Argentina compete for bragging rights to South America's favourite natural wonder, a waterfall of breathtaking beauty and awesome might, held in the clasp of a protected forest filled with hundreds of different species of tropical birds and butterflies.

In a continent full of natural wonders, where spectacular waterfalls are almost commonplace, the Iguaçu Falls inspire a sense of awe. This is South America's most popular natural attraction. Dwarfing Niagara in every dimension, Iguaçu is the most panoramic of the world's great water spectacles. If there were seven wonders of the water world, Iguaçu – which contains 275 cataracts – would be top of the list.

'Big water' spelt three ways

The falls, which span the border between Brazil and Argentina, form a horseshoe 2.5 miles (4 km) wide and 269 ft (82 m) deep. The main force of the flow gets sucked down a cauldron, the Garganta del Diablo (Devil's Throat), itself the world's single most powerful cataract. The name changes depending on which side of the border you are standing on – Iguaçu in Brazil, Iguazú in Argentina, and Iguassú in Paraguay, the border of which lies nearby – but the meaning in the Guaraní language is crystal clear. *I* is 'water' and *guaçu* is 'big', whichever way you spell it.

History books relate how the energetic Spanish conquistador Alvaro Nuñez Cabeza de Vaca discovered the falls in 1541. The local Guaraní people, with longer memories, will tell you that

Confusion of cataracts *Originally formed where the Iguaçu River flows into the Paraná, the falls have cut back 14 miles (23 km) in 100 000 years.*

The Devil's Throat *'An ocean plunging into an abyss.'*

Ruins in the jungle

In a dramatic opening to the 1988 film *The Mission*, a Jesuit priest is strapped to a cross and set adrift above the Iguaçu Falls. The film was a reconstruction of events in the 17th century, when the Jesuits set out to create a theocratic utopia in the jungle. The Catholic order put slave hunters to flight and built about 50 missions, where the Guaraní farmed and worked as craftsmen. The idyll ended with the expulsion of the Jesuits from South America. Jungle ruins and the name of an Argentinian province – Misiones – are reminders of the experiment.

Iguaçu is where the clouds were born. The Guaraní also tell the story of the beautiful maiden Naipú, who was desired by the forest god. When Naipú tried to flee with the handsome warrior Carobe, the forest god scooped out the riverbed ahead of their canoe, then turned Naipú into a rock at the base of the chasm and condemned her lover to an eternity of gazing upon her by turning him into a tree.

The mesmerising powers of the god are apparent still, in the throngs who come to gaze at the top of the falls. There are many ways of doing this, and Brazil and Argentina compete for attention and tourists. Brazil can claim the best overall views, but Argentina has access to more islands and picturesque cataracts. By constructing lookouts and daring *pasarelas* (catwalks) over the water, the two sides bring the experience ever closer to the brink. Below the falls, powerboats of thrill-seekers roar head-on into the spray, spinning at the last moment to create 180-degree arcs of rainbow-coloured spray.

Swifts in the twilight

For many, the image of Iguaçu is of dusky swifts (*Cypseloides senex*) wheeling at twilight in their hundreds, fearlessly darting to their nests behind a curtain of tumbling water. The falls are a gem within a jewel box, the two countries having combined to preserve as twin national parks an 870 sq mile (2260 km^2) patch of subtropical rain forest, reaching upstream on either bank of the river. The land for hundreds of miles around was long ago cleared and the deep, brick-red soil planted with coffee, sugar, soya beans and other crops, leaving Iguaçu an important preserve of virgin jungle. It is heavy with lichens, orchids, and other epiphytes, and harbours a particularly dazzling diversity of birds and butterflies – some 500 species of each. As the thunder of the falls fades into the distance, a hot, humid silence takes over, broken by the drip of water and the sounds of birds and insects.

Shy resident

The bashful tapir (*Tapir terrestris*) is the largest animal of the South American rain forest, weighing around 700 lb (315 kg). Its most distinctive feature is a flexible snout, which it uses to sort through the leaves and water plants that it eats. During the day the tapir rests in the swamps to escape the heat and insects. When startled, it makes a beeline for the nearest water, charging through the undergrowth at breakneck speed. It is a favourite prey of the jaguar, but its major enemy is man. The flesh is tasty, the skin makes leather, the bones were once used to make implements, and the feet turned into a castanet-like musical instrument. Despite declining numbers, the tapir is still hunted for food and sport.

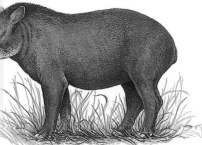

Relic of Utopia *The magnificent mission church of San Ignacio Miní was abandoned after the expulsion of the Jesuits in 1767. The ruins have been cleared of encroaching jungle and are now protected.*

Venezuela's underwater paradise

*Andean mountains, Amazonian jungles...and Caribbean beaches! The stunning variety
that is Venezuela includes 1800 miles (3000 km) of coastline unique in the diversity
of its offshore underwater habitats and desert islands.*

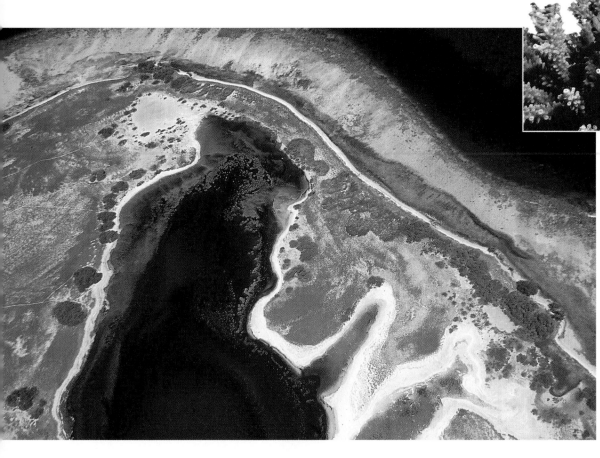

*Desert islands on the doorstep
Angelfish (above) populate the
waters of Los Roques (left).*

Due north of Caracas, a neck-
lace of islands and *cayos* (coral
islets) qualifies for perfect desert
island status, despite being a
mere half-hour hop from the
metropolis. Lack of fresh water
accounts for the pristine state of
Los Roques, an archipelago
lying low in turquoise waters
that teem with parrotfish, angelfish and trumpetfish. Caves at
depths of 80-100 ft (25-30 m)
challenge divers, but less intim-
idating for the novice diver are
the *cayos* of Morrocoy, a three-
hour drive west from Caracas.
There the clear, warm waters are as shallow as 10 ft (3 m). Wholly
different again, and celebrated for deep diving, the rocky islands of
Mochima are a five-hour drive east of the capital.

Pearls as big as eggs – that was the word that reached Seville, and
within months of Christopher Columbus's voyage of exploration in 1499, Spanish fortune-hunters were scouring the offshore islands of what is now Venezuela. Pearls were found in such
abundance that they became fashionable throughout Europe.

Isles of variety

Columbus declared this original stretch of the Spanish Main to
be 'the loveliest in all the world' – a statement made without benefit of the scuba equipment that 500 years later would reveal,
beyond the line of white sand and coconut palms, a stunning
underwater world, full of life and colour.

Parrotfish

Rock beauty angelfish

Paradise under threat

The pearl beds of the conquistadores lie off Isla Margarita, now one
of the Caribbean's best-known 'sun and surf' resorts. The oyster
beds became so depleted that pearling operations were abandoned
decades ago. Some fear that new offshore areas being opened up
could also become degraded through similar
lack of foresight. The waters of Los Roques,
Morrocoy and Mochima are all national parks,
but enforcement of environmental laws, never
strong, deteriorated in the 1990s. A natural disaster that hit 60 miles (100 km)
of the coast near Caracas, when
landslides swept whole towns into
the sea, was blamed in part on mismanagement of the environment –
and tourism took a nose-dive.

Scarlet ibis   A colourful island resident.

The Pantanal – flood and drought

The world's most extensive wetland is an ever-changing panorama, where the greatest concentration of wildlife in the Americas grows fat through the months of flood but struggles to survive the dry season.

Pantanal mascot *The 6 ft (2 m) tall jabirú stork is a familiar sight. It preys on anacondas and other snakes.*

Life literally pulses in the Pantanal, appropriately situated at the heart of South America, where Paraguay and Bolivia nudge up to Brazil. The word derives from *pantano* (swamp), which hardly does justice to this amphibious wonderland. Essentially a land-locked delta – and, like the Amazon, once an inland sea – the Pantanal receives run-off from an upland watershed twice its size (the Planalto) and releases it through the River Paraguay.

Pulse of the seasons

In the rainy summer months (November-March), the Paraguay and its tributaries overflow to form shallow lakes and swamps. In the drier winter season, the waters drop by up to 6 in (15 cm) a day, leaving sediment and stranded fish. There are some 200 species of fish, which help to sustain 600 species of birds and many mammals and reptiles. Despite poaching, there are huge numbers of caiman alligators, or jacarés, and capybaras. Film-producers send their crews here, where animals are far easier to spot than in the Amazon rain forest.

Poacher alert

At least 50 species are threatened or endangered in the Brazilian Pantanal. They include the ocelot, jaguar, puma, giant anteater and giant armadillo. Habitat destruction, poaching, overfishing and the pet trade are all problems. Poaching is endemic throughout the Pantanal and is estimated to account for up to 2 million animals each year. Jaguar, ocelot and caiman skins are prized, while bird fanciers will pay $10000 (£6800) for a hyacinth macaw, largest of the parrot family and critically endangered.

A world in peril

With few people, no towns and only one road, the Transpantaneira (which goes nowhere, because it ran out of funds and into opposition from ecologists), the Pantanal would seem secure, but development is encroaching on all sides. Land-clearance, deforestation and dam construction threaten the delicate ecosystem, as does water pollution. A proposal to open up 2000 miles (3200 km) of the river system for year-round navigation, by straightening, widening and deepening the upper Paraguay also poses a serious threat.

Hidden danger *The waterways look clear but effluent from sugar-refining and mining operations, and pollution by agrochemicals and raw sewage, are a growing threat.*

Super rodent *The capybara can weigh over 130 lb (60 kg).*

Colca Canyon: life under the Andean volcanoes

Over the deepest canyon on earth, the largest of all flying birds circles effortlessly – scanning a landscape of terraced fields, chasms and rock walls almost untouched by modern times.

It is hard to imagine the deepest canyon on earth becoming 'lost', yet this is exactly what happened with the Cañón del Colca, only recently rediscovered as a destination for 'adventure' tourism. Here in the high Andes of southern Peru, condors wheel in the thin, clear air over a panorama that has hardly changed since Inca times. Far to the north, beyond the canyon's rim, lies the source of the River Amazon.

Colca cultivation   *The River Colca cuts through a wide patchwork of fields and ancient terraces where the valley broadens. In Inca times, this area was twice as productive as it is today.*

Dwarfing the Grand Canyon

The gateway to Colca Canyon is the high desert city of Arequipa, where wise travellers pause for a couple of days to acclimatise to the reduced oxygen at 7600 ft (2300 m) before pressing higher. From Arequipa, a bus jammed with people, bundles and the occasional farm animal clambers to 15 600 ft (4800 m) on the dusty *puna* (grasslands) before tumbling into Colca's amphitheatre of patchwork fields and terraced hillsides. A few miles downstream, a dark slit indicates where the river cuts its way out of the mountains through a gorge twice as deep as Arizona's Grand Canyon. At one point, the drop from mountain to river is 13 450 ft (4175 m).

Flight of the condor

The Andean condor (*Vultur gryphus*) is a large black-and-white vulture. A wingspan of 10 ft (3 m) or more enables the condor to soar effortlessly at altitudes of up to 18 000 ft (5500 m). It uses its piercing eyesight to spot carrion on the mountainside. The slightly smaller California condor is on the critically endangered list, having been reduced to a handful of individuals in the 1980s.

Restless land *The riverbed is impossible to chart, being constantly reworked by avalanche, earthquake and erosion. Such stretches are uninhabitable.*

Fortress of God *A massive 17th-century Spanish church dominates each tiny mud-brick village. This one at Lari (below) is the largest.*

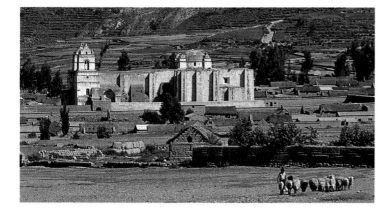

Rediscovery and transformation

When the Inca penetrated the Colca in the 1400s, they came upon the Collagua, a people who worshipped volcanoes and had cone-shaped heads – an effect achieved by strapping a board to a baby's soft cranium. A century later, when the Spanish arrived, more than 22 000 acres (9000 ha) of irrigated terraces and thriving llama herds made the Colca one of the most productive areas in the Inca Empire. But within 30 years, the valley's estimated 70 000 population had been halved through abuse and disease. The survivors were rounded up and placed in regimented *pueblos* (settlements), and the population halved again. By the 20th century, the Colca was all but forgotten, its only contact with the outside world a llama pack train that once a year took alpaca wool down to Arequipa. In 1931, its rediscovery by the Shippee–Johnson air-reconnaissance expedition made headline news in the USA. Today, the Colca is gradually being transformed as tourism expands and power lines extend into the valley. But for now, descendants of the Collagua still live in the 400-year-old *pueblos* and follow an ancient cycle of cooperative labour, cultivating the terraces during the November-May wet season and herding alpacas on the *puna* during the winter months.

Ventures into the canyon

The tourists' primary destination is Cruz de Condor (Condor Crossing), a rocky lookout that affords spectacular canyon views and sure sightings of the great birds wheeling above. Along the way are reminders that the Andes are dangerously alive. At the village of Maca, a church lies shattered from the 1991 earthquake; directly across the canyon, Lari's church was spared, but the village terracing collapsed into the abyss. Intrepid trekkers venture down into the bowels of the canyon, or press upwards to the 17 000 ft (5000 m) level on Mount Mismi. The canyon was not fully explored until 1981, when a Polish expedition succeeded in rafting the 60 miles (100 km) of gorges. In 1983, Alvaro Ibanez became the first Peruvian to run the Colca.

Saving the precious vicuña of the puna

The *puna* grasslands at over 13 000 ft (3900 m) are the habitat of the vicuña (*Vicugna vicugna*), whose long white fleece makes the softest and most valuable of all wools. This fleet-footed little relative of the llama had been hunted close to extinction by the1960s, when it was saved by the creation of wildlife reserves such as Aguada Blanca, above Arequipa, and Pampas Galeras, to the north. Gun battles between guards and poachers cost several lives early in the rescue programme. Light caramel in colour, shading to white, there were millions of vicuña in Inca times, when their wool was used for the garments of the nobility. They are perfectly adapted to their environment, having a high content of red blood corpuscles to cope with the thin air, soft foot pads to protect slow-growing vegetation, and sharp incisors to nip at plants.

Colca girl
From the style and decoration of her hat, it is possible to identify her village.

Desert paradox

*From the border with Ecuador, down the length of Peru
and northern Chile, the 2000 miles (3000 km) of
coastal waters are full of life, but the coast itself is barren.*

Try to imagine a desert that is blanketed by fog for months on
end; or a desert in which you might suffer sunstroke, frostbite,
and altitude sickness, all while standing on one spot. Then try to
imagine three nations going to war over possession of such a desert.

Fog over the desert

To untangle these paradoxes, you need to look at a map of the
west coast of South America. Denied moisture from the Amazon by
the barrier of the Andes, the coastal corridor must look to the
Pacific Ocean as a source of rain – but none falls. Flowing up the
coast, the Humboldt (or Peruvian) current from Antarctica creates
a layer of cold air. This rolls off the ocean and across the arid coast
as banks of thick, chilly fog, especially in winter. This is La Garúa,
known also in Chile as Camanchaca. The only precipitation
comes in condensation from this clammy sea mist; it averages
under 2 in (50 mm) a year, and there are places where it has not
rained for 20 years.

Guano and 'white gold'

Offshore, the Humboldt current stirs up the black depths of the
submarine trenches that run parallel to the coast, causing an
upwelling of nutrients, plankton, and an abundance of fish and
shellfish, sea birds and sea mammals. Basic to the marine food
chain are enormous schools of sardine-like anchovy, gobbled up
and converted by the sea birds into droppings, or guano, which
have built up into thick layers on the rocks. Guano comes from an
Inca word, *wanu* (dung). The Inca knew all about its uses as a crop
fertiliser, hauling tons of it to their mountain terraces centuries
before its exploitation by Europe and North America. In the 19th
century the region was also found to be a source of nitrates – 'white
gold', over which Chile and Bolivia waged the so-called War of

*Guano war   Guano deposits up to 100 ft (30 m) thick on the Chincha
Islands south of Lima caused Spain and Peru to wage war in the 19th century.*

The candelabra conundrum

So large that it can be viewed in
its entirety only from out at sea,
this mysterious design etched into
a barren hillside on the Paracas
Peninsula is known as El Candelabro
the candlestick. Possibly 1500
years old, archaeologists link it to
pre-Inca people whose mummies,
wrapped in richly woven fabric,
have been found nearby. It has
been variously identified as a
marker for ancient navigators, a
sign to the gods, a stylised
representation of the Southern
Cross constellation. or a San Pedro
cactus – a plant from which a
hallucinogenic drug is extracted.
Its similarity to the 'tree of life' of
Biblical cosmology also stirs
speculation. However, its exact
meaning is likely to remain buried
with the mummies.

the Pacific. In the end, it was Chile that emerged victorious, claiming the victor's prize of the northern Atacama, a barren, nitrate-rich
strip stretching along the coast.

Astronomers and archaeologists

Along the coast of Peru, the Humboldt current is occasionally displaced: the fog breaks, warm air spirals into thunderheads and
storms begin. Not so in the Atacama Desert, which is sealed off by
a high coastal range and rises to 13 000 ft (4000 m) on the interior
plateau. There are places in the Atacama Desert where no rain has
been known to fall – ever – even though the blue Pacific visible to
the west and the snow-capped Andes to the east
tease like mirages. With an overall average rainfall

*Guano factory   The brown pelican
(Pelicanus occidentalis), an industrious
Chincha resident, now enjoys the
protection of a nature reserve.*

Atacama fantasy The rippling play of sun on shadow gives a deceptive vitality to the mountainous rim of a desert more arid than the Sahara.

of only 0.02 in (5 mm) a year, the Atacama is a hundred times drier than California's Death Valley; and drier than the Empty Quarter of Arabia. Golden brown under the sun, no hint of organic life issues from this Martian landscape, only rock flashing glints of mica and nitrate. And there is no sound beyond the crunch of gravel underfoot – 'the wild mineral silence' described by Chilean poet Pablo Neruda.

The Atacama is said to receive the highest solar radiation in the world. The clarity of the high, clear, dry air attracts astronomers: some of the world's most sophisticated observatories were in place or under construction at the start of the 21st century. Archaeologists are also drawn here because the desert preserves everything – whether inscrutable messages etched into its crusty surface or mummies twice as old as any Egypt has to offer. Tourists come to view saltpans the size of small nations, watch the sunset in the Valley of the Moon, and get altitude sickness on a sand dune.

Salar de Atacama Flamingos somehow find a living on this 1231 sq mile (3188 km²) saltpan. Their beaks filter out small organisms from the saline waters.

El Tatio The Atacama Desert's surprises include the world's highest geyser field (14 100 ft/4300 m). At dawn, the scalding waters and chill air generate billowing columns of steam.

Pollution and preservation

Then there are the miners, still exploiting the Atacama's rich mineral deposits and creating pollution – arsenic being the greatest cause of concern. A plume of dusty smoke issuing from the heart of the desert marks the site of Chuquicamata, the world's largest open-cast copper mine. Chuqui, as it is known, belonged to the Anaconda Company of the USA until it was nationalised in 1971, a move that contributed to the overthrow and death of Chile's President Allende two years later. Lately, the Atacama's preservative powers have been demonstrated anew, in enabling identification of bodies dumped here in mass graves during the subsequent 17-year dictatorship of General Pinochet.

Land of lakes

Plastered thinly down the western face of the Andes, Chile is a two-way wilderness. As arid as the far north becomes, so the south moistens by the mile – until the Andes themselves meet the ocean, disgorging their glaciers into the cold waters of the Pacific.

Guanaco *Wild relative of the llama.*

No need for directions in Chile – 'the thin country', as Pablo Neruda, the Nobel laureate poet, describes it. From the desiccated depths of the Atacama through the peach-scented Central Valley to the fire and ice of Patagonia, there is no deviating from the gangplank of the Pan-American Highway. Think of driving the equivalent distance from London to Tehran, with the Andes towering over your left shoulder and the breakers of the Pacific Ocean on your right – all the way. Rain, denied to the desert of the north, falls with a vengeance farther south: at Villarríca, annual rainfall is more than 80 in (2 m); farther south, it reaches 160 in (4 m).

Saving the monkey puzzle

Villarríca is a resort of the Lake District, a scenic extravaganza of volcanoes, lakes and forest, very different from its English namesake, but evoking in Chileans feelings of special affection. Most of Chile's 55 active volcanoes are here, glowing like cigar butts in the night and causing frequent disruptions. This is the home of the *pehuen* or Chile pine (*Araucaria araucana*), much better known as the monkey puzzle tree. An ancient species that once provided shade for dinosaurs, it can grow to 160 ft (60 m) and live for more than 1000 years. Monkey puzzle forests draped the volcanoes until the loggers moved in. By 1990 few stands were left intact, so environmentalists and the Mapuche people, who are culturally committed to the tree, persuaded the government to take protective measures.

Glacier's end Debris from the San Rafael glacier in southern Chile. The ice has taken 20 000 years to travel from glacier source to ocean.

A national hero

It is just over a century since this region became safe for outsiders, following 300 years of fierce resistance from the Mapuche people. Villarríca, for example, was wiped out in 1602 and not re-established until the 1880s. Many Chileans have ancestors on both sides of this race war, and Lautaro, the 16th-century Mapuche chief who repulsed the Spanish, is now held in respect as a national hero. The preservation of monkey puzzle trees is not the only concern of the modern Mapuche, who hold title to only about 6 per cent of their former territory, and are in increasing conflict with the promoters of billions of dollars' worth of forestry, mining and hydro-electric projects.

The inundated coast

South of the 40th parallel, lakes give way to the fiords of an inundated coastline mazed with misty waterways. Isla Chiloé is the largest of thousands of islands created over the past few thousand years by glacial melt and rising sea levels. A wild strawberry (*Fragaria chiloensis*) collected from a beach here in the 17th century is the ancestor of the fruit cultivated worldwide today. This was literally the end of the road until the 1980s, when the increasingly wild, glaciated coastline to the south was opened up with the construction of the largely unsurfaced Carretera Austral highway. The purpose of the road was primarily strategic – to facilitate military deployment should Argentina ever

The romantic island of Chiloé

The large and green Isla Grande de Chiloé is where Chileans come to dream. Like an old Spanish galleon that slipped its moorings, it drifts apart from the rest of the country, and is laden with colourful myths and traditions of long ago. For 200 years, the colonists on Chiloé were isolated from colonial Spain, their only link a rare sailing from Lima in Peru. Then, early in the 19th century, the island became the last royalist stronghold, not surrendering to the mainland republic until 1826.

Today the Chilotes are a poor, proud, independent folk with an antique dialect and a unique store of music and dance. Chilote architecture features waterfront houses on stilts, called *palafitos*, and quaint wooden churches, including a lilac-and-tangerine coloured cathedral. Chilote folklore is brimful of tales of wizards and witches, ghost ships and amazing apparitions. But the future may be less magical than the past, as their culture gets packaged for a burgeoning tourist industry.

Torres del Paine at sunrise Some say the name comes from an Indian word for blue; others recall a woman named Paine. The fairy-tale mountains are a wildlife stronghold and backpackers' paradise.

intrude upon this Chilean sliver of Patagonia. For now, the road peters out in glacier country well short of the locked-away jewel of Chilean national parks, Torres del Paine. The Torres are spires of granite, which change colour with the light from slate-grey to rose-pink. They preside over lakes sunk into dark green forests that are shot through with glaciers. Here is the best place in South America to see the fleet guanaco, wild ancestor of the llama, and the endangered ñandú, or Darwin's rhea – a flightless bird. And it is as likely a place as any to catch a glimpse of a puma, or a mountain lion.

Araucarias The magnificent evergreen monkey puzzles get their genus name from Arauca in Chile, and their popular name from being very hard to climb.

Winds of Patagonia

The wind that blows ceaselessly between the Patagonian Andes and the Atlantic Ocean is unquestioned lord of this land that extends across a 1200 mile (2000 km) front between the Rio Colorado and Cape Horn. The Alacaluf Indians had no fewer than 30 words to describe it.

Patagonian penguin
The Magellanic or jackass penguin (Spheniscus magellanicus).

Patagonian Argentina shares with Chile some of the world's most magnificent mountain and lake scenery, stretching down the Andean divide. Surprises include, in San Carlos de Bariloche, a 'Tyrolean' skiing village, complete with chocolate shops and fondue restaurants, and an idyllic lakeside myrtle forest said to have inspired the creators of the Disney classic *Bambi*. Near here, in the Chilole Valley, legendary gringo outlaws Butch Cassidy and the Sundance Kid hid out from 1901 to 1907. The pair's mistake was to come down from the mountains onto the treeless Patagonian plateau, good only for rearing sheep and (they thought) raiding banks.

Haunting desolation

Patagonia covers 400 000 sq miles (1 million km²), and the plateau accounts for three-quarters of this. Scarcely populated, and hauntingly quiet were it not for the howl of the wind, it is strewn with drab, thorny scrub, growing only shin high. 'The curse of sterility is on the land', Charles Darwin declared when he visited in 1834. Years later, he wondered why the arid wastes had taken so firm a hold on his memory. Naturalist W.H. Hudson also wrote of feeling deeply moved by the desolation and not knowing why, while explorer Eric Shipton wrote of 'a strange sense of loneliness as though I were trespassing'. Travel writer Bruce Chatwin famously addressed the mystery with his *In Patagonia*, a series of encounters with melancholy gauchos, decayed expatriates and eccentrics.

Dinosaurs and sheep

Patagonia means 'land of monsters', more or less, and credit for the name goes to the explorer Magellan, who is said to have been impressed by the size of the native Tehuelche Indians. One hundred

Round-up time *It takes about 3 acres (more than 1 ha) of the sparse Patagonian grassland to sustain a single sheep.*

Moonscape with fossils *Petrified trunks lie where they fell more than 100 million years ago.*

Monsters turned to stone

Patagonia is scattered with the petrified remains of the forests that covered it before the Andes Mountains existed. Most of the remains are of giant proaraucarias (*Proaraucarites mirabilis*), an ancestor of trees that grow today in the Andes. Recent finds of dinosaur fossils include a 100 ton sauropod and a carnivore bigger than the famous *Tyrannosaurus rex*.

million years earlier, the name would have been more appropriate, for Patagonia was covered with temperate forests, swamps and dinosaurs. Then the Andes heaved up, pouring forth lethal layers of volcanic ash and setting up conditions for the desiccating winds of today.

Magellan was only passing through. Subsequent attempts to settle Patagonia met with ferocious resistance, celebrated in *La Araucana*, the great Spanish epic poem of the 16th century. The Araucanas, or Mapuches, wore warpaint, rode like the wind and held out for 300 years on both sides of the Andes, until crushed by the caudillo General Roca in a war of extermination called the Conquest of the Desert. What to do with Patagonia proved a problem, until Britons from the Falklands converted it into a vast sheep run. By the 1920s Patagonian wool was as celebrated as Argentinian beef. By the 1970s, the boom was over and plummeting wool prices in the 1990s made making a profit difficult. Ranching dynasties faded and ranch hands and their families were forced off the land and into cities.

Whale of a tale *One of Argentina's 'living national monuments'.*

Tycoons and whales

To the rescue, it is hoped, come tourists. For centuries a byword for all that is strange, remote and inaccessible, Patagonia at the dawn of the 21st century was enjoying a vogue among international travellers of means, while bargain land prices encouraged the likes of media mogul Ted Turner and financier George Soros to purchase *estancias* as ultimate retreats. The authorities in the depressed province of Chubut have turned the bleak Péninsula Valdés into one of the world's leading wildlife showcases, and the province's biggest business. The convergence of a warm current from Brazil and a cold current off the Falklands, coursing round a system of enclosed bays, inlets and cliffs, creates the perfect breeding ground for all manner of marine life, from raucous sea lions to torpid 3.5-ton elephant

seals. A star attraction is the southern right whale (*Eubalaena australis*), proclaimed by the Argentine government to be a 'living national monument'. Adding to the noise of the neighbourhood are an estimated 2 million penguins. Land species include the guanaco, the rhea and the Patagonian hare.

The Péninsula abuts the Chubut Valley, home since the 1860s to a Welsh community, complete with chapels and annual eisteddfod. Directing some of the whale-watching traffic to the valley's Welsh tearooms has provided a fillip for a culture suffering the effects of time and dilution of bloodlines. The late Diana, Princess of Wales, viewed the whales and took tea in the valley in 1995. Her cup, saucer and chair may be inspected.

Valdés sea lions *They are protected from man, but not from orcas (killer whales), which rush the shallows to snatch pups in their jaws.*

Last stand of the Ice Age

Vestiges of the ice sheet that once covered all of the continent's southern cone, the glaciers that reach down the length of the Patagonian Andes to Tierra del Fuego are also a constant reminder of the proximity of Antarctica.

Grinding glaciers, vertical rock spires, winds that scream like jet engines…the Southern Continental Ice Cap is a vast bed of snow, crystallised and compacted into the troughs of the Patagonian Andes between 48°30' and 51°30' S. Covering more than 7000 sq miles (11 300 km²) – about the dimensions of Wales, crushed and squeezed out – its dozens of glaciers are fed by snows from the prevailing westerly winds.

hours. Then calm is restored and the process resumes, normally on a 3-4 year cycle. The event of February 18, 1988, was caught on film by a television crew, but Moreno failed to plug the gap in the 1990s, causing some to suspect that global warming has put paid to a unique performance.

The glacier that explodes

One *ventisquero* (glacier) enjoys filmstar status. The Perito Moreno is one of a dozen glaciers that feeds Lago Argentino. A 200 ft (60 m) wall of ice nearly 3 miles (5 km) wide, it grinds down the mountainside and pushes its snout into the water. Since the 1940s, it has periodically reached the opposite bank, to bulldoze hundreds of acres of beech forest and cut off two arms of the lake. The level of the dammed arms rises until the pressure opens cracks in the glacial wall, which finally – it happened first in 1947 – ruptures. With a noise like the end of the world, Moreno splits asunder and the released waters roar through the gap in a spectacle lasting for

Frozen towers and needles

Moreno even in repose is a star attraction that has transformed this corner of the wilderness into a tourist trap, with catwalks and glacier 'minitreks' for rich retirees, lake cruises and gourmet dining

Iceberg lake *The chalky green waters of Lago Argentino, one of South America's largest lakes (above), are strewn with debris from the Perito Moreno glacier (right).*

Cape Horn *Tip of the Americas.*

Ushuaia *This town, in Argentinian Tierra del Fuego, is the most southerly in the world.*

– and little chunks of Moreno clinking in every glass of whisky. But pristine Patagonia presses all around, a frozen stronghold that remains among the least explored regions of the world. The ice cap was considered impregnable until 1952, when two Argentinians, Emilio Huerta and Mario Bertone, were the first to cross it. That same year, the conquest of its towers and needles began when a French team reached the 11 073 ft (3375 m) summit of sheer, ice-clad Mount Fitzroy. If Fitzroy was daunting, then its neighbour, 10 263 ft (3128 m) Cerro Torre, has been rated the greatest challenge of all. A needle of pink-streaked granite topped by an unstable cap of ice that climbers call 'the mushroom', it continues to claim lives.

In the land of fire

Tierra del Fuego, the Land of Fire and the last landfall before Antarctica, was part of the mainland when people first reached here: rising seas from the Ice Age meltdown rushed in to create the Strait of Magellan in about 7000 BC. The fires that gave the archipelago its name were probably warning beacons set when explorer Ferdinand Magellan hove into sight in 1520. The Fuegans were hardy folk who wrapped up in guanaco skins. They are long gone, killed off by European diseases and genocidal sheep ranchers. Their successors wrap up in fur-trimmed parkas, hands jammed in pockets. Consolations include the landscape's stark beauty and ethereal displays of the aurora australis.

Each year, Tierra del Fuego falls briefly under the Antarctic ozone hole, a fact that worries residents, despite assurances that wearing a hat and sunglasses should take care of the radiation. Scientists say the phenomenon has been stabilised by a worldwide reduction in the use of chlorofluorocarbons (CFCs), and expect the hole to close by 2050.

The beaver problem may be of longer-term consequence. Beavers were introduced from Canada in the 1940s, to create a fur industry. The beavers multiplied and now threaten to gnaw down all the beech trees, while there is no market for the rank pelts they grow in these dank conditions. The beaver make fine bait for catching *centolla* (southern king crab), a delicacy that is greatly overfished.

Capital of the end of the world

Ushuaia, with a population of about 45 000, sprawls untidily on the Beagle Channel beneath the final finger of the Andes. The housing stock is oddly assorted and includes *casa trineos*, shacks constructed on sleds for ease of transport. The last road terminates here: beyond lie ragged islands and Cape Horn, 90 miles (145 km) to the south, where the Atlantic and Pacific merge.

USHUAIA
fin del mundo

There is a golf course and a failed duty-free zone, created in the 1970s to lure manufacturers of electronic goods into setting up assembly plants. A change in economic policy made them uncompetitive, and by the mid-1990s most of the factories had closed. But the duty-free zone endured, preferring French perfumes and Italian leather goods to well-heeled cruise-ship tourists.

Tarzan layer The rain forest is a diverse and fragile multilayered ecosystem. The 'jungle' of popular imagination occurs where trees become laden with rope-like lianas, bromeliads and orchids, lichens and mosses.

Guarana crop The roasted seeds make a stimulating soft drink.

River trade Boats and barges of every description ply the world's biggest river system, bringing supplies and picking up jungle produce such as rubber and nuts.

Exploiting every niche Insect species, many of them unidentified, inhabit the forest – from floor to canopy.

Threatened Eden

It has been called the last unfinished page of Genesis and a processing plant of life. The Amazon basin contains the largest expanse of tropical forests in the world – about 1.5 million sq miles (3.9 million km²) – and by far the greatest diversity of plant and animal species of any habitat. A United Nations Earth Summit in 1992 called for its conservation as a genetic repository for the future and an important control mechanism for the world's climate, but by one estimate cutting and burning has proceeded at the rate of 20 football fields a minute, with a loss of 17 000 species a year, or two per hour. Huge tracts have been cleared for cattle ranches and peasant 'colonisation' schemes. Mining, oil exploration and hydro-electric generation have taken their toll. Lumber companies intensify their cutting, while large-scale soya bean farming is a new threat. With 14 per cent of the forest gone in the last quarter of the 20th century, some experts warned that the Amazon jungle could disappear altogether in the 21st century unless new policies are adopted. Modern satellite imaging gives a clear picture of the rate of deforestation – whether this will have enough of an impact is yet to be seen.

Big fish The pirarucu (Arapaima gigas) is the largest known freshwater fish. It can reach a length of 9 ft (2.7 m) and is commonly speared, but stocks are threatened by overfishing.

1. Howler monkey
2. Emperor tamarin (*Saguinus imperator*)
3. Coatimundi
4. Opossum
5. Puma
6. Anteater
7. Army ants
8. Tarantula
9. Amazon river turtle (*Podocnemis expansa*)
10. Anaconda
11. Para rubber tree (*Hevea brasiliensis*)
12. Harpy eagle
13. Macaw
14. Toucan
15. Sloth
16. Orchids
17. Bat
18. Spider monkey
19. Fuchsias
20. Cacao tree (*Theobroma cacao*)
21. Kinkajou
22. Iguana
23. Jaguar
24. Caiman
25. Morpho butterfly (male)
26. Freshwater dolphin
27. Piranha
28. Giant water lilies (*Victoria amazonica*)

Jungle metropolis Manaus, with a population of 1 million, is the commercial hub of the Amazon basin and an ocean terminal, despite being more than 900 miles (1450 km) upriver, on a bank of the Rio Negro, itself a tributary of the Amazon. A century ago, a rubber boom financed every luxury here, including an opera house. Now it combines chemicals and electronics manufacture with tourism.

Air-strip construction Another tear in the green carpet of Amazonia (right).

Caboclo village Mixed-race caboclos, also called cholos, have displaced Indian tribes along the main rivers. Life follows the annual cycle of the river, with a heavy dependence on fishing.

Amazonia

1 Black and tan The jet-black waters of the Rio Negro flow for miles side-by-side with the silt-laden waters of the Amazon before they eventually mingle.

2 Splash start Cascades fed by the snowmelt of the high Andes give birth to the world's mightiest river system.

3 Mid-course correction The Manu joins the Madre de Dios in the southern Peruvian jungle – a process repeated hundreds of times as tributaries meander and merge.

4 Delta The Amazon enters the Atlantic across a 185 mile (300 km) front of channels, sandbanks and low islands, one the size of Switzerland. The river discharges 3 million tons of sediment daily.

5 Living by the river Levels vary by up to 50 ft (15 m) between dry and rainy seasons. A solution is to build homes on stilts, or float them on logs.

6 Headwater The infant Amazon is called the Apurimac ('Great Oracle') because of the roar of its rapids. The Amazon undergoes seven name changes along its course.

7 River transport A dugout may be 100 ft (30 m) long and still slink through the narrowest inlet.

8 Archipelago The Anavilhanas are a chain of more than 400 islands strung along the Rio Negro. This was held as a world record until satellites mapped a still larger group farther upstream.

Flooded forest *The river and its tributaries create an ever-changing pattern of channels, lakes and backwaters and about 25 000 sq miles (65 000 km²) of annually inundated várzea forest, the most fertile and biologically complex of the region's ecological zones. Most people live here or on its margins. When flooded, the várzea sustains thousands of species of fish, including some adapted to graze on fruit and seeds!*

Out of style *This Tikuna hut reflects a roving lifestyle that is falling from favour. The Tikuna are opting for four walls and villages with schools.*

Yanomami child *The fate of future generations of the tribe is in doubt.*

Yanomami haven *The uncertain fate of the 10 000 surviving Yanomami of northern Amazonia reflects that of Amazonia itself. After coming under sustained attack from prospectors and succumbing to introduced diseases, they found uncertain sanctuary in a homeland set aside by the Brazilian government. The Yanomami live in malocas, communal houses, within palisaded villages.*

Adaptive enterprise *Some Yagua of upper Amazonia support a traditional lifestyle by making seed necklaces and blowguns for tourists. Yagua means red, the tribe's favourite colour.*

Top deck *The sunlit upper canopy 100-170 ft (30-50 m) above the ground is home to many creatures, including monkeys and sloths.*

Flower power A tiny violet-ears (Colibri) hummingbird holds station while it extracts nectar. Amazonia has dozens of species of hummingbird. Brazilians call them 'flower-kissers'.

Undress code Body paint is more congenial than clothing in the jungle. Bixa berries are widely traded for their red dye.

Cloud forest Permanent mists shroud montane forests in Ecuador, long protected by their inaccessibility but now being lost at 4 per cent per year. The Cayambe-Coca Ecological Reserve, near Quito, is an attempt to address the problem.

Endangered Giant otters are killed for their fur.

Xikrin ritual The Xikrin are among 30 tribal groups left in the Brazilian Amazon. In 1900, there were 230 groups; in 1950, they were down to 150. The pre-Columbian Indian population has been put in the millions.

The islands of evolution

The theory of evolution upon which much of modern science is based owes its inspiration to 35 days of leisurely observation among the lumbering giant tortoises and other eccentric creatures of the natural laboratory that is the Galápagos.

Genesis zone *A lava flow from lunar-like Santiago Island – in the background – has engulfed several islets in crossing the path of turquoise-beached Bartolmé Island. This was open water in Darwin's day.*

Early navigators called this strange archipelago Las Encantadas, 'the enchanted ones', for the way it would appear and then vanish within swirling mists and cloud formations. The islands were discovered in 1535, when the Bishop of Panama got blown off course on a voyage to Peru. The Bishop thought that 'God had caused it to rain stones'. The 'stones' are the tips of volcanoes rising 30 000 ft (9000 m) from a geological hot spot on the ocean floor. They form 19 islands and scores of rocky islets straddling the equator, 600 miles (1000 km) west of Ecuador.

A famous menagerie

No island is more than 5 million years old; some are hardly a million years old. In the course of this time, they have been populated by plant and animal castaways, dumped onshore by freaks of wind or current – like the Bishop of Panama, in fact. Despite a scarcity of fresh water for much of the year, hundreds of species thrived, adapted and altered – evolved – to such an extent that a third of the plants, nearly half of the birds and insects, and 90 per cent of the reptiles exist nowhere else. The Galápagos menagerie famously includes seagoing iguanas, cormorants that cannot fly, nippy little penguins that would faint at the sight of ice, and giant tortoises out of the Jurassic Age, a different kind for each island. This was not immediately apparent. The Bishop noted in his journal, 'nothing but seals and tortoises' and birds 'so silly that they do not know how to flee'.

Dash and deliberation *The giant tortoise (left), longest-lived of all creatures, and the blue-footed booby (right) make a study in evolutionary diversity.*

Darwin and the finches

Of all the exotic creatures that Darwin encountered on his five-year journey around the world, it was a group of little finches collected around the Galápagos Islands that triggered his theory of evolution. Religious beliefs of his day insisted, and science dutifully concurred, that species were immutable – fixed forever. The finches of Galápagos provided evidence to the contrary. Descended from a single pair, or a very small group that had somehow reached the islands, Darwin found 13 new types of finch with different beaks and behaviour, each one exploiting a particular habitat and diet. This is a process now known as adaptive radiation. Finches are seed-eaters, but the new forms on the Galápagos adapted to live on plants and insects, and even other birds' eggs. Mockingbirds and giant tortoises demonstrate similar adaptive radiation.

Tool user This Galápagos finch (Camarhynchus pallidus) *uses a tool – a cactus thorn – to hunt out grubs in holes in trees.*

Grown cold   A lava field on Sullivan Bay. The Galápagos is among the most active of all volcanic archipelagoes.

Natural selection

Exactly 300 years later, Charles Darwin was no more impressed. 'Gloomy sky,' he noted in his diary. 'The plants smell unpleasantly …most disgusting, clumsy lizards…such insignificant, ugly little flowers.' As for the tortoises, he wanted only to make 'capital soup' of them. HMS *Beagle,* with the young naturalist aboard, had dropped anchor for what would prove to be a vital five weeks in the course of a voyage that led to a revolution in human perception. But it was only after returning to England and studying his notes and specimens that he observed how species deviated from island to island. It was this observation of natural selection at work that led to the publication, 24 years later, of *The Origin of Species.*

Saving the tortoises

Galápagos is an old Spanish term for tortoise – a reflection of past centuries, when pirates and other mariners called at the islands and hauled the creatures off as fresh meat. They are now down from a quarter of a million to only a few thousand. Scientists at the Charles Darwin Research Station on Santa Cruz, one of four inhabited islands, now work to save the fragile ecosystem from the ravages of invaders – rats, wild dogs, feral goats, pigs, and now tourists, up 700 per cent in the last two decades of the 20th century. The resident human population has also jumped, from 2000 to 14 000. The Galápagos is caught in a classic Darwinian struggle of competing species. Mysterious, stark and otherworldly, the islands and the waters surrounding them have been declared a national park and various programmes have helped contain some of the problems. But many naturalists believe that the only way to restore and preserve the ecology would be to ban tourism entirely.

Sea monster The marine iguana of Galápagos (Amblyrhynchus cristatus) *is an extreme example of environmental adaptation. It can stay under water for several minutes, foraging seaweed and scraping algae off the rocks with specially adapted teeth. The monster look is all bluff. Here an offspring rides piggy-back.*

Robinson Crusoe's islands

The Galápagos has a 'twin' archipelago with a claim to literary fame. The steep, rain-forest clad Juan Fernandez islands, 400 miles (650 km) off the coast of Chile, are another evolutionary hideaway, with birds and plants that exist nowhere else in the world. They also share a pirate past. On one of them, Más a Tierra, Scots sailor Alexander Selkirk was marooned for four years early in the 18th century. A fictionalised account of his adventures became the Daniel Defoe classic *Robinson Crusoe.* Man Friday, Crusoe's castaway companion in the tale, was also based on a real person, though he and Selkirk were not actually marooned together. About 4000 people now live on Isla Robinson Crusoe, as it has been renamed. Lobster-fishing is the main activity.

CHAPTER 2

LAND OF EXTREMES

The Andean cultures that honoured Pachamama, the Earth-Mother, knew her as the guardian of hidden forces that could burst upon the world, spreading destruction. Those forces may explode from volcanoes or from storm-wracked skies. Cities may be destroyed in an instant by earthquakes and mud slides. Once, these forces were seen as the work of gods, or God. Now we understand the physical causes: South America is on the move, and the Andes are its bow-wave, pushed up by the collision of tectonic plates.

The mountain range is both a cauldron brewing up destruction and a frontier that creates extremes of climate. Scientists may explain catastrophes – tracking El Niño across the Pacific, recording earthquakes, monitoring every volcanic quiver – but there is no way to predict or mitigate them. Andean peoples confront the dangers, as always, with fatalism and stoic resilience in the face of disaster.

Devastation caused by floods and mud slides in Venezuela, December 1999.

El Niño, enfant terrible

Peruvian fishermen called it El Niño, the Christ child, because it made its appearance on the coast around Christmas time – a gentle current of warm water that has become a signal for alarm all around the world.

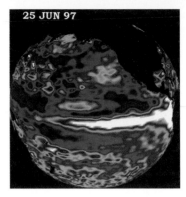

Geologists detect its imprint in sediments laid down 13 000 years ago. Archaeologists blame it for the sudden disappearance of certain prehistoric cultures, daring even to suggest specific years – AD 546 and 576, AD 1100 – when an El Niño event flooded valleys and washed away irrigation systems. Now this intermittent upheaval on the Peruvian coast is credited with sending weather around the world into a catastrophic spin.

First, the fishing failed…

The term *La corriente de El Niño* dates from the 19th century, when the pious fishermen of Paita started referring in this way to a warm southward current that had a tendency to occur off the coast around Christmas time. Paita is located on an arid stretch of coast far to the north of Lima. Early in the 20th century the writer Ernest Hemingway found the marlin fishing in the area to be excellent and El Niño remained only of local concern, even when geographers began to notice that torrential downpours coincided with years when this curious counter-current ran strongest. With the start of systematic ocean study in the late 1950s, scientific interest

El Niño was here   *This scene in Milagro, near Guayaquil, was typical of conditions in Ecuador in November 1997.*

Predicting El Niño: ancient and modern

Ocean detectors enable scientists to predict the onset of an El Niño. They scored their first success in 1997, when they were able to warn governments 4 months in advance. Buoys carrying instruments are strung across the Pacific Ocean on either side of the equator. Via satellite they send daily data relating to surface winds, ocean currents and water temperature, from which meteorologists can prepare computer models. Satellites are also able to detect the height of the ocean to within approximately 1 in (2.5 cm). This is important, because the ocean surface swells under low pressure, warm water conditions – the variation can be as much as 18 in (46 cm). Andean villagers have a more ancient method: they look to the Pleiades star cluster. If the Pleiades do not twinkle brightly, potato-planting is delayed. Researchers who learned of this method checked with satellite data and found that high clouds form around the winter solstice in El Niño years, obscuring the Pleiades and providing a fairly reliable weather prediction.

in El Niño intensified, but the world took no notice until a particularly strong El Niño in 1972-3 knocked out Peru's commercial fishing industry, the biggest in the world. Thereafter, the name El Niño was applied to spectacular happenings, rather than to the original annual event.

On the screen A satellite image (left) captures the Trans-Pacific flow of warm water triggering an El Niño event. Temperatures are colour-registered.

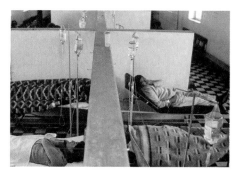

Epidemics in its wake Cholera patients in a Lima hospital. Deadly hantavirus transmitted by a rodent plague added to the toll.

...then came La Niña

El Niño is now known to fit into an oceanic seesaw that scientists collectively refer to as the El Niño-Southern Oscillation, or ENSO. The key factor is the displacement of a pool of warm water, normally in the tropical western Pacific, and much colder water commonly in the eastern Pacific. A shift in air pressure and trade winds can send the warm water eastwards to reverse climatic conditions on either side of the ocean, and by a knock-on effect, to tip climates upside down all around the world. Climatologists call this propensity 'global teleconnections'. A full ENSO runs for 3-6 years, with the intense El Niño phase lasting about a year. When conditions are back to normal, there may be a period of climatic overadjustment that scientists have dubbed La Niña (little girl). Twelve ENSOs were identified in the second half of the 20th century. The El Niño of 1982-3 was stronger than anything previously recorded, with sea temperatures in the eastern Pacific up by 10°C (18°F).

Explosion of life, then starvation

Still more dramatic was the El Niño cycle that began in November 1997 with torrential rains falling along the coasts of Ecuador, Peru and Chile and causing unprecedented dislocation through flooding, washaways and landslides. Before reversing in 1998, the El Niño was also held responsible for record rainfall in China, drought and fires in Indonesia, flooding in East Africa, crop failure in southern Africa and Cuba, and tornadoes in the USA. Events on the Galápagos mirrored the drama in microcosm. Unprecedented rains stimulated an explosion of life – only for the unnaturally warm waters to destroy or drive off plankton, worms, barnacles, clams and fish, and litter beaches with the bodies of sea lions and boobies. Marine iguanas suffered, too, for the warm water halted the growth of the algae on which they existed.

Death from the mountain A landslide following torrential rains destroyed 80 per cent of Santa Teresa, Peru, on January 15, 1998.

Drowned town At Naranjal, Ecuador, flooding associated with El Niño took at least 41 lives and drove survivors from their homes.

Unnatural disasters

While global warming is suspected of increasing the potency of El Niño, there is no question that human activity is compounding the impact of both, by contributing to the capacity of flood and drought to create havoc.

Lima *Like Caracas, Peru's capital is susceptible to earthquake as well as flood.*

On the night of December 15, 1999, along 60 miles (96 km) of coast below the Venezuelan capital, Caracas, relentless rains loosened the sides of the Avila mountain range and massive mud slides carried all before them into the sea. The death toll was estimated at between 30 000 and 50 000. Through lack of urban planning or regulation, deforested slopes notoriously liable to landslides had become crammed with countless thousands of *ranchitos*, fragile squatters' shacks made from scrap and cardboard. 'This was bound to happen, whether set off by an earthquake or heavy rain', commented Teolinda Bolívar, architect and author of a book on the Caracas slums. Other South American cities are similarly ringed by ramshackle slums and under jeopardy from flood or earthquake.

Sechura *An encampment for flood victims in the Peruvian desert in February 1998.*

Flames in the rain forest

A new danger threatening the Amazon was demonstrated in 1998, when the same El Niño that inundated the Pacific coast caused such a drought in parts of Amazonia that the rain forest caught alight. In two months, an area the size of Belgium was reduced to ashes. Fire is not part of the normal ecology of this humid zone, but a recurrence of bad fires in the latter part of the 20th century led some researchers to conclude that the Amazon basin is becoming drier. Human activity contributes to this: a study in 1999 of an area north of Manaus, where the rain forest has been fragmented by roads and agricultural development, found this was sufficient to allow sunlight and hot winds to penetrate. A flaming Amazon releases enormous amounts of carbon dioxide and contributes to global warming.

Putting a price on El Niño

A predicted result of the 'greenhouse effect' of global warming is that a warmer world will be accompanied by an increased frequency of extreme conditions. This is because more heat means more evaporation and more wind energy – hence more violent weather. The cost of natural disasters in the 1990s was put at four times the level of the 1980s. Insurance industry experts attributed 80 natural catastrophes to the influence of the 1997-8 El Niño cycle and put the cost of repairing the damage at over $36 billion.

Amazonia *A fire-ravaged area of rain forest in the Xingu National Park in February 1998, following the drought caused by El Niño.*

The Antarctic winter

Winter in Antarctica – the coldest and windiest place on earth. As temperatures plummet, a thousand scientists are locked into the darkness of a frozen continent that is itself locked into a frozen ocean.

The ancients reasoned that for the earth to remain balanced, there had to be a big continent lending stability down below, so Terra Australis Incognito was entered on the map. This stimulated endless speculation. Alexander Dalrymple, hydrographer to the Admiralty, wanted to colonise it for Britain, seeing here a better prospect than America. He was forestalled by Captain Cook, who tracked a rim of ice right around the southern ocean and reported that beyond must lie 'everlasting frigidness'.

Extreme cold...

Dalrymple never believed Cook and might today find slight solace in the emergence of an Antarctic tourist industry. But the tourists nudging the ice pack in their cruise ships are gone when the sun disappears for the one month of twilight and five months of frigid night that is the Antarctic winter. More than three-quarters of the continent's shifting scientific community also withdraw for the winter, leaving some 1000 specialist and support staff in 40 stations dotted across 5.3 million sq miles (13.2 million km²) of terrain as alien

Emilio – the first Antarctican

The first person to be born in Antarctica was Emilio Palma, son of a commander of Argentina's Esperanza Base, on January 7, 1978. The base, located on the Antarctica Peninsula, has seen territorial rivalry between Argentina and Chile. Both countries sought to name the peninsula after a national hero – making it Tierra San Martin to Argentinians and Tierra O'Higgins to Chileans.

The neighbours   The solidly built emperor penguin also winters over – a lone companion species for the communities of researchers.

and unexplored as the other side of the moon. Whereas the midsummer temperature on the Antarctica Peninsula may climb as high as 15°C (59°F), temperatures in July and August can drop to –30°C (–22°F) on the coast and –70°C (–94°F) on the high interior ice sheet. An all-time low of –89.2°C (–128.6°F) was measured at Vostok, the Russian station at the heart of Antarctica, on July 21, 1983.

...and ferocious winds

More menacing still is the super-cooling factor of wind-chill, often allied with winds of extraordinary ferocity. A French base in Adèle Land, East Antarctica, claims a record with gusts of 200 mph (320 km/h) reported in 1977. The threat is greatest from cold, dense air masses that tumble downslope from the interior heights. Known as katabatic winds, they may turn turbulent in an instant, creating blinding blizzards. Perhaps not surprisingly, 'winter-over syndrome', or 'long-eye' – a combination of anxiety, sleeplessness and depression – is a major health problem.

Wrapped up   At –70°C (–94°F) flesh freezes in under 30 seconds.

Return of the sun   Time to explore the awesome landscape.

Mountains on the move

There are towns in the Andes where ominous cracks in the wall are held to be a good sign. The reasoning goes that if a building has survived one earthquake, then it may very well survive the next. A determined fatalism marks life here.

On February 20, 1835, Charles Darwin and his assistant Covington were in an apple orchard near Valdivia, Chile, when a wind whipped through the trees and the ground trembled. They leapt up, feeling giddy and sick. 'The world, the very emblem of all that is solid, moved beneath our feet like crust over a fluid', Darwin wrote. Sailing up the coast, they found that a chain of volcanoes had erupted, awakened by an earthquake that had demolished the town of Concepción and its port, Talcahuano.

Raising up the Andes

Survivors described how the ground heaved and split along fissures reeking of sulphur; how the sea drained out of the harbour, then swept back in a succession of tidal waves, tossing ships ashore, picking up houses and sucking them back into whirlpools. A survey found the shoreline had risen by as much as 6 ft (1.8 m), and Darwin dared to speculate that the mountains were being raised out of the sea by volcanic activity. He was quite close in this speculation, for we now know that the Andes were formed by sections of the earth's crust colliding – one carrying the South American continent and the other, the Nazca plate, extending beneath the eastern Pacific. The continental plate is subducting (riding over) the oceanic plate. The heaving, buckling and immense subterranean heat generated by the process account for the spectacular rise of the Andes and for the many volcanoes. In 1960, Valdivia was itself hit by an

Earthquake drill *Peruvian schools maintain a constant alert, prepared for quick evacuation in case of an emergency.*

Earthquake aftermath *Survivors shelter among the debris in Armenia, Colombia.*

Armenia, Colombia, January 15, 1999 Unreinforced concrete buildings were deathtraps (right), and lack of drinking water was a problem for the survivors (left).

Cities that topple

Earthquakes have always been a part of Andean life. Archaeologists marvel at the determination of ancient peoples such as the Moche and the Chimú, who continually struggled against tectonic upheavals that kept tilting their carefully calculated irrigation systems out of alignment. The Inca built with monumental blocks, and the other native peoples used clay and straw – both admirable ways of minimising casualties. But the Spanish conquistadores raised European cities, which tumbled in an earthquake, and tumble still. Santiago in 1593, Lima in 1746, Caracas in 1812, Quito in 1587, 1768 and 1859 – every Andean capital has been flattened at least once, so that rebuilding cathedrals has become a practised art. The old colonial seat of Popayán in Colombia lost its cathedral in Holy Week 1983, and was raised from the rubble in record time.

Screams, prayers and looters

To Armenia, in the *zona cafetera* coffee-growing belt due north of Popayán, fell the fate of being the last city to be toppled by an earthquake in the 20th century: it was on January 25, 1999, and the quake registered 6 on the Richter scale. Buildings constructed of unreinforced concrete, one of the least earthquake-proof materials imaginable, collapsed. More than 1000 people died and 30 000 were left homeless. As panicking crowds fled, armed gangs of looters moved in, some disguised as Red Cross workers. Crowds of sightseers hampered rescue efforts and it was not until a week later that heavily armed troops restored order. UNICEF workers used boiled eggs to demonstrate the earth's composition to traumatised children, explaining that what they had been through was natural. In 2001, Peru suffered death and mass injuries due to an earthquake, measuring 7.9 on the Richter scale.

undersea earthquake virtually identical to the one Darwin witnessed, complete with spontaneously ignited volcanoes and 100 ft (30 m) tidal waves, including a tsunami backwash that rolled across the Pacific to spread further death on the coasts of Hawaii and Japan. In 1970, an earthquake measuring 7.7 on the Richter scale triggered one of the worst natural disasters of the 20th century. Most of the 70 000 deaths were caused by rock and ice dislodged from 22 205 ft (6768 m) Mount Huascarán, Peru's highest peak, that dropped onto the town of Yungay, burying it completely.

Earthquakes and volcanoes

Map legend:
- ⇨ Subduction zone
- – – Major faultline
- ▲ Active volcano
- ● Major earthquake
- ● Other earthquake
- ◻ Volcanic island

Map labels: CARIBBEAN PLATE, Nevado del Ruiz, Cotopaxi, Amazon, El Misti, NAZCA PLATE, Juan Fernández Islands, Azul, SOUTH AMERICAN PLATE, SCOTIA PLATE, ANTARCTICA

Watching the Andes grow

It is now possible to watch the Andes grow inch-by-inch, thanks to the space-based Global Positioning System. In 1998, a research team placed 43 radio receivers along the colliding crustal plates and also high in the mountains. By timing signals from the GPS satellite array, the team was able to precisely calculate the positional change of each receiver over the course of a year. Their findings were that the Nazca plate under the Pacific Ocean moved eastwards by 3 in (7.5 cm). Of this amount, 1.4 in (3.5 cm) slid below the South American continental plate and 0.3 in (0.7 cm) rumpled upwards, adding to the Andes. The remaining 1.3 in (3.3 cm) compressed like a coiled spring, ready to release its energy in an earthquake.

Volcanoes of fire and ice

Their often perfect cones, capped with ice, confer a majestic beauty upon the Andes. They are the apu, *lord guardians of the people whose lands they fertilise and water – and who they might at any moment choose to destroy.*

Andean volcanoes explode rather than erupt. Vulcanologists explain that this is due to the chemical composition of their magma, or molten rock. Viscous and relatively cool at under 1000°C (1832°F), it contains pent-up gases that are released at very high pressure, cannoning out the lava in large chunks and pyroclastic fragments, or tephra. Their other characteristic is a consequence of their loftiness and their glaciated cones. When the cannon goes off, the tephra melts the ice cap to create a torrent of mud, cinders and ash, known as a lahar, which surges down the volcano's flanks obliterating everything in its path.

Cotopaxi Lava boils constantly in the monster's crater.

The instant death of Armero

This is what happened to the town of Armero on the night of November 13, 1985, when a comparatively modest, explosive eruption from one of a score of active volcanoes in Colombia's Cordillera Central turned into one of the most lethal in recorded history. The explosion dumped millions of tons of incandescent tephra on the ice cap ringing the 17 717 ft (5 400 m) Nevado del Ruiz. Lahars cresting at between 15 and 50 ft (4.5-15 m) tore down the canyons to almost bury the sleeping town of Armero, 30 miles (48 km) to the east and a vertical drop of almost 3 miles (5 km) from the crater rim. About 24 000 people died in Armero, many of them still in their beds. Another slide, down the western face of the mountain, killed a further 1000 inhabitants of the town of Chinchiná.

Lord of the earthquakes

The Quechua-speaking people of the Andes call the mountains *apu*, 'lord', the same title that was applied to the Lord Inca and to the *apus* who ruled over each quarter of the Inca Empire. To the *runa*, the native Andeans, the mountain is sensed as an ancestor, protector and life-source, sometimes identified with a spiritual entity called a *wamani*. In Inca times, human sacrifices – usually a young person richly robed and left to die of exposure near the summit – were on occasion offered to certain volcanoes. And still today offerings of coca, alcohol or food are left on high passes.

Under the volcano Ecuadorian herdsmen beneath multi-cratered Chimborazo (20 702 ft/6310 m). Their ancestors offered human sacrifices to the mountain.

Bolivian sentinel *Tunupa looms over the Salar de Uyuni, on Bolivia's altiplano.*

Calculating the odds

With thousands of volcanoes making up South America's *Cadena del Fuego* (Chain of Fire) and several score active at any time, the rarity of such catastrophes in historical times has been a miracle. From Colombia to Cape Horn, ranged on the oceanic side of the Andes, are some of the highest densities of volcanoes in the world. The Armero disaster offers a lesson on increasing risk. In 1845, a similar mud flow following much the same path killed about 1000 people, but the town of Armero did not then exist, only farms. Nevado del Ruiz exploded violently in 1595 and geological evidence indicates that the fallout reached all the way to Panama, an appalling prospect nowadays.

Among volcanoes that cast a shadow over major cities, the vulcanologists pick out El Misti, whose perfect snow-capped cone, rising to 19 098 ft (5821 m), towers over the beautiful city of Arequipa, Peru. Misti, which last erupted during an earthquake in 1600, is, they say, a perfect candidate for the unthinkable.

Morning after *The Nevado del Ruiz eruption caused one of the worst disasters of the past 200 years.*

Running the gauntlet

The Avenue of the Volcanoes is a gauntlet of 51 volcanic peaks running through the heart of Ecuador. It includes the world's highest continuously active volcano, Cotopaxi (19 347 ft/ 5897 m), and the most active volcano, Sangay (17 158 ft/ 5230 m). Sangay, brooding over the old Inca highway from Cuzco to Quito, erupts daily. Cotopaxi hisses steam and bides its time. At night, the glow from its crater lights up the clouds. In the 19th century, thousands died when magma exploded from its sides. Pichincha (15 338 ft/ 4675 m) towers over the capital, Quito, periodically dusting it with ash and forcing the closure of the airport and schools. Experts put the likelihood of a future eruption at 90 per cent. Yet another volcano, Tungurahua, brought ruin to the country's most popular resort, Baños, in 1999. The government ordered total evacuation after the volcano awoke, glowing and rattling windows with loud explosions. In 2002, the volcano Reventador, 60 miles east of Quito, erupted but caused no fatalities.

CHAPTER 3

PEOPLE AND RESOURCES

The potential of South America's resources and agriculture is vast. All too often, however, development perpetuates inequalities established under colonial rule, when gold and silver poured from mines worked by Indian labour, and slaves tended coffee and sugar-cane plantations to please European palates. But South America has other growing assets in its ambitious and educated young, in the export of manufactured goods (in which Brazil excels), in its business elites and a new generation of scientists and technicians eager for progress. Their growing economic power may spotlight the gulf between rich and poor, but it also inspires the hope that South America can escape from debt and lessen the colossal burden of poverty.

Steelworks in Ciudad Guayana, Venezuela.

The troubles with oil

Like motorists everywhere, Venezuelans love to complain about the price of petrol. But one thing sets them apart: at less than 40 cents a gallon, petrol in Venezuela is cheaper than bottled water.

Tempting target *Oil pipelines snaking over the Andes have been regularly sabotaged by guerrilla groups. Earthquakes can be a problem, too.*

Lake Maracaibo *Abandoned derricks litter the lake that has been called a 'garbage pail'.*

In December 1922, an exploratory drill bit into rich oil deposits beneath Lake Maracaibo and blew the expectations of Venezuelans sky-high, where they remain to this day. This nation of 25 million people has the greatest oil reserves outside the Middle East. At first, dictator Juan Vincente Gómez grabbed for himself what US oil companies did not take, but by the 1950s oil money was transforming Caracas.

Riots in the city, war in the jungle

In 1960, Venezuela conceived and founded OPEC, the cartel of oil-producing nations, and went on a prolonged binge that earned affluent Venezuelans the nickname 'Saudis of the West'. When the oil price collapsed in the 1980s, decades of self-indulgence among the élite had frittered away the wealth and asphyxiated the rest of the economy, leaving Venezuela with nothing to fall back on. The consequences included runaway inflation, bank collapses, currency devaluations and violent riots. Close to 70 per cent of Venezuelans were left in extreme poverty. 'Columbus discovered us, Bolívar liberated us, and oil ruined us', Venezuelans like to say.

Now oil is welling up in Colombia, Ecuador and Peru, with derricks sprouting in the rain forests of the upper Amazon basin, nudging aside the jaguar and the anaconda and one-time headhunting tribes like the Shuar. The oil finds are major, adding fuel to an explosive situation. For hereabouts is grown the coca leaf for much of the world's illicit cocaine. As well as the drug rings, the coca trade helps fund Colombia's left-wing guerrilla armies and is a lure for ruthless paramilitary forces of the right.

Oil has become the most important commodity for both Ecuador and Colombia, easily outstripping even coffee, as well as a focus of concern for the guerrillas and the region's increasingly politicised underclasses. Oilmen are regularly kidnapped for ransom and pipelines carrying the crude oil to Pacific ports have been sabotaged hundreds of times, adding to an already serious pollution problem. But the stakes are too high for anyone to let go.

Brazil's solution: sugar and the deep blue sea

In the 1970s Brazil inaugurated a programme that substituted sugar for petroleum. By 1990, about 4.5 million Brazilian cars were running on ethanol, an alcohol distilled from the country's abundant supply of sugar cane. The *álcool* costs the motorist less, but not the Brazilian government, which lavished $7 billion (£10.5 billion) on the programme, much of this in subsidies to the *usineiros*, the sugar barons. Brazilian cars now run on gasohol, petrol with just a small amount of *álcool* added. The country is able to meet three-quarters of its petroleum needs, thanks to some of the most advanced offshore drilling technology in the world.

The Brazilian state oil company Petrobras has repeatedly set deep-sea records with oil wells off the Rio coast. By 1999, it was recovering oil from depths of over 6000 ft (1800 m) and preparing to go deeper still.

Fuel sweetener *A pump attendant fills up a car with álcool.*

From wine to rockets

South American nations, long subject to the boom-and-bust dangers of dependence upon a solitary resource, have been expanding their horizons. The results include fine Andean wines and an Amazonian space programme.

Argentina is synonymous with beef, and Chile produces more copper than anywhere else in the world, but lately it is their wines that have become a subject for discussion around the world. Fine wines had been made in Chile's fertile central valley for centuries before experiment turned to fashionable international styles of cabernet sauvignons, sometimes blended with merlot. Over the Andes, Argentina has scored with dark, juicy reds from the malbec grape. Argentine vineyards share Chile's natural advantages. The warm, dry air (excepting calamitous El Niño years) means fewer diseases and growers do not need to graft their vines to root stock resistant to phylloxera, the bane of vineyards elsewhere. Melted snow from the mountains provides perfect, plentiful irrigation.

No country has suffered more from boom and bust than Brazil – sugar, gold, diamonds, cotton, rubber and coffee have all shaken the continent's largest nation through some abrupt reversal in fortune. Consequently, no country has been more intent upon diversification, establishing in the latter half of the 20th century its own petrochemicals, automobile, shipbuilding, aviation and armaments industries.

Brazil's 21st-century ambitions extend to a space programme, with a spaceport at Alcântara on the eastern edge of Amazonia, a joint satellite programme with China, and launch contracts signed with the USA and the Ukraine. A few hundred miles to the north-east, at Kourou in French Guiana, is the launch site used by the European Space Agency. In May 2000, Bell Aerospace of Texas signed a deal to build yet another launch site, in neighbouring Guyana.

Next, a ski resort? Summer scene at a coastal base in Adèle Land. Permanent shore accommodation for tourists is a likely next step for Antarctica.

Argentine wine label La Rural is one of 1200 bodegas (wineries) under the Andes near Mendoza. It is only a short flight from the vineyards of Chile (below).

What to make of Antarctica?

Idealists work to create an Antarctic World Park, but realists suspect the treaty that protects the frozen continent as a preserve of science will hold only so long as its minerals stay beyond reach. Only coal and iron have been confirmed so far, but the copper-rich Andes and gold and platinum-bearing belts of South Africa and Australia all seem to extend into Antarctica, contiguous to where the continents were once joined. Of more immediate interest is the presence of oil, first detected in 1973. Antarctica has been proposed as a deep-freeze storehouse for global grain reserves – and more controversially as the safest place in which to dispose of radioactive wastes. Its icebergs could water the deserts, if only a cheap haulage system could be devised.

Eldorados everywhere

Gold was the sweat of the sun and silver the tears of the moon to the Inca, who had no sense of money and were perplexed by the greed of the Spaniards. It has been sweat and tears ever since.

Mining in South America is not for the faint-hearted. Past centuries of exploitation are best drama-tised by the splendour and hor-ror of Potosí, the city whose mines funded the Renaissance and facilitated the birth of cap-italism. Around two billion ounces of silver were extracted, with each coin minted costing the lives of ten Indians, accord-ing to a 17th-century chronicler.

Opportunities for all   Panning for gold with bateas, *shallow wooden bowls.*

A horror that endures

Bolivia finally closed the Potosí mines in 1985, but unemployed miners trickled back to set up their own cooperatives. Most of Potosí's population of 120 000 are Quechua Indians, who scratch a living from the warren of old workings with pick and dynamite, flickering lamp and no insurance. They toil in extreme temperatures at extreme altitude, chewing on coca-leaf wads to keep going. Most of them have respiratory problems and many will die from silicosis; *palliris,* miners' wid-ows, are a common sight scav-enging near mine shafts.

Something of the Potosí spirit of determined desperation marks all of South American mining. In Chile, it is evident in the *pirquineros,* individuals with their own tiny ore extraction operations, but also in the tough and proud miners in the giant state copper-mining operations. In Brazil, it can get completely out of hand. Ever since 18th-century *bandeirantes* (slave-hunters) from São Paulo found gold in the hilly country north of Rio de Janeiro, prospecting has been a mob activ-ity. Early in the 1980s, a high gold price helped stimulate history's most bizarre gold rush, with 40 000 *garimpeiros* milling like ants around 'the pit', a rich alluvial deposit in the Tocatins valley at Serra Pelada. *Garimpeiros* are transient gold-miners, will-o'-the-wisps who had been panning the rain forest for years, but now as many as 600 000 invaded the Amazon, polluting waterways with the mercury they used in extracting the gold, and spreading disease to remote Indian tribes.

Wresting iron out of the Amazon

The plague of *garimpeiros* was an unwelcome side effect of a grandiose scheme that began in the 1970s with the development of a major iron ore deposit in the Carajá area west of the Tocatins. South America has about a fifth of the world's reserves of iron ore, with the most significant beds in Brazil and Venezuela. In Venezuela, huge open-cast mines and

Massed **garimpeiros**
Traditionally loners, jungle gold-miners swarm where pickings are rich. The child-miner of Serra Pelada (right) has a load of sediment scooped from the depths of the pit.

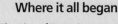

Gold town *A Wild West atmosphere pervades the prospectors' ramshackle settlements. This one is in Venezuela, near the border with Brazil.*

attendant steel, aluminium and iron ore plants at Ciudad Guayana, have transformed the lower Orinoco. Brazil first exploited iron deposits in Minas Gerais, then came Grande Carajás, a multi-billion-dollar scheme to open up the south-east Amazon. As well as the world's richest lode of iron ore, there are seams of gold, copper, nickel, manganese, tin and bauxite; the attendant infrastructure includes a rail link with the Atlantic coast, river ports able to take ocean-going bulk carriers, and the world's fifth-largest hydroelectric power plant.

The dream ticket

The core operation has been well managed, but developments such as dam construction, lumbering, ranching and settlement proved so destructive to the environment that some ancillary projects have been placed on hold. Nothing, however, holds back the flow of poor Brazilians who take their chances with a ticket on the Carajás train – 700 000 travellers a year. Completed in 1985, the 550 mile (890 km) line from the sweltering port city of São Luis runs through landscapes scarred by helter-skelter colonisation. Some halts have mushroomed into boom-towns with belching factories and housing developments; others are still little more than a jungle clearing.

Pay dirt *Extracting Brazil's wealth is no gentle affair at Carajá (inset) and at an alluvial gold operation near Pocone (below).*

Where it all began

The city of Potosí was once as big as London and many times as opulent, but now, says official historian Valentin Abeca, 'It is so poor, it makes you weep'. At 13 045 ft (3976 m) Potosí is the highest city in the world, though its fame rests still higher – in Cerro Rico, the honeycombed mountain of ore that looms over its narrow streets, balconied mansions and ornate churches – all from colonial times. UNESCO has declared Potosí a World Heritage Site and is backing restoration of the city centre and conservation of the mountain. But the Bolivian government thinks that even after 455 years it can get more out of *El Cerro Rico* and has a mind to offer it to the highest bidder – perhaps to level as an open-cast site!

An agricultural revolution

Argentina and Brazil combined represent the world's third largest agricultural market after the United States and China. The old ways of the sleepy hacienda have been replaced by high-powered agribusiness.

Think potatoes. Think tomatoes. Think beans, maize (corn), cocoa, avocados, pineapples, guavas, courgettes and the other squashes, brazil nuts, cashews and peanuts. There is more, but the point is made – the modern world would be hard to imagine without the legacy of the prehistoric South American farmer.

The Fidel Castro factor

Today, the popular image is of vast herds of cattle on the pampa and of sheep in Patagonia – and of bananas, perhaps. It is a reality in transition, however, for farming in South America has been changing faster than at any time since the Spaniards destroyed the agricultural empire of the Inca, 450 years ago. Well into the 20th century, colonial-style peonage remained the rule on large and inefficient agricultural estates, *latifundios* (also *haciendas, fazendas, estancias*) owned by a *criollo* élite at the centre of political and economic power.

It took the 1959 Cuban Revolution to arouse anxieties, embodied in a call from the USA for 'progressive' land reforms. In Ecuador, for instance, Indians were not freed from compulsory agricultural labour until 1964. That was the decade in which most countries began to expropriate land

Bound for sale *Bundles of straw for basketmaking, bound for an Andean market.*

for redistribution to varying effect. The avowed aim was to alleviate poverty and limit class conflict, but more telling was a desire to modernise agriculture as a stimulus for exports. The contrary long-term result was increased rural unemployment, poverty and flight.

Carnations, soya beans and murder

Modernisation meant mechanisation, the removal of small tenant farmers and sharply reduced labour forces. Through the 1990s, for instance, the workforce in the Brazilian sugar industry declined from 1.2 million to 700 000 even as the harvest increased from 13 to 20 million tons, to severely depress the world sugar price. Capital-intensive, large-scale commercial farming evolved inevitably into a new form

Amazon banana market *Bananas were the original agribusiness product. In 1928, machine guns were turned on striking plantation workers in Colombia. The United Fruit Company of the USA was then the biggest corporation in the region: it was nicknamed* El Pulpo, *the Octopus.*

Ploughing the Andes *Without even oxen to help (left), these mountain slopes were more productive in Inca times. Old techniques are under review.*

Gardening on a grand scale *A large 'truck farming' operation outside Rio de Janeiro. Growing vegetables for the big cities is a major industry, often ignored.*

of agriculture, often referred to as 'agribusiness' and frequently involving investment from multinational companies. Thus Colombia curiously becomes the supplier of carnations to much of the world. A supreme example of the triumphs and tragedies of agribusiness is Brazil, where soya beans became the most valuable export crop by the late 1980s, and cattle ranching cut swathes out of the Amazon basin. Brazil has one of the world's most unequal patterns of land distribution: one per cent of landowners own half the agricultural land, much of it idle, bought for speculation. Ranchers with great political power are ranged against millions of 'landless' families backed by a Landless Workers Movement, which lost more than 1000 activists to murder in the 1990s. The 75 million South Americans who still live by subsistence agriculture, under increasingly difficult circumstances, are often forgotten.

Chocolate in the raw *Sacks of cacao beans in a Brazilian warehouse. The cacao tree originated in the Orinoco-Amazon region. Aztec lords sipped xocolati from golden cups, adding spices and flowers to enhance the flavour.*

Round-up *Hereford cattle were first imported to Argentina from Britain in the 19th century.*

Lean times in beef country

Argentina grew rich on the back of its beef herds after the development of cold storage in the 1870s and heavy British investment turned it into the world's largest meat exporter. Today Argentina is among the world's largest exporters of soya beans and wheat, and one of the largest producers of wool and wine, but beef production is in decline, with exports making up only 10 per cent of the total. Changing public tastes and a failure to adapt traditional ways, are two of the reasons why some meat-packing plants have closed and some *estancieros* (ranchers) have gone bankrupt or switched to other forms of farming. Many *estancias* take in 'paying-guest' tourists to help pay the bills.

The *gaucho* and the *llanero*: tough and tougher

South America has nourished two cowboy traditions, each much tougher than the North American variety. The *gaucho* of the Argentine and Uruguayan pampa and the *llanero* of the Venezuelan savannah both originated as hunters of wild cattle. Their heyday ended with the fencing of the plains. For the *gaucho*, this happened more than a century ago, whereas cattle roamed free on the torrid *llanos* until the 1950s. The *gaucho* has been mythologised, whereas *llaneros* are still part of a living tradition, working under extreme conditions. Parched for half a year, the plains then flood and the *llaneros* must grapple with alligators as well as their bucking broncos.

Oceans of fish, with a catch

South America's hundreds of thousands of traditional fishermen get left behind and often forgotten in the race by governments to modernise fleets and compete in burgeoning world markets.

Processing for export *Foreign investment helped Chile become one of the world's leading fishing nations. This plant is in Puerto Montt, a busy port in southern Chile.*

Chimbote, on the barren coast of Peru, was a little seaside village where the fishermen cast their nets from *caballitos del mar* ('little sea-horses'), peapod-shaped boats made from bundled reeds. Then, midway through the 20th century, Chimbote quite suddenly became a rumbustious processing centre for the largest fish catch in the world.

From fish to fowl

By 1970, the catch had reached a record 13 million tons. But, that same year, Chimbote was flattened by an earthquake, then in 1972, the Peruvian fishery collapsed. Down the coast, Chile took Peru's place and learned from Peru's mistakes. What was going on here? As with agriculture, so with fishing – it was the advent of large-scale commercialisation. The catch in question was enormous schools of anchovies, trawled in the famous Humboldt Current, unloaded by conveyor and dumped into hoppers for rendering into fishmeal to feed the pigs and poultry of North America and Europe. And the anchovies were also fed back to fish in Chile, where 'aquaculture' – in this case the farming of salmon and trout – was about to become a major enterprise.

Chilean salmon farm *The fish are raised in submerged cages and are artificially fed. Much of the catch is destined for the Japanese market.*

El Niño and after

The story properly began in 1947, when Chile, backed by Peru and later by Ecuador, was first in the world to challenge an ancient freedom of the seas by unilaterally extending its territorial waters from the traditional 3 miles (4.8 km) to 200 miles (320 km) offshore. Chile at that time was a whaling nation and wanted to drive from its waters the new postwar factory ships of its rivals. But Peru and Ecuador were from the first intent upon protecting their fish stocks, tuna and the sardine-like *anchoveta* in particular. The Californian sardine fishery, made famous by John Steinbeck's novels *Cannery Row* and *Sweet Thursday*, had just then collapsed from over-fishing, and seizing the opportunity Peru went into the *anchoveta* business with a vengeance. Heedless of warnings from marine biologists, the

Waiting for scraps *Pelicans crowd around a fisherman's boat.*

Lesson of the past

Having in the past squandered fabulous guano deposits on the offshore islands over thousands of years, Peru is at pains to facilitate their replenishment by its millions of sea birds. The islands are protected reserves, banned to visitors. Harvesting of the guano is strictly controlled and conducted at times when the birds are not nesting. An estimated 20 million tons of guano was dug from the Chinchas, Ballestras, Lobos and other island groups in the 19th century. Rich in phosphorus and potash, guano is a valuable fertiliser for farming.

Bagging guano *The work is arduous and unhealthy. Ammonia fumes shrivel the skin and can cause blindness.*

Ports

Atlantic Ocean

Pacific Ocean

Atlantic Ocean

■ Principal ports

Peruvians expanded their fleet and doubled their catch to unsustainable levels. In March 1972, the rising water temperatures of an El Niño event depleted the fish stocks and when the schools moved inshore in search of cooler water, the fleet fished them out. For ten years, it seemed the catch would never recover, but it did, as did Chimbote – now a city of 300 000 inhabitants.

Small fishermen squeezed out

Caught in the backwash of such major events were hundreds of thousands of traditional fishermen, marginalised in every sense, though still providing the bulk of domestic needs. In north-east Brazil, for instance, heavily capitalised commercial fleets treated with disdain the *lei do respeito*, customary respect due to local *mestres*, the skippers with exclusive rights to particular fishing locations.

Also, in markets controlled by increasingly powerful middlemen, small fishermen lost out badly. The economic straits of Peru's traditional section became apparent after the 1998 El Niño knocked out nearly 200 jetties and damaged 2000 small fishing craft. Many fishermen could not afford the repairs.

Jangadas *The traditional Brazilian fishing craft are basically big surfboards. Their design is pre-Colombian, and the triangular sail was a Portuguese contribution.*

Ecuador's prawn farms are cause for concern

Ecuador is the world's second-biggest producer of prawns, with one in five inhabitants of coastal provinces reliant on the industry. Its 2000 prawn farms occupy 500 000 acres (200 000 ha), an area the size of the Channel Islands. In 1999 the prawn pools, each the size of a football field, produced 150 000 tons of prawns, reaping $900 million (£600 million), but crowding out ecologically important mangrove swamps and dumping a cocktail of chemicals, fishmeal and prawn faeces into rivers and estuaries. Of all booming forms of aquaculture, prawn-farming is the most controversial.

Chile: miracle or mirage?

Chile became the economic tiger of South America through policies introduced at the point of a gun.
The big question was whether the strategies would endure under democracy.

Santiago *The years of economic boom have lent lustre to Chile's capital – and many tall buildings to its skyline.*

Late in the 20th century, Chile became the model for economic change in South America by being the first country to privatise state enterprises, slash tariffs, liberalise investment and welcome foreign capital. One consequence was a dozen straight years of record growth. This was enough to persuade others to adopt the so-called Washington consensus in support of privatisation, free trade and fiscal sobriety. In Washington and on Wall Street, and in smart new Santiago boardrooms, they called this the Chilean Miracle.

Will 'trickle-down' trickle down?

In 1970, Chile had South America's first democratically elected Socialist government, which gave grave offence by nationalising the copper industry and breaking up the huge estates of wealthy and often absentee owners. In 1973, a bloody coup jerked the country hard right under the military dictatorship of General Pinochet and the ministrations of the Chicago Boys, technocrats schooled in the 'neo-liberal' economics of Milton Friedman at the University of Chicago. Reversing virtually every policy of the past, Pinochet and the Boys created a free-market economy, enforced if necessary by death squads. Subsidies were eliminated and protective tariffs slashed, as was public spending. From the trauma emerged new export sectors, such as fruit and wines. After 1990, when Pinochet relinquished power, the Chilean economy became the envy of the continent. The new civilian government retained the free-market policies and the combination of an educated yet low-paid workforce proved attractive to foreign investors, so that economic growth increased still further, until the Asian market meltdown of 1997 caused a pause.

Neo-liberalism is based on the 'trickle-down' effect: the argument that private wealth naturally seeps down to benefit the worker – but South America entered the 21st century with its highest unemployment rate in 20 years, with poverty rates high, and with education, health and other public services deteriorating rapidly.

Copper bottom *Chuquicamata, the enormous open-cast copper mine at the core of Chile's economy. By 2000, it had not been privatised.*

Tourism – the untapped potential

From 'lost' jungle cities to regions of stunning natural beauty such as the Chilean Lake District, South America has enormous potential to generate wealth through tourism, providing political instability does not get in the way. From the 1970s, for instance, Peru's tourist industry experienced great growth, only for it to suffer a setback when Shining Path guerrillas began to kill tourists.

The petty crime that comes with gross economic disparities is also a problem, while in Venezuela gross negligence and mismanagement brought disaster to its beaches – and consequently its tourist industry – in the mud slides of 1999.

Chilean idyll *Exquisite Lago Llanquihue has been a choice vacation spot since 1912.*

The coffee set

'There's an awful lot of coffee in Brazil', as the old song goes. There's an awful lot of coffee in Colombia, too – but there the similarity ends.

Coffee as agribusiness *A typically large plantation in Brazil.*

Not so hot *'Grab life by the beans', Colombians are advised in a catchy coffee ad, but an export policy denies them the best of their crop.*

Brazil is the world's largest producer, Colombia comes third, and – as many people are aware – the precise timing and intensity of rainfall over the misty hills of Minas Gerais and the rich green mountains of western Colombia can do drastic things to the price of coffee. For the growers of Minas Gerais, the worst that can happen is a killing frost; for the Colombians, it is an earthquake.

A quake grinds the growers

In a one-two punch, the devastating January 1999 Armenia earthquake destroyed more than 7000 farmhouses, processing plants and warehouses, then unseasonably heavy rains hit just as growers struggled to rebuild. In a country wracked by decades of civil war, drug trafficking and poverty, Colombia's coffee zone has otherwise been an oasis of peace and economic development.

Unlike Brazil, which grows coffee on mammoth corporate plantations where much of the crop is harvested with bean-picking machinery, most of Colombia's coffee is grown on a patchwork of hundreds of thousands of farms, each less than 10 acres (4 ha). The deep red berries are plucked individually from the shiny green bushes by 800 000 workers. Coffee has provided enough secure jobs for the left-wing guerrilla groups, active in half the country and in control of large areas, to have had only limited influence here. Another factor is the National Federation of Coffee Growers, a private group so powerful that it forms a kind of shadow government, a state within the state.

Two centuries of growing coffee

Brazil has been the world's largest coffee producer since 1810, when slaves worked the plantations. A century ago, it produced 70 per cent of the world's coffee. The 20th century saw crises of over-production, until quotas were put into operation. In 1989, the quota system collapsed, causing a glut until voluntary quotas were agreed in 1993. Brazil now has a one-third share of the world market and Colombia about 15 per cent. Venezuela, Peru and Ecuador are also producers. With the help of irrigation, Brazilian growers have expanded into the frost-free *cerrado* savannah of the interior, which could again produce more coffee than they know what to do with.

The coffee worker
A 1939 painting by Candido Portinari.

CHAPTER 4

LIVING IN SOUTH AMERICA

Daily life for the ordinary people of South America is often portrayed as impoverished, brutish, and short. Yet for most in this mosaic of cultures and peoples, life has its compensations. The dark side of the drug trade and gang warfare contrasts with the exuberance and passion of festivals, in particular the spangled brilliance of the Rio carnival. A Catholic pilgrimage is mirrored by pagan rituals that originated in Inca times, and both have an intensity matched every week in any football stadium. The struggle for survival in a shantytown is brightened by the brilliant colours and overwhelming variety of goods on offer in a Bolivian market. And in both jungle and highlands, a few tribes still endure, preserving their traditional ways despite the onward march of the modern world.

In Peru, the highest railway in the world criss-crosses the Andes from village to village.

Titicaca: the source

El Lago Segrado, the sacred lake, the sea at the top of the world, is at the core of the Andean experience. Lake Titicaca and its myth-laden islands are in the process of coming to terms with the tourist.

The Inca story of creation begins with the words: 'While all was in utter darkness there rose from this island of Titicaca a resplendent sun…' The island in question is one among 40 that dot Lake Titicaca, a miniature sea lofted high into the Andes. The story goes on to relate how the risen sun created Manco Capac and his sister-wife Mama Ocllo, founders of the Inca dynasty. This calls for no great stretch of the imagination from anyone who has experienced a bone-chilling night on the lake shore before seeing the sun burst over the glaciated peaks, to quickly become a blazing fireball. The skin of lake Indians has the appearance of scorched leather.

Weaving boats, knitting hats
Tourism rescued the reed boat from obsolescence. Knitting the characteristic campesino headwear is a male task.

Birthplace of the sun and the moon

Lake Titicaca, measuring 150 miles (190 km) north to south and up to 50 miles (80 km) across, occupies a trench in the altiplano (high plain) of the central Andes. At 12 500 ft (3800 m), it is the highest navigable body of water in the world. This was authenticated on Christmas Day in 1870, when the *Yavari*, a steamship built in Britain and transported in crates, was hauled up to the lake by mule train and made the first voyage from Peru to Bolivia, nations that share the lake's shores. More than 25 rivers feed Titicaca and there is only one small outlet, yet such are the evaporating powers of the sun and winds at this altitude that the lake level can drop 4 ft (1.2 m) in a dry season. The ancients believed that it had to be connected to the ocean, mother of waters – for had not Viracocha, the supreme being, created the sun and the moon out of this very lake? The Inca, when they learned of this in the course of their conquests, sensibly added Viracocha to their pantheon. Here is where the major indigenous languages come together: Quechua, the language of the Inca, spoken by millions from Ecuador to Chile, and ancient Aymara, spoken in the region of the lake.

A breathless experience

The air is translucent at this altitude, near the upper limit of practical agriculture and of practical living, for heart and lungs have to work on half the oxygen available at sea level. Yet 1000 years ago, the Titicaca basin sustained as substantial

a civilisation as existed in the prehistory of the Southern Hemisphere. The social organisation and ingenious agricultural practices that made this possible were obliterated with the Spanish conquest and the people were reduced to a serf-like state from which they did not begin to be emancipated until well into the 20th century. Even today, with Quechua also an official language in Peru and the *indigena* (native) officially re-designated *campesino* (peasant), the mixed-race *Mestizo* will call the Indian *Hijito* 'boy', or 'sonny', whereas the Indian addresses the mestizo as *patrón* or *senór*.

Steamboat to hydrofoil

The *Yavari*, which could raise a head of steam on llama dung, plied Titicaca's Aegean-blue waters for 100 years, eventually to become a floating museum. In its place whizz hydrofoils and catamarans, heralds of a new kind of invasion, of tourists. Hard as life can be for the farmer-fishermen eking out a living on and around the lake, it makes compelling viewing from the tour boats as they skim past reed shores and potato gardens, scalloped hillsides splashed with adobe villages alive with llama and alpaca, and stepped terraces that predate the Inca.

The Island of the Sun, the Andean Eden, is a short catamaran ride from the small Bolivian town of Copacabana, a halt for pilgrims since before Inca times and dominated now by a cathedral housing the Dark Virgin of the Lake, a miracle-working statue carved, it is said, by an Inca prince.

The *Isla del Sol* does not disappoint. Set in an enchanted landscape are curious ruins, magic fountains, sacred stones and the creation rock itself, and village women in homespun Spanish period costume and bowler hats, cocked just-so. For the time-pressed globetrotter, however, the island's facilities now extend to a 'cultural complex', where the Titicaca experience comes packaged and sanitised as in a theme park. Elsewhere on the lake, tourism provides artificial respiration for an impoverished, dwin-

Copacabana *Veneration of its miracle-working Dark Virgin reached as far as Brazil to account for the name of Rio's world-famous beach!*

dling community inhabiting floating islands of reeds, the Uros. Other societies out on the lake include the Taquile islanders, superb weavers who dress in a jaunty 16th-century style, and the Amantani islanders, tranquil, self-sufficient agriculturalists of another age; a few miles apart, the islands do not even share the same language.

The highest railways in the world

The whistle of the locomotive will awaken the Indian race, a Peruvian president predicted in 1868, when the Andes were opened up with railways. Despite a century of earthquakes, landslides and guerrilla activities,  large sections endure to provide white-knuckle thrills. The Southern Peruvian Line climbs to 14 750 ft (4 500 m) in linking Lake Titicaca with the coast and Cuzco, while the Central Andean Line out of Lima reaches a record 15 700 ft (4785 m).

People of the lake *The Uros islands provide the inhabitants with reeds for housing and boats.*

The Amazon Indians' struggle for survival

Small groups of Indians still wander the rain forest, despite being increasingly beset by settlers, loggers, ranchers, miners and tourists. Primitive in the eyes of the governments that ultimately determine their fate, they are fighting for the right to be different.

Warrior *A Kayapo.*

The Kayapo, Yanomami, Yagua and U'wa are divided by language, national borders and thousands of miles – four among several score of tribal remnants holding onto corners of the Amazon rain forest against increasing odds. The Kayapo, in the south-east of the Amazon basin, were not 'discovered' until the 1930s; the Yanomami, on either side of the Brazil-Venezuela border, not until the 1970s. The Yagua, on the upper Amazon in Peru, have had contact with the outside world since the 16th century. The U'wa, in the cloud forest of Colombia, revere ancestors who in the 17th century leapt to their deaths off a cliff, rather than submit to the Spanish conquerors.

Hunter *A Yagua takes aim with a blowpipe.*

For these four tribes, as for all forest tribes, the crash-development of Amazonia that has taken place since the 1960s has presented a great challenge. Brazil led the charge, opening up the rain forest to let in land-hungry settlers, and with them, disease, alcohol and prostitution. A road driven through Kayapo territory brought prospectors, who in 1980 struck gold. That was the year in which the Kayapo donned warpaint and massacred 20 settlers. It was also the year when aerial surveys found evidence of gold and uranium in Yanomami territory. A decade later, 45 000 prospectors invaded, causing havoc to one of the world's last true Neolithic societies. Lacking immunity to even the common cold, the Yanomami were decimated.

Nowadays deemed 'part of Brazilian society', the Kayapo have an electric generator and a little disposable income from collecting Brazil nuts, but the Yanomami still remain on the critical list. For the Yagua, coping has taken the form of tribal dance-and-barter sessions for tourists taking river cruises. Meanwhile the U'wa became an international *cause célèbre* when they threatened a repeat of the mass suicide jump, rather than be uprooted by oil companies intent on extracting the wealth discovered beneath them.

Weapons inspection *The Yanomami tip arrows with curare, a poison made from jungle plants.*

A study in survival

The Yanomami have become the best-known Amazonian tribe, due to the attention paid them by anthropologists and the drama of their struggle for survival. They live communally in circular dwellings in scattered villages. They hunt, gather fruits and nuts and grow manioc, plantains, tobacco and cotton. Their shamans have a knowledge of medicinal plants that has astounded pharmacologists.

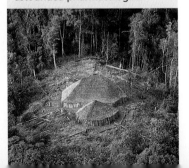

From coca to cocaine

The sacred plant of the Andes was regarded by the Inca as a gift of the Sun god. Processed in clandestine laboratories into a powerful drug, it now destroys lives and undermines societies and economies.

The hardy coca bush (*Erythroxylum coca*) grows wild in the 'eyebrow of the jungle', as Peruvians call the steep eastern slopes of the Andes. It is easy to cultivate and can be plucked for its small green leaves as often as four times a year. For 4000 years, chewing coca leaves has been a part of mountain life, to ward off fatigue and alleviate cold and hunger, and as an accompaniment to social events. 'Mother Coca' is chewed during religious ceremonies and offered up to the deities, be they mountain spirits or the Virgin Mary. Farmers may bury in their fields a potato stuffed with coca leaves to ensure a good harvest. Tourists sip hot, refreshing coca tea, said to be the best cure for *soroche*, altitude sickness. In Bolivia, where about 30 000 acres (12 000 ha) are legally cultivated for internal consumption, coca leaf is sold by the bag in the markets. Unfortunately, coca is also the raw material for cocaine.

Cocaine was first isolated in Germany in 1862 and became the wonder drug of the late 19th century, sold in 'tonics' and hailed as 'magical' by Sigmund Freud. As its properties became better understood, it was removed from over-the-counter tonics and was strictly controlled: its abuse as a recreational drug did not become a major problem in the West until the late 20th century, when craving for the white powder and its derivative, 'crack', fostered an underworld industry said to gross, at street level, more than $50 billion (£33 billion) a year. The Andean peasant farmer receives very little of this, nevertheless coca is several times more profitable than any other crop. The coca leaves are soaked in kerosene, mashed by foot into a smelly brown paste and then processed into 'white dust' with hydrochloric and sulphuric acid in makeshift laboratories.

Coca, cocaine and the drug war

From small beginnings in the 1970s, drug trafficking had spun out of control by the end of the century, drawing Colombia and its neighbours into corruption and violence. Coca became the major cash crop in Bolivia and Peru from the 1980s, with some 200 000 small farmers active before government crackdowns in the 1990s. But this led to intensified planting in Colombia, where guerrilla armies control large areas and provide the *cocaleros* with protection. US-trained anti-narcotic forces went into action in 2001 as part of a $7.5 billion (£4.5 billion) 'Plan Colombia', leaving governments of Brazil and Ecuador fearful of violence spreading.

Coca crop *Most of the coca in the Yungas, in Bolivia, is grown legally for consumption by local people.*

Drug bust *Police destroy an illegal laboratory in the Colombian jungle.*

Over the counter *Coca leaf is sold by the kilo in Andean markets and tiendas,* small stores.

Democracy struggles to take root

First there were the caudillos, *then the charismatic dictators and military juntas. Often crushed in the past, democracy has experienced a rebirth in South America, but resort to the 'strong man' remains for many a compelling option.*

The populist *Hugo Chávez (centre) campaigning for the Venezuelan presidency.*

Hugo Chávez, a dashing paratrooper, failed in a bloody coup to bring down the Venezuelan government. So he tried the other way – and won the presidency in an election landslide by vowing to rout out the flagrant corruption that had plagued the country for decades.

His promise – a golden age

Chávez exploded on the political scene as an answer to troubled times. In 18 months, he rode roughshod over the discredited congress and courts and put in place a new constitution securing greater powers for himself and a hold on the presidency until 2006, at least. The leading political parties, widely loathed for their tolerance of graft and cronyism, had been all but wiped off the map. Declaring a 'peaceful social revolution', Chávez promised no less than 'a golden age'. For many, he represented hope. For others, he reawakened memories of the authoritarian *caudillo*, the classic military strongman, impossible to remove.

Bearing witness *The 'Mothers of the Plaza de Mayo' have demonstrated every Thursday since the late 1970s on behalf of loved ones among the 30 000 who 'disappeared' under the Argentine dictatorship of 1976-83.*

The strains begin to tell

In September 2000, the presidents of all 12 South American republics met, the first such gathering in history. They committed themselves to economic stability and to democracy. It was a moment to savour. Through the 1980s, the continent had divested itself of dictatorships, including that of the brutal Alfredo Stroessner in Paraguay and military regimes in Brazil and Uruguay, Chile and Argentina, but after a decade of ascendant democracy, the strains were showing as aspirations clashed with governments unable to provide an equitable sharing of wealth. Even those countries that had experienced impressive growth had been unable to narrow the gap between rich and poor. Overall, the gap had widened and discontent was focused more upon social reform, and less upon types of government.

A new kind of firebrand

Five centuries have blurred racial boundaries and yet deep social inequalities run broadly along ethnic lines, with South America still largely governed, managed and owned by whites. This seemed on the point of being challenged by a new breed of firebrand, as exemplified by the proudly *pardo*, or brown-skinned, President Chávez. However, a short coup in 2002, a 63 day national strike in 2003 which crippled the economy by stopping oil production, and accusations of increasing dictatorship imply that many Venezuelans are now unhappy with Chávez's leadership.

September 11, 1973 *General Pinochet (seated) takes power in Chile after the military coup.*

Tele Globo, the empire of images

In a semi-literate land as large as Australia or the continental United States, television is all-powerful and Globo is the great communicator.

Light in the night   *Globo reaches 99.8 per cent of Brazil.*

Nestled in the lush Rio hills above Ipanema Beach and within blessing distance of the huge statue, Christ the Redeemer, a giant satellite dish beams up to the Brasilsat the signal of TV Globo. Fifth-biggest in the world in terms of audience size, Globo is the largest privately owned television network outside the United States, and the world's biggest producer of television programming – 4500 hours a year. It has been said of Globo that its signal is Brazil, defining problems and promoting ideas as it provides the enormous nation with its dreams and distractions.

Fast-paced, shiny and bright

Globo's stock-in-trade are steamy serial melodramas known as *telenovelas*. Globo broadcasts three each evening, starting at 6 pm. The 7 pm production is sure to be spicy and glamorous; 10 pm is the 'noble hour' prime time, which calls for something more hard-edged. In the middle, the national news broadcast at 8 pm is the traditional time of government pronouncements.

Television has been called the *miçanga* of Brazil, an Indian word for anything bright and shiny – and Globo is very *miçanga*, its productions visually striking, fast-paced and brightly lit, as though to lighten up the darkest corners of the jungle. Though illiteracy continues to fall, many adults can do little more than write their name. As a consequence, newspapers

Fantasy factory   *A giant sound stage at a Globo production complex opened in 1995. Globo also has a 320 acre (128 ha) 'scenographic' outdoor lot.*

are read by a tiny minority and most people get their news and views from television or radio. Globo also owns the country's dominant radio network.

Progress of the king-maker

Globo is the creation of Dr Roberto Marinho, who in 1925 inherited a newspaper from his father. This he slowly built into Rio's largest daily, adding radio stations and magazines in the 1940s and 1950s, then moving into television in 1965. He thrived under a military dictatorship that saw him as the man to mould Brazil into a model consumer society. Globo looked the other way during the *Diretas-já* campaign for the restoration of democracy, but picked up on the public mood as the campaign swept the country. Dr Roberto gained a reputation in the 1980s as king-maker, for Globo's ability to influence presidential elections. He faltered only when he stopped showing the Rio Carnival, which he considered vulgar. That momentarily cost Globo 85 per cent of its audience, a mistake it would not repeat. Having reached his 90s in the 1990s, Dr Roberto handed on power to his three sons. With almost as many employees as the BBC, Globo remains a family business.

The *telenovela*, a Brazilian passion

Spicy *telenovelas*, descended from *radionovelas* popularised by Cuban radio stations in the 1940s, are popular throughout South America and a consuming passion in Brazil, where not even football broadcasts are allowed to pre-empt their nightly scheduling. Brazilian *novelas* are lavish soap operas with happy endings, usually after about 180 episodes. They are written and taped at a frantic pace, shortly ahead of transmission. Jealousy, intrigue and betrayal are the classic themes. Strong sexual content and generous doses of nudity add to the appeal. They have been sold to more than 100 countries: a novela about the torrid adventures of a beautiful slave broke audience records in China.

Costume drama   *Cast members prepare for a recording session of the 1999 hit* telenovela Força de um desej.

Fighting bulls

The Spanish bullfight has thrived and evolved in surprising ways – from tail-grabbing contests on the Venezuelan plains to places in the Andes where a giant condor is set upon the bull.

Three hundred years of colonial rule made bullfighting a part of South American culture. It has retreated in places – banned for example in Uruguay, where the Colonia del Sacramento bull-ring has not seen a fight since early in the 20th century. But *la fiesta brava* thrives still in Peru, Venezuela, Colombia and Ecuador.

Taking the bull by its tail

In Lima, large crowds are drawn to the Plaza de Acho, oldest bull-ring in the Americas, while Venezuela's Plaza de Toros Monumental in Valencia is larger than any bullring in Europe. The November to March season alternates with that of Spain, enabling top international *toreros* to participate. While the classic *corrida* tends to draw an élite crowd and the best *sombra* (shaded from the sun) seats can be expensive, Venezuela has also a rustic variation, *toros coleados*, popular on the llanos, where mounted *coleadors* compete to grab a bull by the tail and bring him to the ground. 'All knack', 19th-century witness, Sir Edward Sullivan, called 'this art of throwing bulls', though he also noted how many lose their lives. Nowadays the bull is released into a narrow fenced course, the *manga*, with several *coleadors* in hot pursuit. Points are awarded, as in a rodeo. The crowd cheers, beer in hand.

Grisly spectacle

In the Andes, wild bulls from the altiplano may be set against sometimes intoxicated *diestros* ('dexterous ones', as bullfighters are called) with fatal results. In a practice now illegal, a giant condor may be pinioned to the back of the bull, to rip with beak and talons, while villagers attack with prods. The grisly ritual ends with the bull, symbol of Spain, being killed, sometimes with dynamite, while the 'victor' is fed *chicha* beer and released.

*Raging bull   Spectators come to see some of Spain's best *toreros* show off their skills in the bullring.*

The art of life

Whatever their troubles and woes, the people of South America have an instinct for getting the most out of life by seizing every moment, no matter how insignificant, and enjoying it to the full.

Café society *Watching TV is best in company.*

Evening in the Gran Café Tortoni, on the Avenida de Mayo in Buenos Aires. There is a din of chatter, music, billiard balls banging. A young couple kiss, an old man reads. The music is a tango of lost love. The air is pungent with tobacco smoke.

A warm embrace, a kiss…

Café Tortoni, founded in 1858, may be the most famous cafe in a continent of cafés. The tango legend Carlos Gardel sipped coffee here. So did Argentina's literary great Jorge Luis Borges. There is a tango song, *Viejo Tortoni*, which extols the 'infinite fervour' of this

'faithful refuge of friendship'. Fervour in friendship is important in a continent of so many crosscurrents of culture and race, where everyone's sense of identity can do with a boost. Voluble greetings are in order, a warm embrace, a kiss for reassurance, and beyond that, there is group identity. Supporting the local football team is a commitment for life. A fiesta in the Andes, with local dance troupes dipping and weaving to massed pan flutes and drums, is as fiercely competitive as the Rio carnival parade.

A question of priorities

Machismo and *mañana* – as in, 'what's your hurry?' – might sum up the outsider's image of South America. In fact, South American societies are basically still bastions of the male. In Venezuela, women have advanced with a 'charm' approach, epitomised in the career of a former Miss Universe, Irene Sáez, who in 1998 ran for president. As for *mañana*, it comes down to a question of priorities. In South America, most people are convinced that enjoying life comes first.

Looks count. South Americans take pride in their appearance, sometimes to a fault. A consumer study named Venezuelans the most vain people in the world, after 65 per cent of women and 47 per cent of men said that they thought about their looks 'all the time'. Research found that the average Venezuelan household spent one-fifth of its income on personal care and grooming products. Such attention to detail pays off. Brazil might have won the World Cup four times, but Venezuela can point to five Miss World and four Miss Universe titles!

Hush! *Siesta in progress.*

A South American tea ceremony

Yerba maté…the Guaraní Indians discovered it, the Jesuits cultivated it and the gauchos adopted it – a stimulating brew, stuffed with caffeine and tannin, greenish, bitter, fragrant and heavily herby. *Yerba* refers to the dried leaves of a member of the holly family, *Ilex paraguariensis*, steeped in boiling water. The infusion is properly sucked from a hollowed gourd, the *maté*, with a filtered metal straw,

the *bombilla*, often made of silver, just as the gourd may be silver-mounted. More than just a drink, it is a ritual – the *maté* is passed around a group, each person sipping from the *bombilla* in turn – and an important part of life in Uruguay, Paraguay, Argentina, and parts of Brazil and Chile, particularly in country areas.

The Catholic continent

The conquista espiritual (spiritual conquest) undertaken by the priests who served as commissars to the conquistadores made the Catholic Church the dominant institution of South America. The Church is pervasive still, but less so, and expressions of faith are far from orthodox.

A question of faith Catholicism remains strong in South America.

South America is 90 per cent Roman Catholic, records suggest. The continent is encrusted with saints' names and saintly images. Whereas New York has the Statue of Liberty, Rio de Janeiro has Christ the Redeemer. Christ, again with arms stretched wide, also looks down upon the Inca city of Cuzco and a massive statue of the Virgin overlooks Quito.

Difference in the detail

In claiming South America first for God and second for Spain, the conquistadores made the Church a fundamental part of the power base, but by the 18th century, spiritual energies were

Syncretic ritual Candomblé devotees wash the steps of a Catholic church in Salvador da Bahia, home of this Afro-Brazilian cult.

waning. The 19th century saw formal state-Church bonds severed in Brazil, Chile and Uruguay. By 1945, freedom of religion was extended to Ecuador, where the Church's hold had long been strongest, and in 1994 Catholicism lost its state-religion status in Argentina: a non-Catholic could henceforth be president.

Being a Catholic country has thus come to differ greatly in detail. Uruguay is meticulously secular – so much so that Christmas is called Family Day and Easter is Tourism Week! Chile is strait-laced, with the Church influential in politics and the media, though with some hypocrisy in evidence: abortion is illegal, even when a mother's life is at risk, yet one in four pregnancies ends in abortion according to conservative official estimates. Divorce is likewise illegal in Chile: the rich negotiate annulments, while many of the poor simply avoid marriage – almost half the country's children are born out of wedlock. Brazil is catholic, small 'c', the Church more or less resigned to certain sultry ways (in 1998, thieves in Rio stole shipments of 100 000 condoms, just before carnival began), while millions worship old African gods under the thinnest veil of Christianity. In the mountains of Peru and Bolivia, in the old Inca Empire, Catholicism has absorbed the cosmos of ancient Andean culture. As instinctively as the Argentine bus passenger crosses himself when passing a church, the *runa* will nod in the direction of the sun when speaking of *Hesu Kristu*: God the Son at one with the sun.

Archbishop Câmara The champion of the poor died in 1999.

Challenge from left and right

Around the mid-20th century, the Vatican woke up to a sense that all Latin America could slip away from the Church. Thousands of priests were drafted from Europe and scores of new dioceses were set up. New blood brought an infusion of new ideas. Taking as their lead Pope John XXIII's call for spiritual regeneration, a group of theologians and prelates like Hélder Câmara, 'Archbishop to the shantytowns', championed 'liberation theology', which would have the Church take an active role in fighting social and economic injustice. This 'option for the poor' was seen to smack of Marxism and a new conservative Pope, John Paul II, silenced or replaced leading proponents. Meanwhile missionaries of fundamentalist Protestant sects from the United States stepped up

Power of the Pope   *Only one in five Venezuelans attends church, but it required an airport to accommodate the multitude anxious to participate in a Mass celebrated by John Paul II in Caracas in 1996.*

activities to telling effect – the first serious challenge to Rome's 500-year hegemony. In Peru, Protestant organisations helped Alberto Fujimori win the presidency in 1990. By 2000, 20 per cent of Chile was Protestant. In Brazil, hundreds of 'evangelical' churches sprang up in the 1990s , the biggest being 'Bishop' Edir Macedo's Universal Church of the Kingdom of God, with its own TV and radio stations. In Rio de Janeiro alone, conversions were running as high as 100 000 a year, according to Brazil's Institute for Religious Studies. It called for the Pope in person to stem the tide. In October 1997, 2 million people thronged the Rio shore as he celebrated Mass: men in shorts, women in bikini tops, all swaying to hymns under a fierce tropical sun.

Cuzco procession   *On this spot in Inca times sacred mummies were carried in procession with the same concentration on sumptuous finery.*

The African gods of Brazil

As with Andean Indians, slaves from Africa remained true to old beliefs while embracing elements of Christianity. The result is a variety of voodoo-related cults centred on Brazil, sometimes referred to as Macumbo. These hybrids pair Christian saints with West African *orixás*, deities: Ogum, god of war, becomes St George, and Yemanjá, goddess of the sea, is identified with the Virgin Mary. The cross is a powerful symbol.

Ceremonies feature animal sacrifice, drumming and dancing. Rites are led by mediums who communicate with the holy spirits

The Candomblé crowd   *Intense, rhythmic drumming is a constant feature of outdoor ceremonies.*

while in a trance. *Trabalhos*, offerings, may seek a boon or cast a curse. Brazilians in general treat the sight of a headless chicken or candles burning at crossroads with wary respect. Candomblé, most African of the Macumba sects, is popular in Bahia state, where some of its priestesses are important public figures. Candomblé devotees wear white out of respect for their supreme god Oxalá, whose Catholic equivalent is Christ. Umbanda, practised in Rio de Janeiro and São Paulo, blends Candomblé, Catholicism and 'Spiritism', and its appeal has spread to the white middle class. On February 2, people of every colour and creed throng the beaches of Rio to cast flowers, fancy soaps, bottles of perfume and candles into the sea for Yemanjá, mother of the waters.

A feast of festivals

Patron saints and pagan spirits and combinations of both…too many to count, they are cause for hope in hard times and for constant celebrations in which the dancing and drinking and worshipping may be all rolled into one.

It is the second Sunday in October in Belém, near the mouth of the Amazon. Belém is Portuguese for Bethlehem. All week long, pilgrims have been pouring into this sweltering port city, until the population of 1 million has about doubled. They include suppliants carrying heavy wooden crosses, or crawling on their knees as a penance, or in gratitude for some blessing bestowed. Their objective, the Círio de Nazaré, the biggest religious festival in the country with the largest Roman Catholic population in the world

Christmas in October

The origins of the Círio are a tangle of fact and legend. In October 1700, a woodcutter found an 11 in (28 cm) statue of the Virgin Mary and Child on the bank of a creek; he took it home, but it mysteriously returned to the bank and did so repeatedly, even when the colonial governor had the figure brought to his palace and placed under guard. Adoration was clearly in order. The statue is now held in a basilica on the site of the creek, while once a year a replica

Echo of the past   Each June 24, the Inca Empire is reincarnated for the colourful Inti Raymi *ceremony on the ramparts of Sacsahuamàn, Cuzco.*

is paraded through the streets, borne on a cart attached to a 1300-ft (390-m) rope. The cart takes eight hours to advance 3 miles (5 km) through throngs straining to touch the rope, which is said to be charged with divine energy. Over the centuries, the rope has become as venerated as the image of the Virgin, and the Círio has expanded into a Christmas-like holiday for families to get together, with exchanges of brightly painted wooden gifts, traditional duck dinners, and a parade of decorated boats on the great river.

All aboard the pilgrim bus

On saints' days throughout Brazil, roads are clogged with buses and trucks loaded with pilgrims going to 'pay promises', as they put it, at shrines such as that of the basilica of Nossa Senhora da Aparecida near São Paulo, famous for its accumulation of plaster casts of body parts cured through divine intercession. Popular belief is rarely answerable to dogma. Each year, thousands who throng Juàzeiro do Norte, in north-east Brazil, put their faith in Padre Cicero, a miracle-working priest excommunicated for heresy a century ago. In Argentina, a taste for

Diablada *dancer This devil shares Christian and pre-Inca ancestry (top, opposite).*

Corpus Christi in Cuzco *Altars and effigies of all sorts cram the Plaza de Armas on this hectic feast day.*

Qoyllur Rit'i *A purgatorial pilgrimage to the most enduring of deities, the sacred mountains.*

spiritualism extends to veneration of dead icons like the Peróns and tango star Carlos Gardel.

Meanwhile in Venezuela *La Difunta Correa* – a woman who in 1841 died of thirst in a remote desert region – draws upwards of 100 000 pilgrims to her tomb at Easter, thanks to miracles attributed to her. No one quite knows who María Lionza was: devotees call her simply *La Reina*, the queen, a haughty goddess who draws tens of thousands from all walks of life to altars in the mountains west of Caracas, where she is said to have called upon the services of the Pope, Cleopatra, Simón Bolívar and President Kennedy, among others.

dancing and drinking. The village plays host to the visiting images of patron saints from other villages and there will be daily Masses and processions. There might be a bull-fight and football matches. At night, look for bonfires in the plaza and dancing in the firelight and the chicha beer flowing freely.

Dancing with devils

Such major Catholic feasts as Holy Week and Corpus Christi loom large on every South American calendar, diverging in detail according to cultural influences. On Venezuela's central coast during Corpus Christi, colourful *diablos danzantes* (devil dancers) take to the streets, perpetuating a medieval European folk rite brought over by the conquistadores. In the Andes of Peru and Bolivia, *La Diablada* stars St Michael the Archangel and bug-eyed monsters, but this devil dance is pre-Inca in origin and spirit. On the shores of Lake Titicaca, *Diablada* is one among hundreds of ethnic dances performed in the course of a two-week fiesta in honour of sweet-faced *Mamacita*, the Virgin of Candelaria – a marathon of music, fireworks and Masses that lightens up the harsh highlands and leaves everyone dizzy and tipsy. A big village festival will include multiple activities, with solemn religious observances combined with the

To the sacred mountain

In the Andes, there is a fusion of faith, with each sacred place of the pre-Columbian world associated with a specific saint, and Inca festivals merged with Catholic holy days. June 24, the Feast of John the Baptist, marks *Inti Raymi*, the Inca winter-solstice celebration, now re-created and a big hit with Cuzco locals and tourists. More authentic in terms of continuity and the profound emotion it inspires is the Corpus Christi pilgrimage to *Qoyllur Rit'i* (Star Snow), a glacier on the north side of Nevado Ausangate, a 21 000 ft (6400 m) peak about 50 miles (80 km) south-east of Cuzco. Ausangate is an *Apukuna*, a Great Lord of the pre-Inca cosmos, and by virtue of a miraculous appearance of the Christ Child in 1785, it enjoys Catholic credentials as well. Thousands converge on a sanctuary beneath the glacier, each group with its band and ritual dance troupe.

Ukuku bear dancers *Comic and frightening, they protect Qoyllur Rit'i pilgrims from kukuchis, howling demons of the glacier.*

The Rio carnival

For four days and five tropical nights, the rules governing social behaviour are suspended, transgressed, or inverted, as people take to the streets in bacchanalian revelry. Carnaval in Rio de Janeiro is the most extravagant, self-indulgent, wanton and lewd fancy-dress party in the world.

Carnival, in one form or another, is celebrated throughout South America. Introduced from Europe in the 16th century as an occasion for merrymaking before the 40 day Lenten fast, in the Andes it coincided with *Puqllay*, the start of the harvest season, when offerings were made to *Pachamama*, Mother Earth. It has stayed a great occasion for the *campesinos* to soak themselves as well as their landscape in alcohol and coca, and to join in boisterous dancing and flirtation. In Brazil, it is an occasion for massive street and beach parties, and parading to the pulsating beat of samba, *axé* and passionate *frevo*, while Rio de Janeiro mounts the greatest urban extravaganza, the most carnal bash on earth.

Sin and samba

The better-off gather in clubs for uninhibited costume parties. The masses take to the Rio streets, unleashing an energy and emotion that can be frightening. Police step back, social and sexual barriers are lowered, and for the two-thirds whose normal lives are mired in poverty, carnival provides euphoric release. Centrepiece is the Sambadrome, a street-turned-stadium, where the exotically costumed samba schools strut and gyrate, each vying for recognition as most sensual, its parade the best-choreographed. Each 'school' is up to 5000 strong and moves to a hypnotic samba rhythm set by a *bateria* of hundreds of drummers.

Godfathers out, plastic surgeons in

Rio *Carnaval* becomes bigger and more commercial by the year. The parades were not officially organised until the 1930s and the Sambadrome, designed by Oscar Niemeyer, did not exist until 1984. Celebrities and stars of the *telenovelas* adorn the floats, along with innumerable topless models, many of whom have kept Brazil's plastic surgeons (more per capita than anywhere else on earth) busy redefining their outlines for this ultimate promotional moment. Once bankrolled by the *bicheiros*, local mafia bosses, the schools now seek corporate sponsors and many have their own internet websites, where they will sign up foreign tourists as participating *sambistas*, at a price. Hotel room rates, taxi fares and traffic accidents all escalate over carnival, as does the crime rate.

In the Sambadrome   The giant floats are pushed along by teams reminiscent of the slaves in a Cecil B. De Mille Biblical epic. Whatever the theme, the emphasis is on excess.

They 'school' the carnival

The *escolas de samba*, samba schools, are best described as neighbourhood dance associations. They developed in the Rio slums early in the 20th century, not long after the development of the samba, another creation of the *favelas*. There are 14 major samba schools, and they function much like football clubs – fiercely competitive, each with its own colours, supporters, home ground and manager. As social clubs, they also participate in neighbourhood weddings, funerals, and in religious celebrations of the local patron saint.

Fantasia factory   Each school designs and makes its elaborate fantasias (costumes) based upon an annual theme.

A love of speed

In a continent hungry for heroes and charged with machismo, grand prix motor racing has a special allure – but winning is everything. The death in action of a charismatic world champion spurred a new generation of drivers to emulate his daring.

Argentine hero Fangio at the 1956 German Grand Prix.

South Americans have occupied the front of the grid ever since the creation of the Formula One World Championship. The great Argentine driver Juan Manual Fangio dominated the 1950s, winning the championship five times, to be followed by a succession of Brazilians – Emerson Fittipaldi (1974), Nelson Piquet (1981, 1983, 1987) and Ayrton Senna (1988, 1990, 1991), adjudged, like Fangio, one of the greatest racing drivers of all time.

The Extraterrestrial

On May 1, 1994, the succession was broken when Senna suffered a fatal crash on the Imola circuit in Italy. The Extraterrestrial, as they nicknamed him, was given a state funeral and 2 million people turned out to say farewell. Roads and public buildings were named in his honour in almost every city and town. In Rio, a major freeway bears his name; in São Paulo, where he was brought up, it is the motorway to the airport. The magic Senna name was also slapped on a wide variety of luxury goods and a credit card, with profits going to poor children, so plentiful in Brazil.

Bereft of a winner, public interest in grand prix racing quickly waned, but Senna had left a protégé – a young driver named Rubens Barrichello – plus a new generation of eager emulators.

A claim to aviation glory

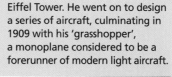

Brazilians argue that a Brazilian flew the first successful aeroplane. Alberto Santos-Dumont was a self-described 'aerostatic sportsman' who in 1901 hitched a petrol engine to a steerable balloon for a flight around the Eiffel Tower. He went on to design a series of aircraft, culminating in 1909 with his 'grasshopper', a monoplane considered to be a forerunner of modern light aircraft.

It flew! This early Santos-Dumont aircraft stayed up for 21 seconds.

Signed to race for Ferrari, Barrichela won the German Grand Prix in 2000 and helped the famous marque to its first world constructors' championship in 21 years. Many other young Brazilians acquired rides in the more accessible US equivalent of Formula One racing.

Juan Pablo Montoya

None had quite the success of a Colombian, Juan Pablo Montoya, who won the major North American championship and capped this by winning the richest race in motor sport, the Indianapolis 500, both at his first attempt. Clean-cut and from a well-to-do Bogotá family, Montoya became the instant idol of his troubled nation and moved to Formula One in 2001, to race for the BMW Williams team based in England.

There is a dark side to such identification with high-speed heroics. With a tenth the number of cars, Brazil has the same number of road-deaths as the USA, about 50 000 each year. In Rio, being run over is the leading cause of death for children. Buses are particularly dangerous, because drivers use them to affirm their manliness.

Doomed idol Senninha, 'Little Senna', endures still as a beloved cartoon character.

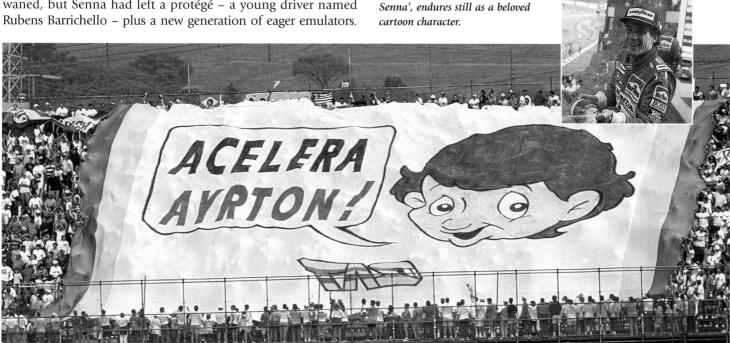

Football mania

'Gooooooal…' South American football broadcasters in their lyrical commentaries are said to be capable of sustaining that cry of 'goal' for up to one minute. It is a cry that unites a continent.

Ronaldo For Brazil's fans, one name is enough.

In 1989, an airline pilot became so engrossed in listening to a Brazil v. Chile football match that he flew in the wrong direction, ran out of fuel and crashed in the Amazon rain forest. The tragedy met with understanding in a continent where soccer is not so much a game as an obsession, with the prestige of district, city and nation all riding upon the fortunes of their soccer teams. From the remotest village in the Bolivian Andes to the teeming *favelas* of Brazil, youngsters kick and dribble and aspire to become the next Ronaldo or Maradona, or the next Pelé, real name Edson Arantes do Nascimento, best-known soccer player (and hence the best-known Brazilian) of all time.

How a game became an art form

Futebol was a gift of the British, incidental cargo brought ashore in the late imperial era. In 1891 there were sufficient numbers of British bankers, investors and engineers in places like Buenos Aires to organise matches with balls, and even the goalposts, shipped from home. In Brazil, the leading São Paulo team Corinthians takes its name from an English amateur club that toured in 1910. Adoption of the game by the urban poor, largely mulatto and black, on empty lots and construction sites, brought about a transformation: in place of methodical British play came improvisation and the agility of the *capoeira* dancer. Progress was such that in 1930 Uruguay hosted and won the inaugural World Cup, beating Argentina in the final. Uruguay won again, memorably, in 1950, and Argentina triumphed twice, in 1978 and 1986. As for Brazil, it won in 1958, 1962 and gained permanent possession of the original cup in 1970, after winning for a third time. They triumphed again in 1994 and yet again in 2002.

A cause of national rapture

'Other countries have their history, we have our football.' This was how a Uruguayan coach summarised the significance of his small country's successes. For Brazil and Argentina, football has assumed a major political dimension ever since populist presidents Getúlio Vargas and Juan Perón grasped the game's potential to harness the masses – Vargas building the world's biggest stadiums, where he could also address 'the people'. Military regimes in their turn sought to use football. In Brazil, the generals adopted the team

Colombian fervour *Football provides relief from economic woes and drug-related violence.*

Street soccer   A moment in Olinda, in north-east Brazil, that repeats itself throughout South America.

anthem, *Pra Frente Brasil* (Forward Brazil), as the theme tune of the junta and made a disastrous attempt to curb natural flair in the interest of 'discipline', only for the Corinthian star Sócrates to lead a campaign for the restoration of 'joyous' soccer – and free elections.

For Argentina, the World Cup victory in 1986 was cause for national rapture, incorporating as it did sweet revenge over England, its foe in the Falklands War four years earlier, and now defeated thanks to a controversial goal by their national hero Diego Maradona, whose fisting of the ball he later attributed to 'the hand of God'. In 2000, Maradona dedicated his published memoirs – to God.

Darker side of passion

Like all passions, this one has a dark side. In Argentina, hooligan elements known as the *barra brava* caused stadiums to be equipped with moats and fences to keep rival fans apart and off the field. In Colombia, the drug cartels gained control of several leading teams: when the national side suffered elimination from the 1994 World Cup, one of the players was assassinated as 'pay-back' for a defensive error. In Brazil, where soccer officials known as *cartoles*, top hats, attain great power and wealth, there is a history of scandal, but nothing compared with the malaise of 2000, when a series of humiliating defeats and dismissal of the national coach amid allegations of corruption were capped by emergency government hearings into the state of the *scratch du ouro*, the 'golden team', as Brazilians call their country's most cherished possession.

England's nemesis   Argentines adored 'Diego of the people'.

Maracanã, stadium of dreams

Boom-boom-boom-boom…the voodoo beat of the samba drums reverberates under the concrete canopy of the Maracanã stadium in Rio de Janeiro, home of *o jogo bonito*, the beautiful game; of *jinga*, the feline grace unique to Brazilian soccer stars; of Pelé, the 'man of 1000 goals'. The stadium was constructed for the 1950 World Cup on a scale grander than anything before or since. Brazil beat Sweden 7-1 and Spain 6-1 to reach the final with little Uruguay. Near the whistle, Brazil was 1-0 up, then Uruguay scored twice to leave 200 000 faces peering unbelievingly into the abyss. There were heart attacks and suicides. Fifty years later, Maracanã was showing its age, its chance of a reprieve denied when Brazil lost a bid to host the 2006 World Cup.

Maracanã   Rio's football stadium

Market life

Places to meet and to trade, heavy with scents and flavours, the markets both set and reflect the rhythms of daily life. All colour and chatter, they fill and spill out of the village plazas or sprawl on the edge of town.

Buoyant outlook *Quibdó, on the Rio Arato in western Colombia, has a picturesque floating market.*

Dawn breaks fast over Otavalo, on the equator and 8300 ft (2530 m) up in the Ecuador Andes. But not fast enough to catch this engagingly friendly town asleep. The livestock market is already busy, owners gossiping, bargaining. By 8 am they are done, while in the town centre, in the Plaza de los Ponchos and spilling in every direction, another market is in full swing. This one is famous.

Sweatshop to cottage industry

Poncho Plaza is a feast of colour and texture: rolls of cloth, softly napped wool blankets, ponchos and distinctive tapestry wall hangings, all hand-crafted by the Otavaleños in surrounding villages. The Otavaleños are present in numbers, the men, handsome in dark ponchos, beige felt hats and long braided hair; the women striking in embroidered white blouses, blue wraparound skirts, dark headcloth and gold necklaces.

They are descended from a tribe conquered by the Inca, then oppressed by the Spanish, who used them in *obrajes*, weaving sweatshops, under a forced labour system not wholly abandoned until the 1960s. Over subsequent years the Otavaleños contrived to put together a cottage industry that has uniquely enabled them to thrive without compromising their cultural integrity or traditional craft ways.

The achievement of the Otavaleños needs to be set against the millions who have abandoned the land for the cities – taking with them their markets. La Paz, the Bolivian capital, is rich in markets, none more intriguing than the *Mercado de los Brujos* (Witchdoctors' Market), with an unparalleled choice in charms and potions. Across the continent in Rio de Janeiro, the Afro-Brazilian lifestyle finds pulsating expression on Sundays at the Nordeste Fair, a cacophonous conjunction of food stalls, bric-a-brac vendors,

A few pesos buys every dream

Ekeko is a cheerful, tubby little god of luck, prosperity and happiness who is the nearest thing to an Inca Santa Claus. In Bolivian markets during the Alacitas Fair of late January, a few pesos will purchase tiny toy houses, kitchen utensils, domestic animals, even a miniature airline ticket. The hope is that Ekeko will in due course bestow upon the purchaser the real thing. Ceramic statues of Ekeko pre-laden with good-luck charms are also sold in Andean markets. There is a snag, however. They only work when received as a gift.

Chinchero market *Peruvian smallholders surrounded by their produce.*

Lotions and potions *A vast selection of roots, potions and charms are on sale at the Witchdoctors' Market in La Paz.*

Exotic harvest *The star fruit, ribbed outside, juicy inside, grows on the carambola tree.*

sellers of cheap hammocks and fine leather vaqueiro hats. In steamy Belém, there is the *Mercado Ver-o-Peso* (check-the-weight market). Here, in a market hall dating from 1688, fishermen dump their catches from the Amazon delta near to piles of jungle plunder, from miracle-working herbs to gaudy parrots theoretically protected from such commerce. Upriver, at Manaus, a modern, duty-free shopping zone in the heart of Amazonia adds a new dimension to the 'jungle' experience, but hard by on the murky waterfront the Mercado Municipal is as it should be, exotic.

'They walk home zigzag'

'The people wake up at 4 am and work in the field till 4 or 5. They go to bed early. That's why they have many children. They rest on Sunday and drink a lot of chicha. They walk home in zigzag but work very hard next day.' A tourist guide describing the life of Andean *campesinos*.

Sunday is market day in the Sacred Valley of the Incas, its sanctity lessened slightly by the presence of tourist buses, but all the better for business. Chinchero is 10 miles (16 km) from Cuzco. An Inca wall forms one side of the market, which is ablaze with bright colours. At nearby Pisac, the market is set beneath splendid Inca ruins: a rollicking affair, egged on by a brass band that falls blissful victim to the beer tent as the day proceeds. Everybody walks home zigzag.

For the potato gourmet *Papas – potatoes – come in more than 200 varieties and are served in nearly as many dishes. Peppers are often used to add zest.*

The perfect 'bife' steak, and conger eel soup…

Spices, peppers and aromatic herbs are a feature of many South American dishes, but are disdained by the most famous and simplest of them all – the *asado* of the pampa. This granddaddy of barbecues is a near-religious experience for devotees to bife, Argentine beef. The huge grills are called *parrillas*. For the perfect flavour, coals made from logs of quebracho, a hardwood, are recommended. The ocean's answer to the pampa is the chill Humboldt Current up the west coast, which makes possible such Chilean dishes as *caldillo de congrio*, a conger eel soup and *ceviche*, raw fish

marinated in a piquant sauce made with lemon juice, onion and hot fresh peppers. With shellfish added it becomes *ceviche mixto*. In Peru, the adventurous try *cuy*, guinea pig stewed, fried, or spit roasted.

CHAPTER 5

CITIES OF SOUTH AMERICA

In contrast to the great cities of ancient Andean cultures, today's cities have modern roots in European military and administrative headquarters. After independence, the old colonial patterns endured. Estate-owners who seized the fertile land forced immigrants into the cities, where they scratched a living in shantytowns. Huge towns grew up around the perimeter of South America, while immense hinterlands remain virtually uninhabited. In Argentina, Chile, Uruguay, Brazil and Venezuela, almost 80 per cent of the population live in towns. São Paulo, with some 20 million inhabitants, is the world's third largest city. Each of these huge entities has its individual character: Buenos Aires feels European, Bahia African, Cuzco Indian, Caracas American. Together, they encapsulate the continent's diversities and contradictions.

The courtyard of the Museum of Arts, Lima, Peru.

Chaotic Caracas

Venezuela poured its oil wealth into transforming its capital Caracas along North American lines, without thought to the consequences. Now 5 million people cram a narrow valley, stacked in high-rise apartment blocks or perched on the heights in squatter shanties…with more arriving every day.

City contrasts 'Caracas I love you!' reads the giant mural juxtaposed between apartment blocks and barrio slums.

It was known as the city of Santiago de Léon de Caracas, charming, bucolic, nestling in a narrow, verdant valley with an ideal climate; warm, but never too hot. Simón Bolívar, the Liberator, was born here. His statue, cast in Europe, was its centre of gravity.

Then came oil, lots of it, and a transformation so comprehensive and spinning so out of control that it is a wonder Bolívar has not fallen off his horse. From hardly a building over two storeys in the 1950s, the valley floor now bristles with skyscrapers, and while the setting is spectacular, with the green wall of El Avila national park on the city's north flank, this only serves to highlight the contrasts of wealth and poverty. From the air, the scene is startling: whole hillsides blanketed with squatters' *ranchos* (shacks) encasing a dynamic central core of steel, concrete and glass. Within the core, there is only one escape from traffic gridlock – down, into the excellent French-built metro.

Rescuing the concrete jungle from itself are the *Caraqueños* themselves, young and in love with life. Just as the big avenues are decked with flowering trees, so bright blossoms peep from window boxes. Outdoors is where to be, on Sabana Grande, a pedestrian boulevard lined with boutiques and bookshops, perfume shops and pavement cafés. This is the pop culture capital of South America, sophisticated and 'hip'. Looking good is a major concern: the *Caraqueños* would rather not eat than not look elegant; sure enough, during the deep recession of 1999, sales of cosmetics increased.

Local hero A statue of the Liberator on his horse dominates the Plaza Bolívar. Simón Bolívar was born in Caracas – just a short walk from the square that bears his name.

Black Forest in the cloud forest

Up in the cool, misty mountains an hour's drive from Caracas, the atmosphere is authentic Bavaria. In 1843, a community of German farmers from the Black Forest settled here and re-created all they had left behind. They kept their language, customs, costumes and architecture, their sausages, bread and beer, and they married within the community. Their isolation ended when a motor road arrived in 1963, and then their prosperity began. Their village, Colonia Tovar, is now a busy 'Black Forest' resort, immensely popular as a weekend retreat from the smoggy city – so much so that the average income is the highest of any community in Venezuela.

Cartagena, fabled port of the Spanish Main

Tucked into a corner of the Caribbean, the gateway to Spain's South American empire looks much as it did in the days of the buccaneers and treasure galleons – even if the principal export now is oil. 'Cartagena de India' is the most striking colonial city in the whole of South America.

Medellín: orchids and drugs

With a climate that is often described as 'eternal spring', a delectable location in a fertile mountain valley famed for its orchids, and a population approaching 2 million who are noted for their dynamic approach to life, Colombia's second city would seem to be most favoured – but Medellín is synonymous with cocaine. The notorious Escobar drug cartel of the 1980s left the city with the image of murder capital of the world. This charge is no longer applicable, but the spanking new high-rise glass towers, broad boulevards and three universities need to be considered against a surround of shanty slums.

Old Cartagena The major slave market of the New World was once round the corner.

Sacked in 1586 by Sir Francis Drake, who made off with 100 000 gold ducats, Cartagena was rebuilt with magnificent walls and fortresses to secure the gold and silver shipped from here to Spain. Far from the mainstream by the 19th century, it found new purpose with the discovery of nearby oilfields and now it is Colombia's second-largest port. Nevertheless, the old walled town has hardly changed, its narrow winding streets, palm-shaded plazas, palaces, monasteries and houses with elaborate wooden balconies are all more Spanish than Spain. The cathedral, whose completion was delayed by the attention given it by Drake's cannon, is understandably on the massive side. The Palace of the Inquisition still contains racks and thumbscrews, and the fortresses are still used occasionally, by film-makers. As for the old bullion vaults, these make excellent craft shops.

Very old gold This Calima pendant is one of 33 000 pieces from pre-Hispanic cultures in Bogotá's unique Gold Museum. Indian pan pipes provide background music for the displays.

Splendour and misery in Bogotá

Santa Fe de Bogotá (to give the city its full name) is the South American experience in caricature. The capital of troubled Colombia was once an Indian village called Bacatá, which was razed by a conquistador who had a keen sense of location. In colonial times, it was the seat of Spanish viceroys ruling an area that also included modern Ecuador, Venezuela and Panama, but the exponential growth that drove its population to over 6 million by 2000 all came in the second half of the 20th century. The people of Bogotá live in the clouds, 8670 ft (2642 m) up in the misty northern Andes, taking pride in their culture and the purity of their Spanish accent. But the polluted, traffic-jammed metropolis is an explosive mix of extremes – futuristic skyscrapers and vast shantytowns, vibrant intellectual life and rampant crime, opulent restaurants and bands of homeless children.

Bogotá street urchins Shared drugs dull the pain.

Quito, in two worlds

Life seems more intense in Quito, from the manner in which the restless volcano Pichincha looms over everyone's affairs, to a climate that can run the gamut of all four seasons in 24 hours, thanks to the city's location on the equator at an altitude of 9250 ft (2775 m).

Plaza de la Independencia
Also called Plaza Grande, it stands at the heart of colonial Quito. Old gentlemen read their newspapers and packs of shoeshine boys hunt tourists.

There are two different worlds in Quito, encased within the confines of its narrow Andean valley. North means modern high-rise buildings, upmarket shopping malls, mobile phones and the atmosphere of money. Then there is the Old Quito, best-preserved of the continent's colonial capitals, all whitewash and red-tiled houses, cobblestone streets, colonial mansions, cathedrals and churches – more than 80 of them, including La Iglesia de San Francisco, oldest church in the Americas, its plaza teeming with tourists and worshippers, hawkers, beggars and police. With medieval zeal, vendors sell incense, rosaries, saintly images and wax models of limbs, their business brisk. The church interiors often reflect a *mudejar* Spanish-Moorish style, and are a dizzy mélange of spectacular carving and gilding, brightly coloured paintings of the saints and gruesome crucifixions; the air is heavy with incense and Mass seems always to be in progress. The Old Town has the protection of UNESCO World Heritage listing and seems secure, Pichincha and earthquakes permitting.

The middle of the world

A favourite afternoon excursion is to *La Mitad del Mundo*, the 'middle of the world', where a monument and a yellow line mark the equator as first determined in 1736 by a party led by the French aristocrat Charles de la Condamine. Skipping from one hemisphere to the other and posing for a photo complete the experience.

Old Quito side-street *The old town's charms do not extend beyond sunset. When tourists and others retreat to modern Quito's restaurants and bars, crime takes over the cobbled streets.*

Guayaquil, a story of perseverance

Cut through the humidity and pollution, the street crime and the bumper-to-bumper traffic, and Guayaquil turns out to be a hospitable, progressive city with good restaurants, a lively nightlife and shady waterfront walks. Pirates, fires and natural disasters – the last one an earthquake in 1942 – have necessitated its rebuilding from scratch numerous times. It has persevered to become a major Pacific port and Ecuador's largest city. Its population of more than 2 million is twice that of the capital, Quito. Guayaquil was the site, in 1822, of the historic meeting between the liberators Bolívar and San Martín, cause enough for days of city-wide partying each July to mark Bolívar's birthday.

Cuzco, city of the sun

Cuzco – the name means 'navel' – is the former Inca capital and the oldest continuously occupied city in the Americas. Vivid and alive, with plenty of evidence of the extinct empire and its Spanish usurpers, its cobbled streets are filled with foreign tourists who come to gawk at the Peruvian descendants of the children of the sun.

Hat conscious Each style is a badge of identity.

On November 13, 1533, Francisco Pizarro and his men plunged into this fertile valley 11 000 ft (3300 m) up in the Andes and paused briefly to marvel at 'this greatest and finest city' before stripping it of its gold and other riches. But the Inca masonry would not be budged, not even by the earth tremors that periodically shake loose the Spanish city set on top of it.

The latest tourist destination

Noted for its sublimely exotic setting by an earlier generation of travellers, Cuzco is having to make adjustments. The Catholic nuns occupying accommodation originally built for Inca 'chosen women' now have as neighbours a cyber café and a travel agent offering helicopter rides to Machu Picchu. Credit-card signs hang over Inca stonework, and the main plaza, sacred core of the Inca Empire, is loud with discos and bars. With 300 000 inhabitants, Cuzco welcomed almost that number of tourists in 1999 and substantial further growth is anticipated. Anthropologists may fret, but abrupt change and odd cultural mixes are nothing new – the inhabitants are taking matters in their stride.

Rock solid   Colonial adobe rests on Inca masonry in Hatun Rumiyoc – the massive blocks as close fitting as the day they were built.

Lima, city of the viceroys

Shrouded in sea mists except for the short summer, when smog is a problem, the one-time capital of Spanish South America, and now capital of Peru, has a dismal climate. Founded in 1535 by Pizarro, who needed to be close to his ships, the 'City of the Kings' enjoyed centuries of grandeur as the seat of the viceroys. Some sense of this has been reclaimed by a restoration programme, but Lima has been overwhelmed by Andean migrants, many arriving in the 1980s, when a merciless struggle between Shining Path guerrillas and the military made the mountains unsafe. The city moved into the 21st century with a population of 8 million, many living in *pueblos jóvenes*, in fact shantytowns lacking basic facilities. The population in Lima's imperial heyday was 25 000.

A new menu for the Last Supper

Dominating the plaza, on the site of an Inca palace, Cuzco's 16th-century cathedral bears witness to a time of far greater culture shock.

Inside, in the gloom and glitter, you see the extent to which religious fusion has occurred, with pre-Hispanic symbols – mountains, suns, snakes – becoming part of the church imagery. Here is a version of the Last Supper, one of the most famous examples of the Cuzco School of painting, an extensive body of work by Indian artists under Spanish tutelage. Visitors looking closely at this huge painting will note how Christ and the apostles are dining on roast guinea pig, hot peppers and Andean cheese!

Cross-cultural archangel   Cuzco School (18th century).

Itaipú: modern-day wonder

Economists raised their eyebrows at the staggering cost, but an international panel of civil engineers voted this breathtaking power project one of the seven wonders of the modern world.

Major bridges and dams

Itaipú spillway   Itaipú means 'singing rock' in the Guaraní language. The dam is 643 ft (196 m) high and backs up the river for 100 miles (160 km). It sank without trace the spectacular Sete Quedas, or Guaira Falls, said to have carried the greatest volume of falling water in the world.

They are close enough to be almost within sound of each other … the thundering Iguaçu Falls and Itaipú, its man-made rival. Itaipú, on the Paraná River at the Brazil-Paraguay border, is the world's largest hydroelectric plant, and when one of its sluice gates is opened, the cascade rivals that of Iguaçu.

To create Itaipú, the *barrageiros* had to shift the course of the seventh biggest river in the world, removing 50 million tons of rock to dig a bypass. Then came the concrete – 15 times as much as was used to build the Channel Tunnel. Then the powerhouse, half a mile (0.8 km) long and half underwater, containing 18 enormous turbine generators, each one gulping 160 tons of water per second. Built over 18 years with the last turbine in place in 1991, Itaipú has the capacity to generate 12 600 megawatts of electricity and light cities as distant as São Paulo and Buenos Aires. It has more generating capacity than Grand Coulee in the United States; six times more than Aswan in Egypt. The construction job, with work crews of 28 000 and a total on-site population of 150 000, transformed the region. On the Paraguayan side of the Paraná, a small village grew into the country's second city, Ciudad del Este, 'City of the East'.

Itaipú capped an era of dam construction for Brazil and its neighbours, with enthusiasm at its height in the 1980s. But attitudes sobered with the restoration of democracy, when questions were asked about Itaipú's $20 billion (£13.5 billion) cost, and how it had drowned a set of cataracts rivalling Iguaçu in splendour. A blackout throughout southern Brazil in 1999 gave further cause to ponder over-reliance on hydroelectricity – the planners had failed to calculate the effects of a drought!

Rio-Niterói Bridge   Constructed in 1974, it crosses Rio de Janeiro's Guanabara Bay.

Putting water to work on a grand scale

Pending completion of China's Three Gorges project on the Yangtze River and a monster Russian scheme being built in Siberia, South America had three out of the world's top four hydroelectric power stations. Ranked in size after Itaipú are Venezuela's Guri Dam on the Caroní River (10 300 MW) and the Tucuruí Dam (7960 MW), largest of Brazil's Amazon projects. Downstream from Itaipú is Yacyretá (2700 MW), a joint project of Argentina and Paraguay. Salto Grande (1600 MW) is another Argentinian project, this time jointly with Uruguay. This region has also seen a spate of large-scale bridge construction.

Mighty São Paulo

This is the financial, business and industrial capital of Brazil and anyone expecting to find the laid-back ways of the rest of the country is in for a shock. As Ronald Reagan exclaimed upon first visiting São Paulo, 'I had no idea you had things like this down here.'

São Paulo is what powers Brazil. With a population approaching 20 million, it is not merely the largest city in South America, it is the largest in the Southern Hemisphere and also the richest, its financial centre representing the greatest accumulation of wealth in what used to be called the Third World. Aggressive, sprawling and resourceful, it is a city of immigrants and claims to have the largest Italian population of any city outside Italy, the largest Japanese population outside Japan, the largest Lebanese and Syrian populations outside the Middle East – claims substantiated by the make-up of its vast array of restaurants. The metropolitan sprawl covers 3000 sq miles (8000 km²) and more than half of Brazilian industry is located here. 'São Paulo works so the rest of Brazil can play', say *Paulistanos*, with immense pride. Clamorous, congested, polluted, twice as expensive as the rest of the country – they take pride in that also.

Melting pot   *Immigrants from 60 countries flocked to São Paulo.*

Stealing, but getting things done…

São Paulo is up in the hills 30 miles (48 km) from the coast and 220 miles (354 km) from Rio, with a climate that benefits from the 2690 ft (820 m) altitude – all thanks to the Jesuits who in 1554 chose the spot for their first

The other Chicago   *Called the Chicago of South America, São Paulo is six times as populous. Once it was a sleepy Jesuit mission, with a population of only 200.*

It's a job   *Migrants from the impoverished north-east compete for casual work as they eke out an existence in the vast slums.*

venture into the interior. It was from here in the 16th and 17th centuries that the plundering *bandeirantes* mounted the expeditions that defined Brazil's vast frontiers. Much later, coffee cultivation spread into the region and a planter élite graced the little city. With slavery abolished, the planters formed companies to bring in European peasant labour and immigration in the 1890s became a flood. With the coffee boom faltering, the planters reinvested their wealth to stimulate industrial growth, which became and remained relentless. *Paulistanos* like to think that the *bandeirante* spirit is with them still: sometimes, too much so. The city has a tradition of corruption, long excused by the phrase *rouba mas faz*, roughly meaning, 'he steals but he gets things done'.

An eclectic list of attractions

São Paulo has been consolidating its status as cultural capital since the 1920s. The *Museu de Arte de São Paulo* (MASP) has the best collection of fine art in South America. There is also a fine MAM (modern art museum) and MAC (contemporary art). The *Bienal,* an international art show, is held every second year. Other attractions are a major symphony orchestra, a snake farm, gigantic soccer stadiums, a famous motor-racing circuit – and more live music than Rio!

Pulsating Rio de Janeiro

On the top of Corcovado, an immense statue of Christ, arms open wide, holds vigil over Sugarloaf Mountain, the beaches edged with skyscrapers and the islands scattered on the sea. The effect is spectacular, the influence of the sacred image less evident. Too beautiful to be other than sinful, this city dabbles in every excess.

The last piece to the picture postcard that is Rio de Janeiro was added in 1931, when the 700 tons of Christ in concrete were set atop Corcovado, 'Hunchback', the precipitous 2300 ft (709 m) peak with tremendous views. Directly in line with *Cristo Redentor* (Christ the Redeemer) and half as high is the cheeky hummock of Sugarloaf, Rio's signature image. Reached by a spectacular cable-car ascent, Sugarloaf's summit offers the reverse angle view of the conical hills, called *morros*, which give the city its inimitable anarchic look. Clinging to their steep flanks, suspended over increasing affluence as one moves southwards, are the rickety *favelas*, the shantytowns. The *cidade maravilhosa*, 'marvellous city', all *Cariocas* agree to call it. A *Carioca* is a Rio resident: there are 11 million *Cariocas*, some in penthouses, a lot more in *favelas*.

Manhattan with bikinis

The mountain range that incorporates Corcovado splits Rio in two, between a *Zona Norte*, where tourists rarely venture (unless they are drawn to some big soccer match at the Maracanã Stadium), and the more affluent, safer *Zona Sul*. At the foot of the mountain is *Centro*, the business hub, which is congested by day but almost deserted at night.

Centro is the oldest part of Rio, where the museums, galleries and major churches are located. On its fringes are picturesque colonial neighbourhoods, including hilly, cobbled Santa Teresa, connected to the centre by trolley cars running on top of an 18th-century aqueduct. Middle-class Flamengo and Botofogo form a corridor to *Zona Sul* and the most famous beaches in the world.

The great South American body contest

Beauty contests are an industry in South America, particularly in Venezuela and Colombia, where the election of a 'queen' can bring the country to a halt. Brazilians are no less body-conscious, with Rio's beaches a mecca for golden bodies strutting in the latest near-nothing from Salinas or Bum Bum, while he-men throw themselves into volleyball or beach soccer with self-conscious vigour. For the less-than-perfect, help is at hand from Rio's 1000 plastic surgeons – more per capita than any other place on earth. They include Ivo Pitanguy, who is a national celebrity. The word has spread. Women – and men – come to Rio from around the world on 'plastic surgery vacations'.

Hectic, colourful Copacabana has been called a Manhattan with bikinis. Around its classic crescent run Avenida Atlântica's mosaic pavements, hotels and cafés – this is the essential Rio experience. These days, however, Ipanema and Leblon beaches are rather more chic. Everywhere, tropical vegetation spills onto the streets to provide that final exotic touch to a city that, like the vegetation, will not stop spreading.

Clinging to hope
Each favela *takes on an organic life of its own.*

The city of pleasure

On January 1, 1502, a Portuguese navigator dropped anchor in a prospective harbour and made a famous mistake. He mistook a bay for an estuary and named it Rio de Janeiro – January River. Rio thrived anyway and in 1763 replaced Bahia as colonial capital. The city's lush botanic gardens are a gift of King João VI of Portugal, in exile here from 1808. Once the king had sailed home, Rio, in 1822, became capital of Brazil. In 1900, the population reached 1 million. From the

Free riders *Carioca commuters put public transport to the test.*

Beach trader
From hats to sun cream – all the essentials of life.

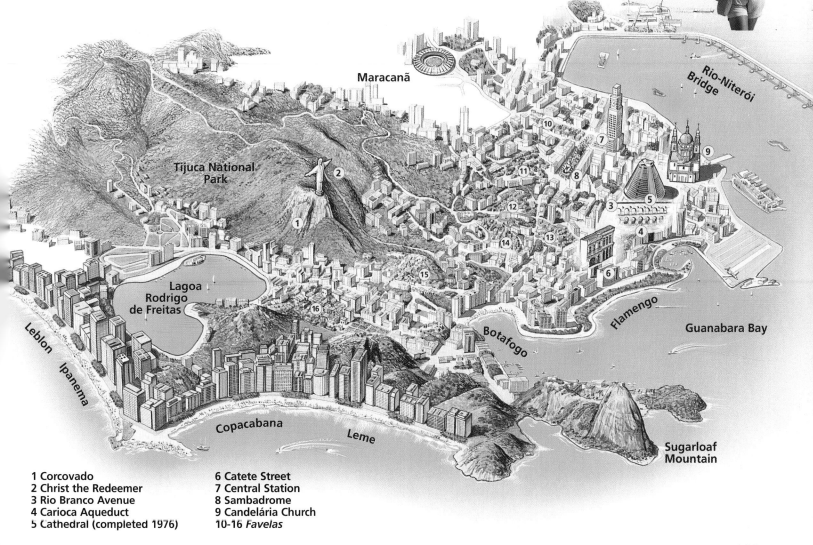

1 Corcovado
2 Christ the Redeemer
3 Rio Branco Avenue
4 Carioca Aqueduct
5 Cathedral (completed 1976)
6 Catete Street
7 Central Station
8 Sambadrome
9 Candelária Church
10-16 *Favelas*

Copacabana Beach *The most famous beach in the world fills with locals and tourists during the week. On weekends it is besieged by the masses who live in the favelas.*

1930s to the early 1960s was a golden age, a euphoric period of social cohesion, it appears in hindsight. Private beach villas made way for apartment towers and new beaches were claimed from the sea. Cultural life was intense. This was the time of the soft-and-sensual union of samba and jazz called *Bossa Nova* (New Trend), and of the fervent, exploratory *Cinema Nôvo* (New Cinema). In 1964, the military coup d'état was a terrible blow to Rio, which four years earlier had suffered the loss of its capital status to Brasília.

Then the grave economic crisis of the 1980s drove industries to São Paulo. The city of pleasure was left having to make pleasure its business.

Death squads and shanty tours

Eight children gunned down by off-duty policemen as they slept outside the Candelária Church in 1993 drew international attention to the other face of the most beautiful of cities: chronic violence, corruption and the armies of street urchins, *pivetes*, surviving from petty theft, washing windscreens, running errands, or as *avaiôezinhos*, 'little airplanes', runners for drug dealers. A 50 per cent drop in tourism between 1986 and 1992 spurred a clean-up campaign, particularly in tourist zones. The present annual homicide rate of 6000, equivalent of a medium-sized war, stems from violence that can go undetected by a visitor who sticks to the bright lights.

For millions in the straitened circumstances of *favela* life, fear is directed equally at the drug gangs and the police in their helicopters. Yet nothing is quite as it seems in this unpredictable city and the *favelados* are forever optimistic. They know they are needed, as maids, drivers, cleaners, and the opulence of the setting makes poverty less oppressive. Even the poorest can enjoy the view and the beaches, which are all public. In 2000, Rocinha, an enormous *favela* perched precariously above a select beach neighbourhood beyond Ipanema, opened itself to tourists with a reception centre and jeeps to take visitors up the steep, narrow, twisty lanes and into the lives of 200 000 spirited people. They wanted to show how the other half lived, they said.

Rio by night *For many Cariocas, nightfall marks the start of a second day.*

One more *chopp* and it's off to the dance hall

In Rio, much of life is lived out of doors, and nothing brings more people together than *botequims*, open-air neighbourhood bars that are an essential part of the city's fabric. Typically, there will be a few bar stools inside, but people usually prefer a table outside on the pavement. Draught beer, known as *chopp*, is the mainstay at most bars, along with such typically Brazilian drinks as *caipirinha*, made from pure cane spirit with infusions of tropical fruit juices. Not surprisingly, Rio has no shortage of nightlife options, from raunchy cabarets to dance clubs featuring MPB, short for *mûsica popular brasileira*. Dance halls include *forrôs* and *gafieras*, throwbacks to the time of waltz, polka and bolero.

The girl from Ipanema

Nothing has come to be more identified with Rio than *Garota de Ipanema* ('The Girl from Ipanema'), the 1960s Bossa Nova hit, soft and sensual as the warm breeze on the Ipanema beachfront. The song was inspired by a schoolgirl, Heloisa Pinheiro, who caught the attention of songwriter Antônio Carlos 'Tom' Jobim and lyricist Vinícius de Moraes when she walked past their favourite bar.

Recife, tropical Venice

On Brazil's eastern tip, the capital of the state of Pernambuco derives its name from the barrier reef of white coral that protects this part of the Atlantic coast and reveals natural swimming pools at low tide.

Founded in the middle of the 16th century by the Portuguese for its relative proximity to Europe and Africa, Recife was little more than an anchorage until the arrival in 1630 of the Dutch, who encouraged its development. Prosperity, based mainly on sugar, lasted into the 18th century. Charles Darwin, in 1835, was not impressed with Recife. He thought it 'disgusting…filthy'. He did not like the people, either, but he was nearing the end of a very long voyage, which might explain his grumpiness. Today, Recife's rank as the major port and principal city of the *Nordeste* cannot assuage the problems of the region, which are made manifest in the dilapidated state of some structures, modern as well as ancient, and in a plague of pedlars. On the Street of the Benevolent Jesus, just off the docks, archaeologists have found the remains of the first synagogue in the New World. Chased off by the Inquisition after 1654, when the Portuguese regained control from the Dutch, the Recife Jews took passage for New York to found what is now the largest Jewish community in the world.

Olinda: a colonial gem

When Duarte Coelho Pereira first saw Olinda in 1535 he exclaimed '*O linda!*' ('Oh, beautiful!'). Set on a hill overlooking the ocean, the town flourished as the stronghold of Pernambuco captaincy until superseded by Recife, 5 miles (8 km) away. Today, Olinda is an artists' stronghold, with ornate architecture, Moorish fountains and cobbled alleys that plunge down to the ocean.

City of water *A confluence of rivers and consequent accumulation of waterways and bridges led to Recife being labelled the Venice of South America. This Venice comes with white sand beaches and coconut palms, but also economic problems.*

They know how to party
Throngs clog the steep streets of Olinda for the 11-day carnival.

A full festival calendar

Recife and Olinda rival Bahia in the number of annual festivals and the zest of their carnivals. By January, when Nossa Senhora do Cormo, Recife's patron saint, blesses the *jangadas*, the traditional fishing craft, preparations for the pre-Lent *Carnaval* are already in full spate, with *blocos*, neighbourhood groups, holding practice sessions in the streets and on the beaches. A single *bloco* has been known to turn out in a force 20 000 strong. The major carnival dances here are the frenetic *frevo*, a cousin to the samba, and the intense *passo*. Olinda's carnival is famed for its length and unique atmosphere, causing many to prefer it to that of Rio and other big cities.

Brasília: utopian vision

A capital built by political decree, Brasília has been described as yesterday's vision of tomorrow. This 1950s hymn to the motor age and to reinforced concrete was intended to forge an egalitarian utopia through architecture. Instead, it became a monument to the follies of urban planning.

The idea was an old one – to open up the country by building a capital in the vast, empty interior. In Juscelino Kubitschek, Brazil had a president with ego and ambition enough to act upon it. He would build a shining 'city of the future' in the *cerrado* hundreds of miles from the coast.

The Warriors Giogi's sculpture honours the builders of Brasília.

Costa's doodles

The story goes that urban planner Lúcio Costa doodled his winning scheme five minutes before entries closed in the 1956 contest to pick a design for the new capital. It took the form of a bird with outstretched wings, or a jet plane, with a 'fuselage' of government buildings crossed by curving wings of residential buildings and embassies. To design the major buildings, Costa chose Oscar Niemeyer, a one-time pupil of Swiss modernist Le Corbusier, whose functional visions were a

Alternative voices

Innumerable religious cults and New Age communities flourish in Brasília. Many believe the city to be a conduit for cosmic forces, due to its supposed location at the centre of a magnetic field. These include The Legion of Goodwill, a sect that has built a pyramid with a large crystal at its summit. Dom Bosco, a 19th-century Italian priest who prophesied the coming of the 'promised land of milk and honey', draws a large following. Brasília also has a designated religious sector for the location of all manner of churches and temples.

Pietá Inside the cathedral

Crown of thorns Oscar Niemeyer's semi-subterranean cathedral (foreground) appears menaced by the advancing ranks of towering office blocks.

Mellowing among the superquadras

Brasília's sweeping express lanes and feeder roads with no pavements and few stop-signs are still deadly to pedestrians. Its streets still have numbers, not names; residential zones are still called *superquadras* and the expanses between Niemeyer's spectacular structures continue to exhaust the feet.

Yet there has been some mellowing. Vines soften concrete walls; flowering trees lend scale and colour to monumental vistas; the national cathedral leaks, endearingly. Blessed with a more temperate climate, easy commuting and a lower crime rate than its big sisters on the coast, Brasília has become popular

prime inspiration, even though nothing could have been more at odds with Brazilian tradition. Earth-movers were air-lifted in; labour was recruited from the poor north-east, and work proceeded at such a pace that Brasília was built in three years. The dedication ceremony was in April 1960. To induce civil servants to move from Rio de Janeiro, the government had to double their salaries.

with young professionals as a place to raise a family. The egalitarian utopia that Costa and Niemeyer envisioned never came to pass. Instead, the central zone – their 'Brasília' – is a class-structured, white-collar enclave of 400 000 privileged residents, while five times that number, including those poor migrants who built Brasília, are settled in 18 ramshackle 'satellite cities' on its peripheries.

Bahia, source of the Brazilian beat

Salvador da Bahia, capital of the state of Bahia and once capital of all Brazil, is the most African city in the Americas. Rich in architectural treasures from colonial times, and famous for its spicy cuisine, for its beaches and for an exuberance of spirit that impresses even other Brazilians, this is where Portuguese culture blended with that of the slaves to create much of what is thought of today as expressly 'Brazilian'.

You can call it Bahia for short, or Salvador, or you can be very proper and call it *São Salvador da Bahia de Todos os Santos*. The setting, a bluff overlooking the Bay of All Saints, is properly sumptuous. For almost 300 years, this was the most important city in Brazil, second only to Lisbon in the Portuguese world. The bay forms a deep natural harbour and here fortunes were made on the simple formula, slaves in, sugar out. On top of the bluff, the planters built residences and endowed Baroque churches. To pay for all this they brought in more and more slaves, so that Bahia is today at least 80 per cent Afro-Brazilian.

Up and down the elevador

Once the formula failed, Bahia lapsed into a century-long siesta. Lately, it has experienced rapid population growth, to well over

Capoeira : dance, sport, martial art

Almost as much a martial art as a dance, *capoeira* originated with slaves from Angola – some say it was a strategy for escape. It developed into a lethal sport in which the high-kicking, somersaulting participants might have knives attached to their ankles. The modern dance is a graceful, acrobatic mock combat performed in time to the throbbing rhythm of the one-string *berimbau*. The effect is hypnotic and completely mesmerising. The various *capoeira* schools in Bahia pursue the art with dedication.

2 million, but the relaxed mood has not been compromised. Energy needs to be conserved for the taxing cycle of fiesta-partying that, together with its beaches, makes Bahia a favourite holiday choice of Brazilians themselves. Much of the focus is on the historic city centre, part on top of the bluff, part down below, and linked by the *elevador Lacerda*, a fantastic lift in service since 1872, and surely the best 2 cent trip in the world today. Here *Baianas* in flowing white lace dresses and turbans cook and sell on the street spicy and sweet items out of the Bahian cookbook. A blend of Africa and Brazil, this cuisine uses plenty of coconut milk, ginger, hot peppers, coriander and *dendé*, palm oil, which is used in almost every dish.

The Afro-Brazilian cults: religion with a musical message

Colourful syncretic cults thriving in Bahia are the inspirational source of much of the music and dance that give Brazil its distinctive 'beat'. An important element in Candomblé and other Afro-Brazilian cults is possession by an *orixá*, an African deity usually associated with a Catholic saint. In such a state, the believer 'becomes' the *orixá*, or *santu*, and receives *axé*, a vital energy force. Pulsating music and dance are agents in the process, and from the turn of the 20th century these gave rise to secular forms, most famously the samba. This flow has not abated. Distinctive Bahian *axé* music has lately gained popularity around the country.

Making the old new

Pelourinho is the lively heart of the old city, a collection of 17th and 18th-century buildings that glow in every pastel hue, thanks to a major renovation that did not please every architectural purist. The name derives from the pillory that once stood here.

Cities torn by opposing forces

Communal life in South America is evolving fast, as country-dwellers migrate to towns, and cities rush into a future that seems destined to be a struggle between wealth and poverty, between high-rises and shantytowns.

The frantic pace of urban change leaves open the question of whether anything of the old communal past will be preserved. It is still possible, though, to work your way into the heart of a culture by tracing history through local architecture, from pre-colonial times to modern cityscapes, especially if you are prepared to search for the roots of community life in the countryside.

Villages out of time

Outside the large cities, the feel of the past is most evident in the Andes, where the roots of civilisation are deepest. Wherever you go, from

Standing high *The shacks in the shantytowns of Guayaquil, Ecuador, are built on stilts to avoid the disease-ridden floodwaters of the Guayas river.*

Glass wave *The 'flapping flag' shape of Oscar Niemeyer's Copan Building in São Paulo was one of Brazil's many postwar urban masterpieces.*

arid mountain to lush tropical valley, you will stumble on villages that seem frozen in time. Walking along mud roads that are nothing but furrows defined by their stone gutters, you see lines of pretty thatched houses. These little, single-storey terraced boxes have façades painted either in bright contrasting colours or immaculate white. Often, their doors and windows are out-of-true. The rooms are usually arranged around an interior courtyard or garden, or even a little grove of fruit trees, which acts as a focus for family life. If the roofs are flat, leading in a line from one to the other, the owners may grow cacti round the edges to discourage thieves and stray animals. Occasionally, the ground floors stand on huge jointed blocks inherited from Inca days.

Cuzco, in Peru, is an example of a town which contains fossilised remnants of its past. The 10th Inca monarch, Pachacuti, turned it into his capital in the 15th century, with the Temple of the Sun as its focal point. Around two squares – one of which is today's Plaza de

Ancient charm   Indifferent to modernity, many Andean village houses, like these in Los Nevados, Venezuela, still have earth floors.

A good life on the grasslands

On ranches – *fazendas* in Brazil, *estancias* in Spanish-speaking areas – the buildings are traditionally set in a circle, as befits what were at one time self-centred little communities of farm-workers. Around the *casa grande* – the 'big house' where the estate-owners live and work – are the old slave-barracks (*senzalas*), which were adapted to house workers and their families when slavery ended. In the late 19th and early 20th centuries, the agricultural revolution created by barbed wire and farm machinery increased the wealth of the landowners. Nowadays some ranches have been upgraded to accommodate tourists, who come to fish, watch wildlife, ride or to take part in one of the many great popular celebrations or festivals.

Rich retreat   Arroyo Dulce, an Argentinian estancia once worked by slaves, now lives up to its name – 'Gentle Stream'.

Armas – ranged palaces and the stone-built residential areas of the nobility and their servants. Beyond, in a sort of suburban sprawl, were the wood-and-straw dwellings of the lesser nobility and artisans. Those buildings have vanished, and much else lies beneath colonial architecture, but the feel of the Inca capital endures in the maze of little alleys, where people stand at their doorways, chatting with passers-by.

The two worlds of the city

Roots like this are hard to see in the larger cities, for during the second half of the 20th century they evolved into two worlds, both of which obscured the past. In business centres and rich residential suburbs, the better-off built solidly in pursuit of modern comforts that symbolise success and status. At best, this has produced stunning architecture, particularly in Brazil. In 1956, the decision to build Brasília as a new capital from scratch inspired a generation of architects led by Oscar Niemeyer. His creations – the Palace of the Dawn, the Cathedral, the Plaza of the Three Powers – won international acclaim, as did the schools, hospitals and universities designed by him and others.

But the building boom had its downside. It is rare now to find a colonial quarter preserved in the face of galloping development.

Among the offices, apartment blocks and skyscrapers, only a few old houses remain, with their painted wooden blinds, iron window-grills and interior patios that form little havens of greenery and peace.

Away from the rich areas, peasants flooding in from the country-side in search of a better life were condemned to slums. The slums, some of which have achieved international notoriety, are known as *favelas* in Brazil, *villas miserias* (misery towns) in Argentina and elsewhere as *chabolas* or *barrios de las latas* (cardboard-box districts). Whatever the name, they share the same things: lack of drinking water, walls made of bits and pieces scavenged from dumps, and corrugated iron roofs. The shantytowns, once seen as temporary, have become fixtures. They ring almost all the major cities of the continent, and often penetrate their hearts, the result of an uncontrolled rush in which rootless suburbs suck life from villages and their traditions.

Tradition preserved   Houses with tiled roofs and whitewashed walls make a backdrop for stall-holders in a Peruvian village marketplace.

Old and new   Colonial classic contrasts with grim modernity in a Rio street.

Rich oases or rich ghettos?

As the privileged began to feel increasingly threatened by the shanty-dwellers, they started to build enclaves that were totally enclosed by protective walls: *barrios carrados*, or 'locked areas'. For the security-minded, the ultimate in self-protection is to build a house in a country club. These huge green areas, entirely surrounded by fences or even armoured concrete bastions, have carefully vetted access. Inside are club houses and grounds with every conceivable facility: leisure areas, swimming pools, golf courses, football pitches, tennis courts, shopping centres, banks, and libraries. In exchange for a vast entry fee – up to £30 000 – the upper-crust and *nouveaux riches* can live in luxury villas in artificial paradises, all in the cause of safety and at the cost of being segregated from the realities of city life.

The Moneda Palace *Traditionally, but no longer, the presidential residence, the Moneda Palace was reinaugurated in 1981, following its restoration in the wake of the 1973 coup, when it was heavily damaged by air attacks. Moneda means 'coin', a reflection of the building's original role as a Spanish royal mint. Designed by the Italian architect Joaquín Toesca and completed in 1805, its distinctive low profile was Toesca's way of lending it resistance to earthquakes.*

Sun and smog in Santiago

A Mediterranean climate with vineyards in the suburbs, ski resorts a short drive in one direction and Pacific beaches in the other – if everyone would only switch off their car ignitions, things might be perfect in this capital city that is home to more than 5 million Chileans.

At noon on weekdays, a cannon booms from the little hill where the doughty conquistador Pedro de Valdivia sat down and planned a capital for Chile. 'Life here cannot be equalled', he wrote to his king. A brief winter, delicious summer breezes, fertile soil…he went on to set down all the wonders of this valley site, dramatically framed by the snowcapped Andes on the one hand and the coastal cordillera on the other. Today his lookout makes a charming park, Cerro Santa Lucía, rising out of a sea of traffic and overlooking the Plaza de Armas, the square that he traced out in 1541 and which now harbours pleasing gardens and a bandstand. Charm is a word often used in describing this well-tended city without the chaos associated with some other South American capitals and retaining an air of intimacy despite its size. This is explained in part by an unusually compact core, which is

augmented by a sprawl of more than 30 *comunas*, distinctive communities, the richest of them nestling in the foothills of the Andes.

The founder's instincts for the ideal location were perfect, but for a failure to anticipate the invention of the internal combustion engine. The Santiago Valley makes a perfect trap for engine emissions and levels of air pollution are among the worst in the world. Starting in the 1990s, emergency restrictions on car use have become a regular occurrence through much of the year. Escape is close at hand, however. Chile's wine country starts in the suburbs; the best skiing in the Andes is just 30 miles (50 km) away by road and the beaches of the Pacific are within 90 miles (150 km).

Valparaiso: rickety thrills and enchantment

Valparaiso lives dangerously. Chile's colourful second city, legislative capital and major port, 75 miles (120 km) from Santiago, is subject to earthquakes (those in 1906 and 1971 did particular damage), yet a shortage of foreshore obliged residential areas to spread into the *cerros*, precipitous hills separated by yawning gulches. By dint of daunting stairways, zigzag paths and a rickety network of *ascensors* (funiculars or cable tramways) the *cerros* have been scaled and strung together. Coping with gravity and the exigencies of earthquakes was left to the ingenuity and daring of individual builders.

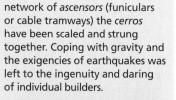

Life on the edge *Taking an* ascensor *shrinks the city's climbs.*

Bellavista *This is where Santiago kicks up its heels. The city's 'artistic' neighbourhood of galleries, theatres and restaurants has numerous late-night haunts. Pablo Neruda wrote some of his best poetry while living here.*

Montevideo, the vintage capital

'It is necessary to take time to take time,' goes an old Uruguayan proverb. The capital of the Oriental Republic of Uruguay, South America's smallest Spanish-speaking nation, is in the process of putting this maxim to the test.

The only thing fast about Montevideo is the *buquebus,* the high-speed catamaran ferry from Buenos Aires that leaps across 80 miles (130 km) of Rio de la Plata to the amiable, shabby-elegant capital of a land where cows outnumber humans three to one and sheep outnumber cows two to one. To step ashore is to seem to go back in time. Old British Leyland buses and electric trolleys ply this retro-metropolis, loaded with neoclassical, Italianate, beaux arts and other European architectural styles, amid a traffic stream of scooters, bicycles and vintage motor vehicles. Unselfconscious and unpretentious, the Uruguayans (they number 3.2 million, of whom 1.8 million live in the city) have been through hard times and few can afford the high import duty on cars, so the streets have become moving museums. The easy pace of the city seeps into the bones. Jorge Luis Borges once wrote it a poem: 'You are the Buenos Aires we once had, That slipped away quietly over the years…' In Montevideo, quite the latest thing has been a renaissance of – the tango!

Plaza Independencia *In the graceful heart of Montevideo, the camera is vintage, naturally.*

Asunción for short

The capital of Paraguay – poor, subtropical and wedged between Brazil, Argentina and Bolivia – began existence in 1537 as a stockade overlooking the Paraguay river. Nuestra Señora Santa María de Asunción did not have a piped water system until 1955 and despite a construction boom it still lacks the feel of a capital city. European and Indian societies melded here as nowhere else in the continent and most people are bilingual in Spanish and Guaraní. Tropical butterflies and black market money-changers flit about the Plaza de los Héroes, where the dictator Stroessner used to have his name flashing in neon and where the National Pantheon of Heroes, modelled on the Invalides in Paris, holds the remains of assorted leaders and soldiers from the country's wars with its neighbours. A few blocks away is the Estacíon Ferrocarril Central, where some of the oldest steam engines still in use are to be found. The station is a Victorian gem, once British-owned and run.

Government Palace, Asunción
The interiors came from Paris.

Punta del Este: for an expensive sun tan

Call it 'Punta' and people will know you belong. Occupying a small peninsula 86 miles (138 km) east of Montevideo, Punta del Este is the most fashionable beach resort in South America. It started with families from Montevideo and Buenos Aires building beach chalets.The chalets became holiday mansions, discreetly set behind tall pines and mimosa. A series of high-level international conferences held at a resort in the 1960s added panache. Residential complexes proliferated, along with hotels and casinos and superior boutiques bearing names like Gucci. In January and February – the polo season – tournaments attract some of the world's best players to Punta. In winter, much of the resort closes down.

Sky-high La Paz

It has been said that the capital of Bolivia is the only city in the world that it is impossible to imagine without experiencing it in person. Recent developments make the imagining even more difficult.

The highest capital in the world! The thrill of flying into La Paz, skimming over the Cordillera Real and making a landing on a lunar-like landscape at 13 179 ft (4018 m) carries the possible penalty of a day or two of *soroche*, the nausea otherwise known as altitude sickness. Even when the body has adapted to the thin atmosphere, it takes a local to get about this fascinating city without apparent effort. A Captain Alonso de Mendoza came this way in 1548, bent upon the usual quest for gold. What he found was more valuable – a route through the mountains from the silver mines which had been discovered three years earlier. A little over 40 miles (65 km) beyond the eastern shore of Lake Titicaca, the Choqueyapu River has carved a gaping canyon

Upper class redefined *Conditions at the canyon rim contrast starkly with those down below, as exemplified by the spacious Plaza del Estudiante (above) near the centre of La Paz.*

about 1400 ft (430 m) deep. At its base La Paz was able to develop in comparative comfort, protected from the bone-chilling winds of the Altiplano and the high Andean plateau – until the thrust of urbanisation from the 1960s onwards caused population-creep up the canyon walls.

Out on the barren plateau beyond the lip of the canyon sprawls a littered, jerry-built city of the poor, many of the inhabitants are without water or electricity. This is Alto La Paz, alias El Alto, which accounts for nearly half of the city's burgeoning population of 1.5 million. Here wealth is measurable in descending altitude: from 13 452 ft (4100 m) on the exposed rim to 10 171 ft (3100 m) where the finest homes occupy the most sheltered land.

Potosí: cursed by riches

There is a Spanish figure of speech, 'as rich as Potosí', that masks bitter irony. Potosí, in the eastern cordillera 300 miles (480 km) south-east of La Paz, was founded in 1545 following the discovery of Cerro Rico, the 'rich mountain' of silver ore that became Spain's primary source of wealth. To extract it, countless Indians were forced to toil, while Potosí became the largest city in the New World. In 1650, the population reached 160 000; records list eight fencing schools and 36 gaming houses. After the silver gave out, Potosí survived on tin-mining, until the tin price collapsed. Potosí today is an eerie city filled with crumbling colonial architecture and occupied in part by impoverished miners who pick at the old workings.

Rescue mission *UNESCO is backing restoration projects for about 2000 buildings in Potosí.*

Sucre: the forgotten capital

Legally speaking, Bolivia's capital is not La Paz, but Sucre, a beautiful old university town that is sometimes called La Ciudad Blanca, the White City, for its dazzling appearance – a local regulation requires buildings to be given a fresh coat of whitewash each year. A move to replace Sucre, the original capital, caused such offence in 1898 that civil war broke out. The upshot was a compromise. Sucre remained the constitutional capital and it retained the supreme court, while all other arms of government moved to La Paz.

Sucre *Consolation in a dab of whitewash.*

Tough and tender Cochabamba

In the 'valley of eternal spring', in the heart of the Bolivian Andes, Cochabamba is reputed to have the world's finest climate. But troubles mount for this Shangri-la as poor migrants strain its resources beyond endurance and drug-trafficking offers a drastic way out.

Market force *Loading up for La Cancha, the big daily market.*

Cochabamba – the sound of the name is enough to conjure the brightly clothed Indian women selling fresh fruit in the plaza beneath the 16th-century cathedral. Cochabamba nestles in its mountain bowl at 8200 ft (2500 m) above sea-level; skies are crystal clear, the climate constantly spring-like. Fertile soil has made this Bolivia's agricultural centre. Cochabamba boasts a Christ-statue that is 10 ft (3 m) taller than Rio's and its *chicha cochabambina* is considered as fine an example of traditional Andean brewing as one can find. Here, early in the 20th century, the tin baron Simón Patiño lavished some of his vast fortune on building for himself a palacio, now a culture centre.

Drinking the valley dry

There are no Patiños today, only unemployed miners and too many rural migrants drawn to a city without the means or the infrastructure to cope. A population of 20 000 early in the 20th century had grown to well over a half-million by its end, with 800 000 projected for 2005. Coupled with a drying climate, this is turning the once lush valley into a parched and dusty place. Farmers cannot get what they need for irrigation, while drinking water is rationed or unavailable to half the population. Due east, where the mountains drop into jungle terrain known as the *Chapare*, those with enterprise or desperation enough grow coca for processing into cocaine, though the risks following a crackdown are great.

The Patiño palace *The mansion has a replica of the Sistine Chapel on the first floor.*

All aboard the death train

Its official title is the Expreso del Oriente, a 30-hour journey from Santa Cruz in Bolivia to the Brazilian town of Corumbá. It is better known as the 'Death Train' for the gun battles that have taken place on board between feuding drug traffickers. Much of the cocaine produced in the *Chapare* is brought out in the train's luggage wagons – from Corumbá, the railway provides access to Atlantic ports. Santa Cruz, in the hot lowlands east of Cochabamba, is a booming city whose flamboyant mansions, luxury cars and nightclubs reflect a lifestyle unknown elsewhere in South America's poorest country.

The government thought it had a solution – to privatise the water supply and approve a London-based consortium's plan to end shortages forever by driving a pipeline through the Andes. But the idea of foreigners owning their water – and charging for it – enraged people already smarting from coca-containment measures. Riots shut down Cochabamba, then all of Bolivia, until the government dropped the plan.

In the steps of Che Guevara

The famous poster with the handsome, scowling face is still brandished during demonstrations in Bolivia, where the prince of guerrillas met his death. Ernesto 'Che' Guevara, from a well-to-do Argentine family and aide to Fidel Castro in the Cuban revolution, was betrayed, wounded and captured on October 8, 1967, and shot the next day. Excursions 'in the steps of Che' are organised from both Cochabamba and Sucre. The trips include visits to Camiri, site of his last base camp, La Higuera, the tiny village where he was shot by his army captors, and Vallegrande, the town where his body was taken.

The legend lives on *Che berets, T shirts, posters…*

Avenida 9 de Julio A span of 460 ft (140 m) makes this the widest avenue in the world. The obelisk was erected in 1936 to mark the city's 400th anniversary.

Passionate Buenos Aires

San Telmo, Palermo, La Recoleta, Belgrano, La Boca, Barrio Norte, Once, Constitución… recite the names of the 47 barrios, or districts, of the Argentine capital and it sounds like an incantation, or a playbill for this most theatrical of cities.

Buenos Aires is a city of 11 million people, who call themselves *porteños*, or port dwellers. It spreads ceaselessly over the *pampa* on the western bank of the River Plate, a checkerboard of *cuadras*, 300 ft (100 m) blocks piled with the architecture of successive waves of European immigration. Its boulevards, cafés and bookstores swirl all night with a tide of humanity – between 10 pm and midnight is when *porteños* commonly begin dining out. This is a cosmopolitan city with grand hotels and wide boulevards, a seven-tier opera house and the best rib-steak in the world. It is a city polarised between two of the world's best football clubs, Boca Juniors and River Plate; a city with its own argot. This 'Paris of South America', built upon the beef boom of the 1880s, also has its problems – pollution, decay and *villas miserias*, creeping shanty land.

Two ends of town

Northern Buenos Aires is the wealthier end of town. La Recoleta is the most fashionable place to stay, to while away hours in chic cafés and galleries, to walk poodles in the park; and when it's all over, it's the place to end up. Recoleta Cemetery is the most exclusive address of all, a walled necropolis of extraordinary ostentation. Evita, Eva Perón, is here surrounded by the rich she despised and who despised her. Flowers never stop arriving, and neither do tourists: some simply ask the way to Madonna.

Wander south of the Plaza de Mayo, the political and historical heart of the city, and the streets become more crowded and more like old movie sets. San Telmo is a *barrio* of small shops, antique

dealers, bars and artists. On summer evenings, the plaza fills with couples dancing the tango, the song and dance form created in the slums a century ago and seen to convey the Buenos Aires spirit as nothing else.

Loneliness, jealousy, despair Singing tango in the street, San Telmo. Tango is said to reflect the Argentine character, as samba is the spirit of Brazil.

La Boca, barrio of The Candybox

Bounded by rusting freighters and abandoned dockside cranes, and dominated by *La Bombonera* (the candybox), the home stadium of Boca Juniors, La Boca is a vibrant working class *barrio* believing only in the invincibility of its soccer team and the divinity of Eva Perón. Settled by sailors and dockers from Genoa in the late 19th and early 20th centuries, and still sometimes referred to as 'Little Italy', it is famous for its *pizzerias*, for its rowdy *cantinas* where everybody sings loudly, and for its houses of corrugated iron that are painted in the brightest colours possible; also for the stench of the Riachuelo channel. Upriver is Puerto Madero, a redevelopment of 19th-century waterfront buildings, new tower blocks and exclusive restaurants.

Mar del Plata: the pearl

In summer, Argentines head for the beach – any beach – but they head in greatest numbers for Mar del Plata, otherwise known as the 'Pearl of the Atlantic', or simply 'Mardel' to its 3 million or more regulars.

Star turn *Geraldine Chaplin leaves her handprints.*

Despite cheap and easy access to the beaches of Brazil, the Caribbean or Mexico, *porteños* retain a fierce pride in their own Costa Atlántica. When high summer hits the capital, the *barrios* empty to reassemble *en masse* 250 miles (400 km) away, where the hills drop down to the sea. Through December and January, Mar del Plata becomes Buenos Aires in sunshades and deckchairs.

No half measures here

Mar del Plata was founded in 1874 by a developer named Patricio Peralta Ramos and it was planned as a resort from the very start. The distance from the capital assured exclusivity, and by the turn of the century rich patrician families were building lavish villas that vied with each other in their extravagance. In pursuit of authenticity, they would import from Europe the genuine article in prefabricated form. The British 'Victorian villa', picturesque 'Silvina' villas in a French style, and Scandinavian-style homes from Norway all found favour. The resort was served by rail and the middle classes began to arrive.

In the 1930s, major road improvements were accompanied by the opening of a casino: with 36 roulette tables, it was the biggest casino in the world. Foreshore development reached its most intense in the 1960s and 1970s, while other smaller resorts, each with a distinctive appeal, have sprung up along the coast in either direction. Mardel is now half-an-hour from the capital by air.

On the beach *Overpopulation can be a problem.*

La Perla del Atlántico has 5 miles (8 km) of beaches, parks and several golf courses; attractive plazas and pedestrian shopping malls; all-night dance clubs and theatrical shows on transfer from Buenos Aires through high summer. It has a fishing port and plenty of seafood restaurants. But probably the biggest single attraction is the casino, still one of the world's biggest.

The *Ombú:* an 'Oscar' for South America

The turbulent history of Mardel's International Film Festival reflects both Argentine passion for the cinema and the crises that have dominated the country's modern history. From its founding in 1954, the festival was a success. Notable winners include Ingmar Bergman in 1959 for *Wild Strawberries* and François Truffaut in 1962 for *Jules et Jim*, while the appearance of stars such as Paul Newman and Natalie Wood testified to its influence. But economic and political upheaval, and the censorship of authoritarian regimes, forced its cancellation for 26 years, from 1970 to 1995. Since its resurrection, the festival has regained its place on the international calendar and draws more than 100 000 film fans to Mardel in late November. The screenings last a week, concluding with a grand jury awarding trophies known as *ombúes*. The Golden *Ombú* is awarded for best feature film. Silver *ombúes* go to best director, actor, actress and screenplay. The film festival is one of a series of national events staged in Mar del Plata each year.

The Plaza de Armas

When it came to urban planning, one thing Spanish and Inca agreed upon was the importance of the plaza, or public square. In Cuzco, it marked the precise centre of the Inca Empire, a ceremonial ground covered with white sand mixed with flakes of gold, silver and coral – and soils brought from conquered lands.

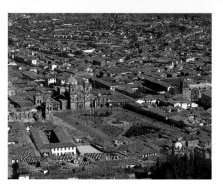

Plaza de Armas, Cuzco *The plaza was twice as large in Inca times.*

The Inca had individual names for what is called a *pata* in Quechua – Square of Joy, Square of Weeping, Square of War are some of those that have come down. To the Spanish conquistadores, who were under orders to strictly follow procedure, *plaza de armas* (meaning arms, weapons) was the term for their defensive perimeter, with a fort their priority construction. Procedure further called for church and public buildings to be grouped around the plaza, and in no time another 'city' would be born. In a remarkable number of instances, the name has stuck, so that today there is a plaza de armas in many South American cities.

Progress of a plaza

The Plaza de Armas in Santiago, the Chilean capital, is a typical example. After more than 450 years, the city remains firmly anchored around the plaza and the well at its centre that was Santiago's first water source. Through the Spanish colonial period, this was the marketplace and focus of public activities, from religious processions and military parades to public hangings. By the 1830s, it had gardens and a marble monument to liberation. Nowadays, the Plaza de Armas is a popular retreat from the surrounding bustle, with a constantly changing cast of buskers and street artists, shoeshine boys, lovers and loungers, and bandstand performances twice weekly. The cathedral on the plaza is the fifth to occupy the site, earthquakes having demolished most of its predecessors.

Plazas for every purpose
The Plaza de Armas in Santiago has a corner for chess lovers (left), while in the small Bolivian village of Challa (below) it is the setting for weekly markets.

The Jesuit plaza: salvation by example

The plaza principle was adapted by the Jesuits as a feature of their system of protected Indian villages in the 17th and 18th centuries. In this case, the Indians were housed on one side of the plaza, while the church, stores and all community facilities, even the cemetery, were set on the opposite side, with a statue of the village's patron saint set to dominate the plaza itself. In this regimented way, the Jesuits converted to Christianity 700 000 Indians between 1610 and 1767.

Córdoba, core of Argentina

The second city of Argentina is a city of the heartland in every sense.
It provides an important economic, political and social counterweight to
the far-off capital across the pampa.

Pride in tradition
A gaucho in his
baggy breeches.

Strike inland from Buenos Aires, across the immense, flat pampa, and after eight or nine hours' driving through vast expanses of grain and sunflowers and enormous herds of cattle, a line of rolling hills breaks up the horizon and you are entering Córdoba, a city of about 1.2 million, midway between the Atlantic and the Andes. With a background steeped in piety and learning, and with immediate concerns that range from the cattle industry to car plants, Córdoba is a stimulating place to explore, its streets filled with students and factory workers, lawyers, seminarians and ranch hands in town in their best *bombachas*, baggy breeches.

It felt just like home

Founded in 1573 and named after the Spanish city of the same name, Córdoba prospered when Buenos Aires was no more than a smugglers' retreat. The Jesuits arrived in 1599 and made it their headquarters; in 1613, they founded a university, now the National University of Córdoba. Fortunes were reversed after 1776, when Buenos Aires was named capital of a new viceroyalty, and Córdoba became mired in conservatism and resentment. The modern

Enduring scene Student life has flourished in Córdoba for 400 years.

Scratch the surface *Beneath a bland surface, Córdoba is intriguing.*

city can trace its origins to 1869, when the railway and the first immigrants arrived. A hundred years on, in 1969, students and factory workers joined forces to almost bring down a military government in the *Cordoblazo*, the Córdoba coup.

Charm amid the bustle

In Córdoba, colonial charm and modern bustle combine easily, with help from a lively student population. *Peatonales* (pedestrian ways) are lined with bookstores, boutiques and cafés and close to the city centre a tree-lined canal, *La Cañada*, offers shady walks. In summer, streets are decked out for craft fairs and music festivals.

Corrientes, a focus of Argentine traditions

Six days after its foundation in 1588, Corrientes was attacked by Indians and miraculously saved – according to local legend – by a cross that the colonists had placed at the centre of their small fort. Celebration was therefore in order from the very start, and Corrientes has not let up since. An annual feast in honour of the *Santisima Cruz del Milagro* (Most Sacred Cross of the Miracle) is one of a number of celebrations that enliven this provincial capital located below the confluence of the Paraná and Paraguay rivers, 635 miles (1025 km) north of Buenos Aires. The city's *Carnaval Correntino* attracts big crowds, while residents even accord the *chamamé*, a dance related to the polka, its own festival. These are opportunities to dress up and take to the streets in lively bands known as *comparsas*, while missing no chance to stop and share a *maté*, the famous herb tea.

CHAPTER 6

SPLENDOURS AND ENIGMAS OF SOUTH AMERICA

Never has there been a more brutal clash of cultures than when Spanish conquistadores toppled the Inca Empire in the 16th century. The legacy of that culture clash is still present. Politically, the countries of South America face formidable challenges: the deep gulf between rich and poor; the drugs problem; inflation; a record of brutal military dictatorship. In other ways the legacy has been far happier: the mingling of Spanish and Indian traditions, with later infusions from Black Africa, has created a cultural vitality that leaves the rest of the world open-mouthed with admiration. And there are relics from the past to remind us that it can still be a place of mystery: Machu Picchu, the city that time forgot; the strange outlines etched into the Nazca desert; pre-Columbian pyramids. If the past is shrouded, at least partly, in mystery, and the present is not without its perils, the exuberance of South America's people holds out great promise for the future.

Overlooking Cuzco the remains of the Inca fortress provide a good viewing point at festival time.

Souls of the dead in the Valley of Statues

In the high valley of the River Magdalena, in southern Colombia, lies a natural fortress, protected by two ranges of volcanic mountains. In this awesome setting, a forest of statues commemorates the souls of the dead.

Enigma in stone *These mysterious statues at San Agustín may represent the eternal battle between good and evil.*

The silent stone faces in Colombia's Valley of Statues hold secrets that may never be revealed. Who were the people who carved them? Where did they come from and why did they vanish?

The riddle of San Agustín

Hundreds of stone gods, animals and men lay hidden in the valley for centuries, and might have remained undiscovered had they not been stumbled upon by tomb-robbing herdsmen more than 200 years ago. The statues appear to be linked with a cult of the dead, but little is known for certain of the culture that created them. The only clues are traces of circular bamboo huts, once roofed with thatch, that could have been either homes or workshops. The San Agustín culture appears to have developed between 500 BC and AD 1100 – a stretch of time that included a period of remarkable population growth in what is now southern Colombia, based on the cultivation of maize, potatoes, sweet potatoes and beans. Certain details of the statues and tombs appear to show the influence of distant cultures: the cat-like fangs on the eternally grimacing faces appear also in statues from the Peruvian Andes; the representation of an eagle devouring a serpent recalls a creation legend of ancient Mexico; while the brooding heads are reminiscent of Easter Island statues.

Within a circle some 15 miles (25 km) in circumference are nearly 500 statues and tombs. Inside the tombs, with their coffins of wood and stone, are offerings to the dead – trinkets, pottery and other objects that might prove useful in the afterlife. A culture that could treat its dead with so much respect was clearly one with firm beliefs about the next world. Clearly, too, the statues show an acceptance of pain and fear as part of life in this world. Some of the statues, half men, half beasts, are devouring tiny human beings. Others bear the features of pumas or wild cats. Yet others, endowed with feline fangs, have sprouted a second head on their shoulders.

Cult of the jaguar

Amid a profusion of frogs, snakes and crocodiles sculpted in the rocks, the waters of the river are diverted into a series of conduits and canals that wander through the site. It is not yet clear how this water cult fitted into the belief system of the vanished people of San Agustín, but the water may have been a means of easing the passage of the souls of the dead into the bodies of animals. Almost certainly, the fangs are linked with the cult of the sacred jaguar: called by the Indians the 'swallower of the moon', it was held to possess the power to link the everyday world with the spirit world.

More to come? *Archaeologists believe the statues that have so far come to light represent only a small part of what remains to be discovered at San Agustín.*

The brooding statues of Easter Island

Dwarfed only by the immensity of the surrounding Pacific Ocean, the giant statues of isolated Easter Island have for centuries kept their secrets locked deep in their stony hearts.

On Easter Day 1722, Dutch Admiral Jakob Roggeveen sighted, on an uncharted speck of an island in the South Pacific, what he took to be an army of giants lined up on the shore. Drawing nearer, he saw that they were colossal statues raised on platforms. Easter Island, 2400 miles (3800 km) off the coast of Chile, has more than 300 such statues, called *moai*, standing 10-72 ft (3-22 m) high and weighing up to 51 tons. Those on the shore have their backs to the sea; others are on the slopes of Rano Raraku, an extinct volcano, and inside the crater are the remains of another 400 unfinished statues. By the late 19th century the island's population had been reduced by Peruvian slave traders and by European diseases to little more than 100. Tribal warfare had long called a halt to the building of statues, and many had been toppled. Their purpose is as enigmatic as the solemn gaze they turn on the island's treeless landscape.

In the navel of the world *The Polynesians had a poetic way of describing nature. Easter Island was the 'navel of the world', and the blue lakes scattered over the crater floor of the Rano Kau volcano (right) were the 'eyes that gaze upon the sky'.*

The first discoverers of Easter Island

Easter Island, a dot in the vast Pacific, was discovered by the Polynesians, master navigators who spread over 7 million sq miles (18 million km²) of uncharted ocean without compasses, sextants or chronometers. They explored from island to island, guided by the sun and the stars, and by observing seabird movements, cloud formations and flotsam. Above all, they were able to 'read' the waves. Just as ripples on a pool are broken into intricate patterns by rocks at the surface, so waves at sea take on a pattern that can reveal the location of far-off islands The Polynesian sailors crouched in their boats to feel the waves beneath their feet.

Eternal vigil *Lined up at the foot of the volcano Ranu Raraku, 15 gigantic statues survey the present – and conceal the past.*

Cult of the Birdman god

Today's Easter Islanders depend heavily on tourism for a living. The population numbers about 2500, and they are concentrated in the village of Orongo, situated at the island's southern tip. A traditional race used to take place nearby. Every year, at the first signs of the approach of spring, athletic young men, each the chosen champion of a competing clan, would dash into the sea and swim for one of the offshore islets where the graceful, fork-tailed sooty tern laid its eggs on returning from migration. The winner of the race was the youth who seized the first egg of the year and carried it back, again braving the sharks and currents, to offer to Tangata-Manu, the islanders' Birdman god. The winner's reward was to be treated with great honour for the rest of his life. After living in total seclusion for a year, he became the instrument through which the voice of the Birdman god was heard. On his death, the Birdman victors who had succeeded him would attach living cockerels to his feet. The feathers they shed were believed to represent his soul.

The origins of the Birdman cult are as mysterious as that of Easter Island's statues, but it is possible that, exhausted by warfare, and no longer able to to vie with one another in erecting statues, the islanders decided to turn to a less lethal form of competition.

Birdman of Orongo *Near the village of Orongo, images of the Birdman god have been carved on blocks of basalt, a hard volcanic rock.*

The lost city of Santa Marta

In 1975, in the forest-covered mountains of Colombia's Sierra Nevada, a tomb-robber discovered a long stairway beneath a tangle of entwining jungle plants. Some 1300 steps led the way to a city that had been abandoned centuries earlier.

Seeing the light *Ancient terraces, won back from the jungle.*

Santa Marta is the oldest city in Colombia, founded in 1525 by the Spaniard Rodrigo de Bastidas. But in the jungle-clad mountains a score or so miles from its busy port and its tourist beaches is another, much older, city that lay forgotten for centuries.

Terraces in the jungle

The lost city of Santa Marta, shrouded in mist on the flanks of the mountain of the same name, is slowly being won back from the enveloping arms of the jungle. Called Buritaca-200 by archaeologists, and Teyuna in the local Indian language, the city was discovered by chance in 1975. It is built on a series of terraces between 2900 ft (900 m) and 3900 ft (1200 m) high. There are 140 terraces in all, connected to each other by stone staircases.

The Tairona civilisation built the terraces, erected temples and other buildings on them, and grew crops using a complex irrigation system. The effort of winning flat land out of the side of a mountain, the irrigation system, the stone highways and aqueducts are all

Imprisoned by nature *Archaeologists face the task of rescuing the lost city from a tangle of lianas and undergrowth.*

strong evidence of a highly organised society. Archaeologists have reconstructed spaces that once lay smothered under creeping vegetation and rescued ruined temples from the strangling roots of giant trees. This marvel of the past is now finally coming out of the shadows, but it still has secrets to reveal.

Survivors in the heart of the jungle

What drove the Taironas to leave their terraced city is not yet known, but they did not die out or abandon the region totally. Their descendants, the Kogui Indians, still live in the surrounding jungle. There are some 6000 of them, existing on the margins of survival in a closed and shrinking world. They have preserved some of the traditions of their ancestors in their personal trinkets and in the white tunics they wear. The Koguis, who have long, jet-black hair, carry their personal possessions in a *mochila*, woven bag. So intimate is their relationship with the jungle that they can move through it with the ease of a jaguar. From mountain to coast is no more than a day's journey for them.

Machu Picchu, forgotten city of the Incas

Isolated on a grey-green ridge of granite in the Andes, Machu Picchu escaped discovery and destruction by the conquistadores and is today an outstanding example of Inca architecture.

When Pizarro was plundering Peru, Machu Picchu was the one Inca city that escaped his notice. Perched on a mountain ridge in the Andes, and surrounded on three sides by 1000 ft (305 m) deep gorges, it was protected by its remoteness and inaccessibility. For nearly 400 years the city was forgotten, until its discovery in 1911 by the American Hiram Bingham.

A great feat of engineering

Bingham found a royal fortress dominated by a sugar-loaf peak that looked down on houses, palaces and temples. Great blocks of stone, higher than a man, had been shaped to dovetail together precisely, without mortar. Ground had been won to grow maize, beans and potatoes for a population of up to 2000 by hacking 100 terraces out of the granite mountainside. The soil for crops had been carried up by the basketful from the valley below, and the terraces were watered by reservoirs and irrigation. Even for the Incas, superb engineers as they were, this was a remarkable feat – for the wheel, which might have eased the task of moving the heavy stone blocks into position, was unknown to them. Instead, they hauled the blocks on sledges.

Machu Picchu was built around 1450 on the orders of the Inca emperor Pachacuti. About 100 years later it was abandoned, for reasons that are unclear, though the collapse of the Inca Empire was clearly an important factor. On a later visit, Bingham discovered 174 skeletons in a burial chamber – 150 of them female. He theorised that they had been Chosen Women, or Virgins of the Sun, selected to serve the emperor and the priests in the temples.

Living quarters *Nobles and priests lived behind the inner city walls.*

The professor's mistake

When Hiram Bingham, guided by an Indian, stumbled across Machu Picchu, he was looking for a different city entirely – Vilcabamba, the last stronghold of the Incas. After Pizarro's conquest, a rebel group made it their capital, taking with them the Chosen Women, who were dedicated as 'brides' of the sun god. Bingham was convinced this was the city he had found, and for years archaeologists went along with this view. In fact, Vilcabamba, which lies 62 miles (100 km) downhill from Machu Picchu, was not discovered until 1964.

A city restored *Machu Picchu, saved from the Spaniards and now won back from the jungle.*

Mysteries of Peru

Some civilisations are reluctant to give up their secrets, and where facts are few, theories abound. We know what the pre-Columbian cultures of Peru created, because of what they left behind. But we do not always know why a temple was built, or why strange patterns were etched onto the face of the desert.

Well before the Incas carved out an empire in what is now Peru, some cultures had left a record of astonishing achievements. That of Chavín de Huántar, which arose around 1000 BC and spread widely in the highlands, is now considered by archaeologists to be the foundation of Andean civilisation. The builders of Chavín had no knowledge of the arch, so they built pyramids, reducing the weight that had to be borne by walls and lintels as storeys were added – a style that is widely found in the ancient Americas. The principal building at Chavín, the Castillo, was 50 ft (15 m) high and 230 ft (70 m) wide at its base. Inside, it is honeycombed by passages, stairways, ramps and small rooms. Outside, monumental heads form a striking sculptural frieze. The heads have human-like features mingled with those of the jaguar. Everything points to the conclusion that Chavín was not a city for ordinary mortals, but was sacred to the gods – possibly even regarded as their home.

Strangers beware   A menacing head, half human, half jaguar, carved on the outer wall of the Castillo at Chavín de Huántar.

The lady of Nazca: a life dedicated to a conundrum

German by birth and Peruvian by adoption, Dr Maria Reiche devoted nearly 50 years of her life to the Nazca mystery. She concluded that the lines were a huge calendar. With royalties from her best-selling book, *Mystery of the Desert*, Dr Reiche was able to pay for wardens to protect the lines from damage by over-zealous tourists. Having done most of her own surveying from stepladders, she was also able to afford to build a viewing platform. In the museum at the site she shared her knowledge with visitors from all over the world. Dr Reiche was a legend in her own right, and the Peruvian government and air force helped in the research she carried on until her death in 1998, aged 95.

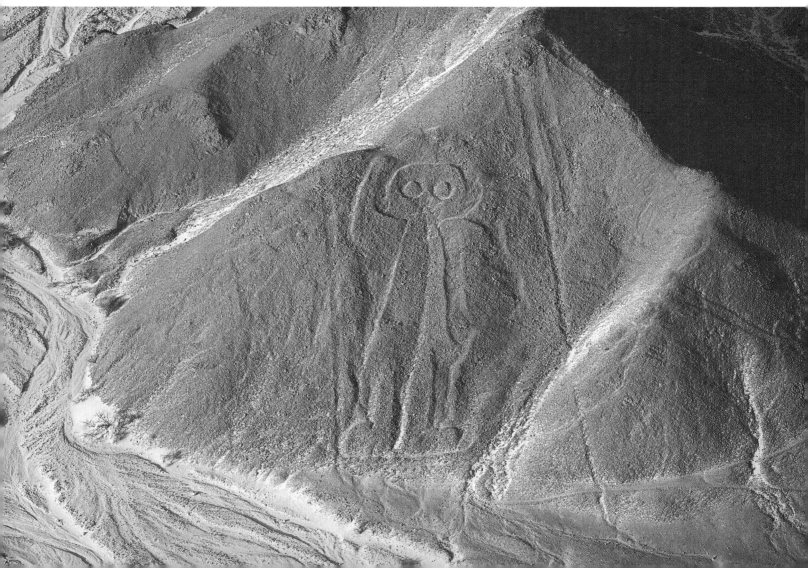

Centre for sacrifice *Pachacamac, a centre for ritual, sacrifice and ceremony until it was destroyed by the Spaniards, has been restored and in parts entirely reconstructed, thanks to painstaking work by archaeologists.*

The jaguar cult has led some archaeologists to suggest that the people of Chavín came originally from forests, where the animal is found. Others point to the Olmec culture of Mexico, which also had a jaguar cult, and believe there may have been trade between the two regions. All that is known for certain is that around 300 BC the Chavín civilisation vanished as mysteriously as it had arrived.

Nazca: baffling lines in the sand

It was supplanted by a number of local cultures, among them one that arose in the Nazca Valley in southern Peru around 350 BC. The earliest of the nearby 'Nazca lines' – large-scale geometrical figures and outlines of animals and plants etched in the stony desert – had already existed for centuries. They are believed to have been created by the Paracas, Nazca and the later Ayacucho cultures. Among the shapes are birds, a dog, a monkey, a spider, a fish, a lizard and a tree. Some are more than 1.25 miles (2 km) long, and they make sense only when seen from the air. This has led to a frenzy of speculation about their origin. According to some, they are a landing ground marked out to guide the spaceships of extra-terrestials. In another explanation, the lines connected important burial sites on the ground – a theory that sounds plausible, except that no such burial sites have been found.

Scientist Paul Kosok, who discovered the lines when standing on a nearby hill, believes they were intended to be an astronomical calendar, giving guidance on when the peasants should sow their crops. So did German-born Maria Reiche, who devoted her life to studying the lines and seeking the purpose behind them. Reiche put it expressively: 'This work was carried out so that the gods could see it and, looking down from their celestial

Puzzle in the desert *This weird outline in the Nazca desert (facing page) has led some commentators to speculate that it might be an astronaut, welcoming his companions from outer space.*

The devastation of Pachacamac

When Francisco Pizarro arrived in Peru, Pachacamac was the largest, and reputedly the richest, city on the coast. For centuries it had been a major shrine, where priests foretold the future by examining the entrails of sacrificed animals. Pilgrims who consulted its oracles showed their gratitude with rich offerings. The city, which pre-dated the Incas, was built for the worship of the god Pachacamac, who supported the world. One of the reasons for the Incas' success was that they tolerated the gods of other cultures, so long as the sun god was accepted as supreme. Around 1533, Pizarro sent his half-brother Hernando on a mission to strip the city of its gold and other treasures. Among the buildings Hernando found was the Temple of the Sun, which housed the Chosen Women. The Spaniards also found a wooden idol, spattered with blood, sheltered in a dark room whose walls were hung with sheets of pure gold. The conquistadores found less booty than they had hoped for, but they killed the priests, smashed the statues, which they regarded as idols, and left behind a city in ruins.

home, help the Nazca Indians in their farming, their fishing and their other activities.'

Some of these theories are more convincing than others, but even if the purpose of the lines were to be established beyond doubt, there remains the mystery of how they could have been constructed on such a vast scale without an aerial vantage point.

One theory is that the Nazca made hot-air balloons to carry them aloft so that they could direct workmen on the ground. The closer investigators come to grasping the key, the further it seems to recede.

Workers in stone *The skills of the Chavín builders were expressed in sculpture, as in the portrayal of a warrior (left), and in architecture, as in the gateway of the Castillo (below). Chavín's artistic style spread widely.*

Art ancient and modern

Even the conquistadores could not totally destroy the temples and treasures of America's pre-Columbian cultures – so called because they predated the voyages of Columbus. The relics that survived inspired the artists who followed.

Golden girl   A Mochican 'Venus'.

After the mysterious eclipse of the ceremonial centre of Chavín de Huántar, with its temples and its disquieting jaguar god, it was the turn of the Paracas, Mochica and Nazca cultures to flourish. All three showed outstanding skills in the arts of pottery and of textile weaving.

Mummies clad in splendour

The Paracas, named after a peninsula on Peru's southern coast, were particularly good weavers. Evidence of this first came to light in the 1920s, with the discovery of 429 mummies, unearthed in a remarkable state of preservation, thanks to the extreme dryness of the climate. In life, they had clearly been important people – high-ranking priests and nobles – for they were wrapped in splendid cloaks embroidered with birds, fish, gods and other figures. Instead of building imposing temples, the Paracas seem to have devoted their energies to a cult of the dead. They also left behind some fine examples of pottery, painted with resin.

Farther to the south, the Nazca, too, were accomplished weavers, decorating their textiles with bold, abstract motifs. But it was in producing multicoloured pottery that they excelled. It was decorated with, and often shaped to resemble, birds, insects, fruit, animals and humans with animal features. In what may be a link with Chavín and the jaguar cult, many show the head of a cat.

Bloodthirsty warriors

The Mochica, who flourished on the northen coast of Peru from around 200 BC to AD 900, spun cotton, vicuña and llama wool for their textiles, and the men, with richly embroidered shirts, were more gorgeously attired than the women. A remarkable record of their daily lives is preserved in their pottery and – for they were also skilful goldsmiths – in golden goblets, cups, statuettes and headdresses. It shows a bloodthirsty society that was often at war, and sometimes collected heads as trophies. The chief weapon of the warriors was a copper-headed club. Children, as well as prisoners of war, were

Treasure from the grave   A golden doll, with feather headdress and embroidered cloak, found near a mummy in Peru.

Links with the past

In South America there is an unbroken tradition of vitality and energy that links the artists of today with the craftsmen of the pre-Columbian era. Their inventiveness and sense of humour is clearly evident in the work of Colombian sculptor and painter Fernando Botero. His style of painting, with its broad-beamed, slightly grotesque figures, has been compared to the prose style known as 'Magic Realism'. This same liveliness is also seen in the painting of murals, inspired by the work of the Mexican artist Diego Rivera. Just as pre-Columbian art was for the most part on public display, so murals bring art out of the galleries and into the streets. The widest audience of all is available to the talented young avant-garde graffiti painters of Brazil, who have turned the walls of São Paulo into true works of art.

Botero   Self portrait, 1987.

Pyramid of the moon   All that remains of the mighty pyramid temple raised by the Mochicas to the glory of their moon deity.

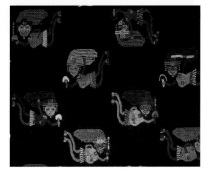

Flying figures from Paracas
Embroidered burial cloak from
Paracas. The design skills and
sheer dexterity shown in
Paracan textiles are unsurpassed.

Pushing out the frontiers of art

Jesús Rafael Soto is a Venezuelan artist who spends his time between Paris and his workshop in Caracas. His work, which falls into a category known as 'kinetic art', has been shown at galleries and in exhibitions all over the world. Its vibrant colours recall those of pre-Columbian pottery and textiles. Soto's paintings are spectacular arrangements of colours, patterns, shadows and materials, and the character of the work changes for the observer, under the influence of movement and optical illusion.

sometimes sacrificed to the gods of the sun and the moon, to whom the Mochica built enormous pyramid temples. The Pyramid of the Sun, in the Moche Valley, stood 60 ft (18 m) high, on top of a massive platform, and the Pyramid of the Moon, though on a smaller platform, was 10 ft (3 m) higher, for the moon god (or goddess) outranked all other deities. Even their sport, which took the form of ceremonial races, was dedicated to the gods.

Traditions that did not die

The engineering talents of many of the pre-Inca societies were little short of stupefying. Suspension bridges constructed over dizzyingly high gorges, aqueducts, irrigation canals, terraces for growing crops – all were within their scope, and all represented a triumph of human ingenuity and applied effort over the hostility of the natural terrain. Spanish chroniclers of the 16th century marvelled at the underground wells dug out by the Nazca – wells that are still in use today.

When the Incas set out on their path of conquest in the 15th century, their engineers did not need to start from scratch: they were able to build on the achievements of those who came before them. They, too, had skilled craftsmen who carried on the tradition of making vases, bowls, headdresses and cult objects in precious metals. And even the shock of invasion could not wipe out the creative urge. Traditions that go back to the Incas and beyond can still be detected in South American art today.

A world of music

If music is a universal language, it is one in which Latin Americans appear to be fluent from birth. It pervades all of life, from the samba-based rhythms of Brazil's national football side to the tango of a Buenos Aires nightclub.

The music of Latin America is a complex mixture of many styles, yet it is instantly recognisable. The same influences that helped shape the people and their history have gone into it – folklore, conquest, slavery, defiance and an irrepressible delight in life.

Haunting flute music of the Andes

The earliest of these influences can still be heard today, in remote mountains and forests from Bolivia to Tierra del Fuego. Indians speaking Aymara, Guaraní, or Quechua, the language of the ancient Incas, have kept their traditions alive in their music. In pre-Columbian South America, music played an essential role in innumerable rites: magical incantations to prepare for hunting; feast days; even, among the Jivaro Indians, special chants for the shrinking of human heads. On the high plateaus of the Andes, the haunting, melancholy sound of the shepherd's flute, with its pentatonic (five-toned) scale, is a heritage from their Inca ancestors. Creole music developed as a fusion of Spanish and Quechua traditions with the songs brought from Africa by

Voice of South America   Mercedes Sosa, whose warm and passionate songs reached a world audience.

black slaves. In our own day, musicians like Atahualpa Yupanqui and Mercedes Sosa have spread the folk music of Latin America throughout the world.

The world dances

Since the Roaring Twenties, people in many lands have danced to Latin American rhythms. From Brazil came the samba, from Cuba the rumba and the conga, and from Argentina the tango. Latin American dance bands gave the world the cha-cha-cha, and in the 1960s came the bossa nova, which held out the promise of a glamorous lifestyle on the beaches of Brazil. Tom Jobim and

---

Villa-Lobos: a bridge between two musical worlds

The Brazilian composer Heitor Villa-Lobos (1887-1959) found his inspiration in two different musical traditions: the heady excitements of Afro-Brazilian folk music and the sublime genius of J.S. Bach. Taught by his father to play the cello at the age of six, Villa-Lobos went on to master the guitar, the piano, and several wind instruments. In his youth he travelled in the Brazilian interior, steeping himself in folk music. A trip to Paris in 1922 added a European sophistication to his style. Operas, ballets, quartets, symphonies and concertos – some 2000 works in all – poured from his pen. The two passions of the master musician were combined in his *Bachianas Brasileiras* suites.

The magic of carnival   Drums, dance and a swirl of colour in Rio.

Vinícius de Moraes produced the song that epitomised the appeal of the bossa nova, 'The girl from Ipanema', and North American jazz saxophonist Stan Getz sent the song around the world.

Enter The Beatles

Latin music was clearly open to influences from the rest of the world. In one case, it even imported its own music: the erotically charged salsa was born in the 1970s in the tenements and clubs of New York, among Cuban and Puerto Rican immigrant communities.

Musical comedy increased the popularity of these new and irresistible rhythms. South America lived also to the beat of international pop music. Television, radio and the records industry made The Beatles as popular in Buenos Aires as they were in Liverpool. Rock, punk, disco, techno, heavy metal, released the energies of the young, whether played at pop concerts or, almost as deafeningly, on 'ghetto blasters' in the shantytowns. Classical composers, such as the Brazilian Heitor Villa-Lobos, drew heavily on folksongs and legends, and this same tradition was taken up by left-wing composers in Chile and Peru during the 1960s and 1970s.

A musical spree

By the 1980s it had become difficult, sometimes, to draw lines between what once were clearly distinguishable styles of music.

Such was the exuberance of the South Americans that classical and pop, modern and folk, native and foreign, tango and jazz, samba and rock, spilled over into one another in a spree of cross-cultural borrowing. To Latin America, music is music is music.

Festival in Bolivia *The drum and the flute summon the very spirit of the Andes, their peaks circled by condors.*

The music of rebellion

The music of protest was an exception to this general rule, for politics cannot be kept out of music. The life and death of singer-songwriter Victor Jara (1938-73) became a powerful illustration of this truth. Jara was a patriot and a communist, who used his songs to denounce social injustice and political scandal. He played an important role in the *Nueva Canción* (New Song) protest movement, and was implicated in revolutionary activities. When the Marxist Salvador Allende won Chile's presidential election in 1970, Jara gave a concert in a football stadium to celebrate. In September 1973, General Augusto Pinochet led an army coup against Allende, who was killed in the fighting. The army, in a demonstration of its power, staged a massacre of Allende supporters in the very stadium where the victory concert had been held. Jara, imprisoned for five days, had his hands cut off before being executed.

The Martyr *Homage to Jara 25 years after his execution.*

Literature and cinema: protest finds a voice

After independence, writers in South America began to search for a voice of their own. When they found one, it was a powerful voice of protest against injustice – and the same struggle was to become a theme of politically committed movie-makers, too.

Literary great   The poet and storyteller Jorge Luis Borges.

Literary creativity in South America both shaped and was shaped by politics. Apart from the 15th-century Spanish missionary Las Casas, there had been few in colonial times who cared, or dared, to speak up for the Indians. But that was to change.

Writing for a better world

With independence came the expectation that words could be used to change the world for the better. An early protest was *The Slaughterhouse* (1838) by Argentinian Esteban Echeverrin, a satire on the rule of dictator Rosas. As the 19th century ended, the protest movement gathered pace. *Birds Without a Nest* by the Peruvian Clorinda

Matto de Turner drew attention as early as 1889 to the plight of landless Indians. Argentinian Alcides Arguedas, in his *Race of Bronze* (1919), took up the theme of Indians cheated by land-grabbers. Peru's José Carlos Mariátegui, writing in the 1920s, looked back on the Inca state as an early version of socialism, because it saw to the needs of the poor. Tensions in a changing society were a theme taken up by other writers. *Don Segunda Sombra* (1926), by the Argentinian Ricardo Güraldes, contrasted the simple life of *gauchos* on the pampas with the less satisfying life on offer in the cities. Chilean poet Pablo Neruda, who joined the Communist Party and left Chile when it was outlawed, wrote movingly

The Master   Gabriel Garcia Márquez (far left), whose work is rich in fantasy, won the Nobel prize for Literature in 1982.

Spellbinder   Paulo Coelho (below), brilliant writer from Brazil.

Fantasy and magic realism

The love of fantasy that is one of the strongest elements in Latin American writing can be traced back to the ancient Incas or to the Mayans and Aztecs of Central America. Their myths and legends have fired the imagination of such writers as Paraguayan Augusto Rao Bastos, who served in the Chaco war of 1932-5 and wrote of its horrors. The vein of fantasy runs through the work of Argentinian Jorge Luis Borges. In the tales of Colombian Gabriel García Márquez it evolved into 'Magic Realism', which stands logic on its head and deals with happenings that fly in the face of reason. Argentinian writer Julio Cortázar juggled fantasy, time, place and characters to create an atmosphere of uncertainty.

Writer and politician The author Mario Vargas Llosa runs for president of Peru in the 1990 elections. He lost.

about the Inca past. Argentinian poet and storyteller Jorge Luis Borges was demoted from his job as a librarian for opposing pro-Nazi policies during the Second World War.

For some writers, literature took on the nature of a political manifesto. Dictatorship, exile, oppression and a disturbing sense of alienation featured in their work. Peruvian writer Vargas Llosa's *The Time of the Hero* (1962) enraged the authorities to the point that the book was publicly burned. A short story by Argentinian Julio Cortázar was turned into the hit film *Blow Up*, which revealed the emptiness at the heart of Swinging London in the 1960s.

One of South America's most important contributions to world literature was the concept of Magic Realism, the acceptance of irrational or impossible events as if they were commonplace. It is present in the work of the Colombian Gabriel Garcia Márquez, whose *100 Years of Solitude* (1970) was hailed by critics as one of the greatest novels ever written in the Spanish language. Women writers, too, made their mark. Isabel Allende, niece of the overthrown Chilean president Salvador Allende, was acclaimed as a dazzling new talent for her story of exile, *The House of the Spirits* (1985).

At the movies

Early film-makers in South America tended to be overshadowed by Hollywood, the colossus to the north. Even so, the remarkable silent film *Limit* (1930), by Mario Peixoto, was admired by no less a commentator than Orson Welles. Romantic films and melodramas dominated the 1940s and 1950s, but there were still a few

Seekers in the fog   Scene from The Cloud, *an exposure of the sufferings of the Argentinian people, directed by Fernando Solanas.*

A hit with the critics   Central do Brasil (Central Station) was a road movie, Brazilian-style, that won the Golden Bear award at Berlin in 1998.

films that offered a bitter social protest – notably Argentinian Hugo del Carrill's *River of Blood* (1952). Fidel Castro's revolution in Cuba, in 1959, inspired film-makers throughout the continent. The Bolivian director Jorge Sanjines drew an unforgiving portrait of imperialism in *Blood of the Condor* (1969). Chilean Miguel Littin told of the defeat of a socialist community in *The Promised Land* (1974). In *The Hour of the Bonfires* (1968), director Fernando Solanas compressed the entire history of Argentina into less than four hours of screen time.

Brazil's new wave movie-makers

In the late 1950s, a number of young Brazilian directors turned their backs on the prospect of making big-budget movies in well-equipped but artistically sterile studios. They wanted to film new subjects, in a fresh way. The new style, *Cinema Novo*, found its settings in the slums, among the overworked peasants.

The working classes were taken seriously, rather than being treated as comic relief. As the leading young director Glauber Rocha put it, the purpose of *Cinema Novo* was to 'make the public aware of its own misery'. *Cinema Novo* was extinguished in the 1970s when Brazil was ground under the heel of the military.

137

MAPS, FACTS AND FIGURES

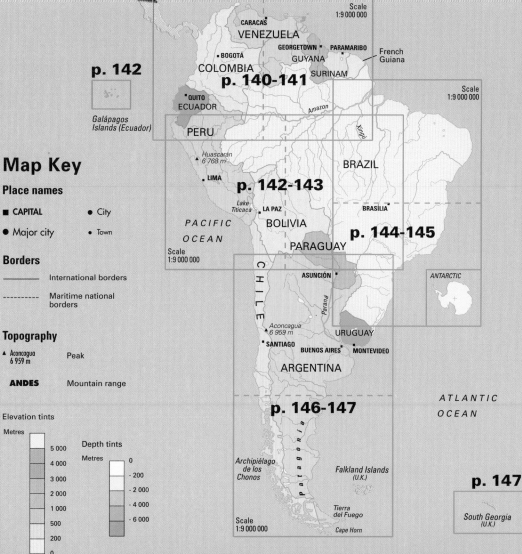

Map Key

Place names

- ■ CAPITAL
- ● City
- ● Major city
- • Town

Borders

——————— International borders

- - - - - - - Maritime national borders

Topography

▲ Aconcagua
6 959 m   Peak

ANDES   Mountain range

Elevation tints

Metres

5 000	
4 000	
3 000	
2 000	
1 000	
500	
200	
0	

Depth tints

Metres

0	
- 200	
- 2 000	
- 4 000	
- 6 000	

Map labels

p. 142

Galápagos
Islands (Ecuador)

Scale
1:9 000 000

CARACAS
VENEZUELA

GEORGETOWN ■ ■ PARAMARIBO
BOGOTÁ   GUYANA   French
COLOMBIA   Guiana
p. 140-141   SURINAM

QUITO
ECUADOR   Amazon

PERU

Huascarán
6 768 m   BRAZIL

LIMA
p. 142-143

Lake
Titicaca LA PAZ   BRASÍLIA

PACIFIC   BOLIVIA   **p. 144-145**
OCEAN
Scale   PARAGUAY
1:9 000 000

Scale
1:9 000 000

ASUNCIÓN   ANTARCTIC

CHILE

Aconcagua
6 959 m
Parana
SANTIAGO BUENOS AIRES ■ ■ MONTEVIDEO
URUGUAY

ARGENTINA

p. 146-147

ATLANTIC
OCEAN

Archipiélago
de los   Falkland Islands
Chonos   (U.K.)   **p. 147**

Patagonia

Tierra
del Fuego   South Georgia
Scale   (U.K.)
1:9 000 000 Cape Horn

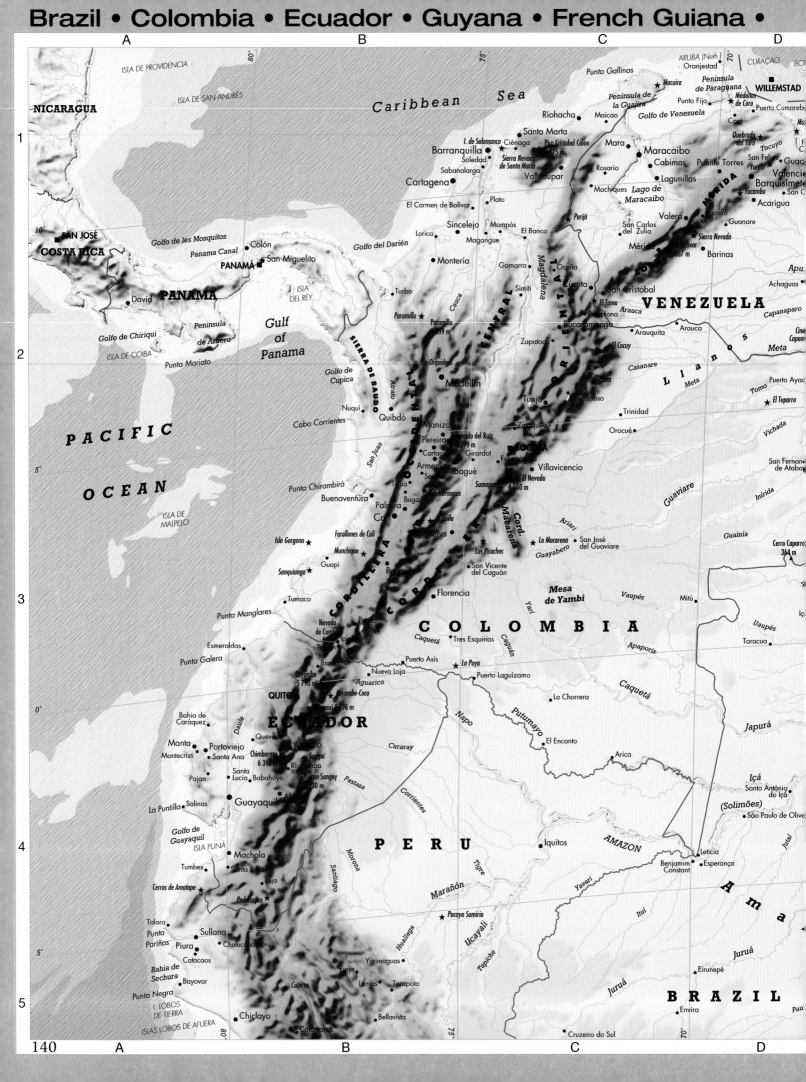

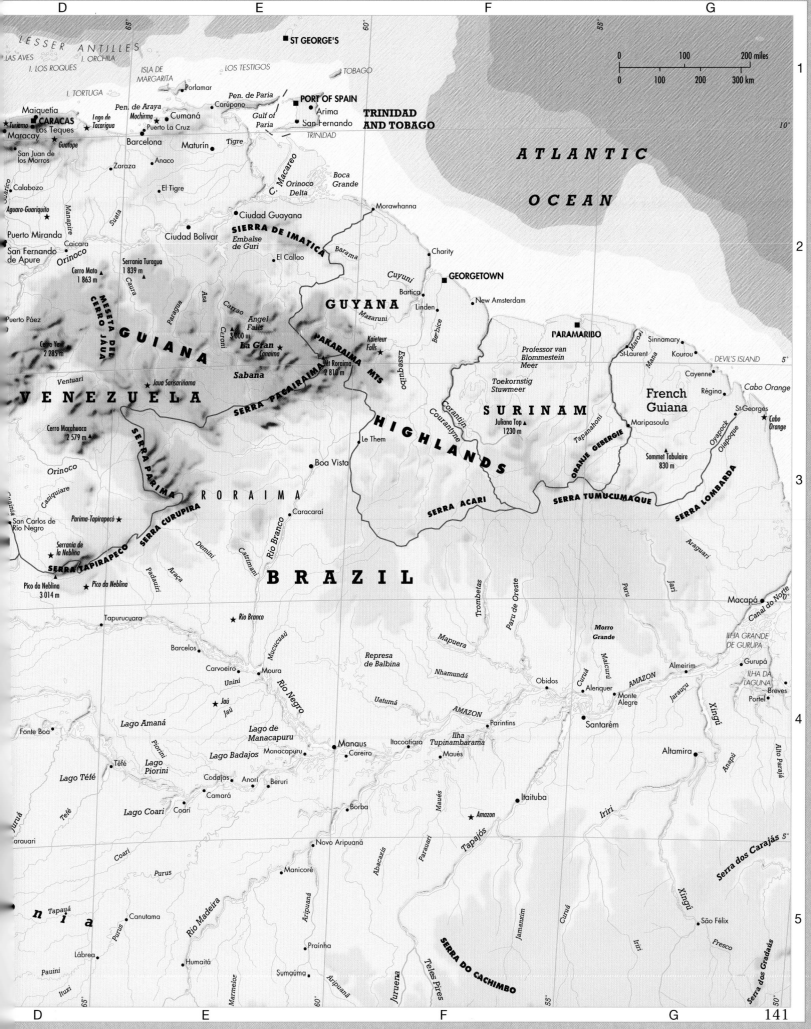

D · E · F · G

LESSER ANTILLES
LAS AVES
I. ORCHILA
I. LOS ROQUES
I. TORTUGA
ISLA DE MARGARITA
LOS TESTIGOS
TOBAGO
■ ST GEORGE'S

Maiquetía
CARACAS
Los Teques
Turiamo
Maracay
San Juan de los Morros
Guatope
Calabozo
Aguaro-Guariquito
Puerto Miranda
San Fernando de Apure
Puerto Páez

Pen. de Araya
Mochirma
Cumaná
Puerto La Cruz
Barcelona
Maturín
Anaco
Zaraza
El Tigre
Tigre
Anaco

Porlamar
Pen. de Paria
Carúpano
Gulf of Paria
Arima
Port of Spain
San Fernando
TRINIDAD
TRINIDAD AND TOBAGO

C. Macareo
Orinoco Delta
Boca Grande
Morawhanna

ATLANTIC OCEAN

Ciudad Guayana
SIERRA DE IMATICA
Embalse de Guri
Ciudad Bolívar
El Callao
Barama
Charity

Serranía Turagua 1 839 m
Cerro Mato 1 863 m

Cuyuni
Bartica
GEORGETOWN
New Amsterdam
Linden
GUYANA
Mazaruni
Berbice

MESETA DEL CERRO JAUA
GUIANA
Cerro Yaví 2 285 m
Jaua Sarisariñama
Angel Falls 3 000 m
La Gran Canaima
Sabana
PAKARAIMA MTS
Mt Roraima 2 810 m
Kaieteur Falls
Essequibo

PARAMARIBO
Professor van Blommestein Meer
Sinnamary
St-Laurent
Mana
Kourou
DEVIL'S ISLAND
Cayenne

VENEZUELA
Cerro Marahuaca 2 579 m
SERRA PARIMA
Serra Pacairaima
Le Them
HIGHLANDS
Corantijn
Courantyne
SURINAM
Juliana Top 1230 m
Toekornstig Stuwmeer
Tapanahoni
ORANJE GEBERGTE
French Guiana
Régina
St-Georges
Cabo Orange
Maripasoula
Sommet Tabulaire 830 m

Orinoco
Casiquiare
San Carlos de Río Negro
Parima-Tapirapecó
SERRA PARIMA
SERRA CURUPIRA
RORAIMA
Boa Vista
Caracaraí
SERRA ACARI
SERRA TUMUCUMAQUE
SERRA LOMBARDA
Oyapock
Oiapoque
Araguari

Serranía de la Neblina
SERRA TAPIRAPECÓ
Pico da Neblina 3 014 m
Pico de Neblina
Demini
Cetrimani
Rio Branco
BRAZIL
Trombetas
Paru de Oreste
Paru
Jari
Macapá
Canal do Norte

Tapurucuara
Rio Branco
Mucucuaú
Mapuera
Nhamundá
Morro Grande
ILHA GRANDE DE GURUPA
Maicurú

Barcelos
Carvoeiro
Moura
Unini
Jaú
Jaú
Rio Negro
Represa de Balbina
Uatumã
Obidos
Curuá
Alenquer
Monte Alegre
Almeirim
Gurupá
ILHA DA LAGUNA
Breves
Portel

Lago Amaná
Fonte Boa
Téfé
Lago Téfé
Piorini
Lago Piorini
Lago de Manacapuru
Lago Badajos
Manaus
Manacapuru
Careiro
Itacoatiara
Maués
AMAZON
Ilha Tupinambarama
Parintins
Santarém
Altamira
Xingú

Codajás
Anori
Beruri
Camará
Borba
Itaituba
Iriri

Lago Coari
Coari
Novo Aripuaná
Amazon
Maués
Tapajós
Anapu
Alto Parajá

Juruá
Téfé
Coari
Purus
Manicoré
Abacaxis
Parauari
SERRA DOS CARAJÁS
Xingú

Purus
Canutama
Rio Madeira
Aripuanã
SERRA DO CACHIMBO
Jamanxim
Iriri
São Félix
Fresco

Lábrea
Humaitá
Sumaúma
Teles Pires
SERRA DOS GRADAÚS
Juruena

D · E · F · G

141

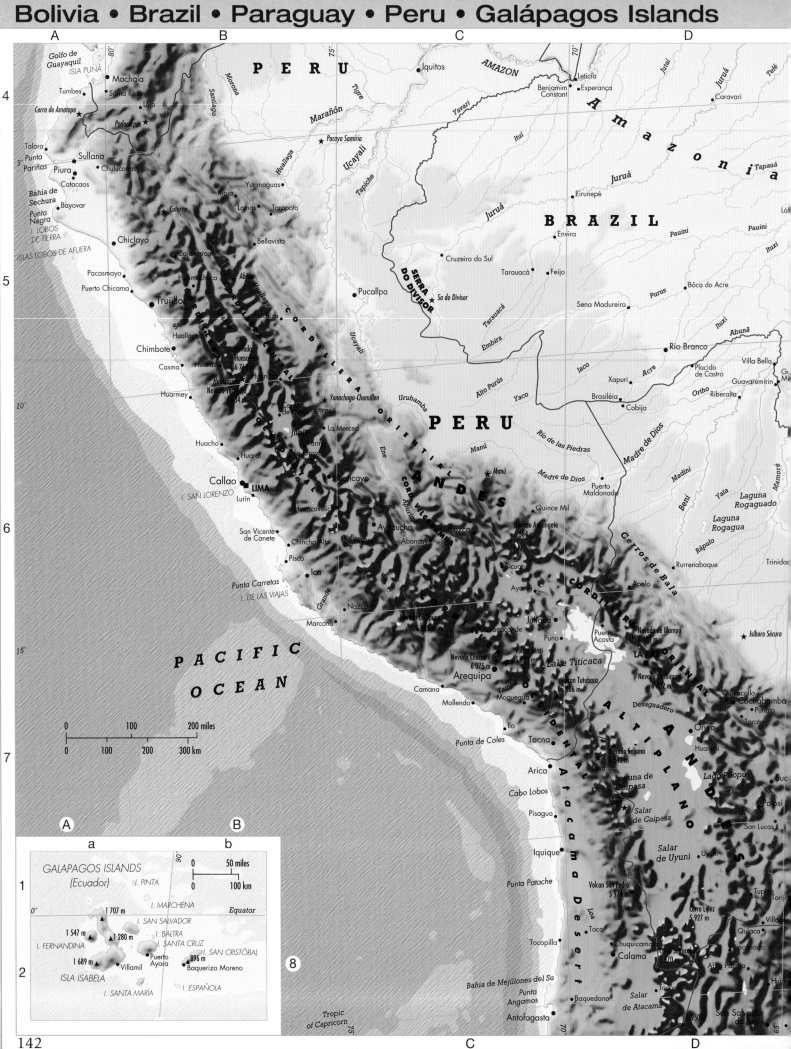

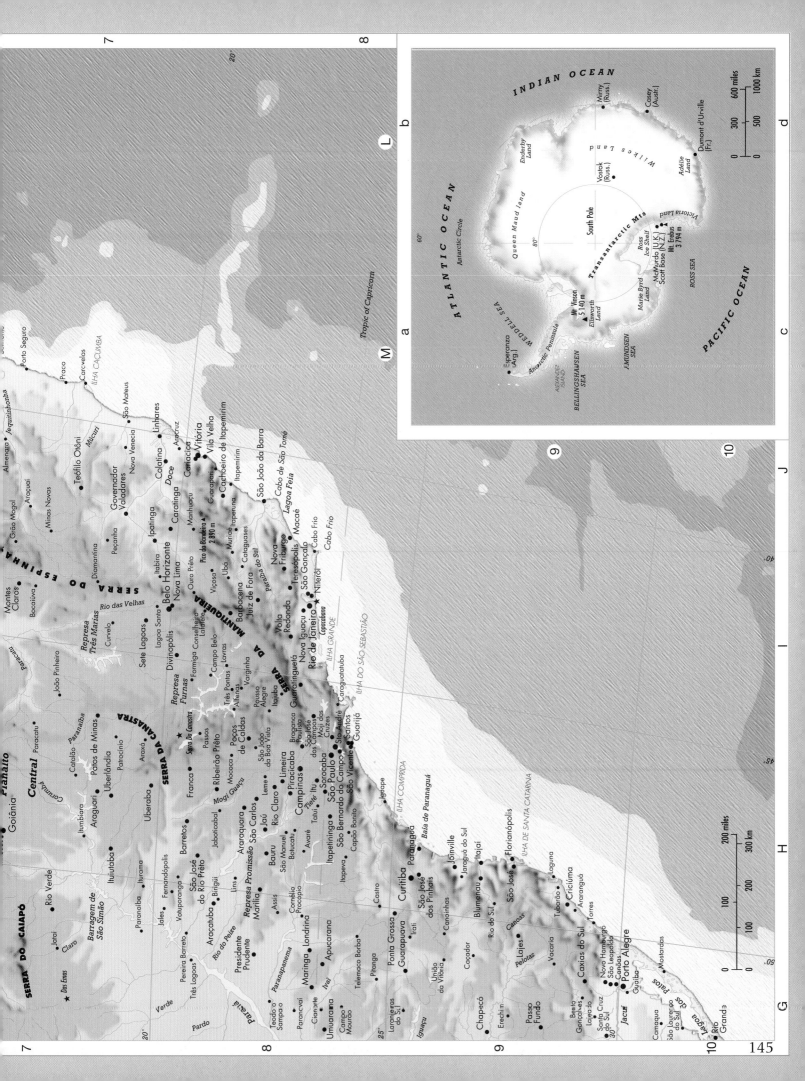

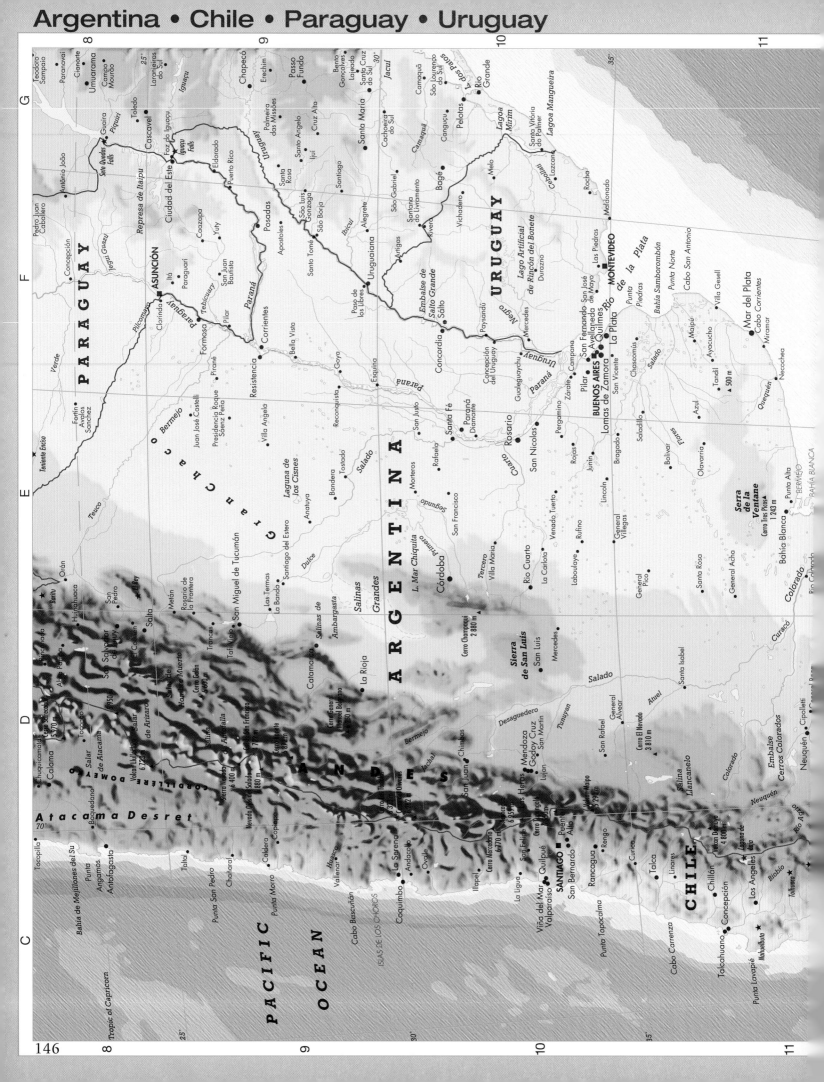

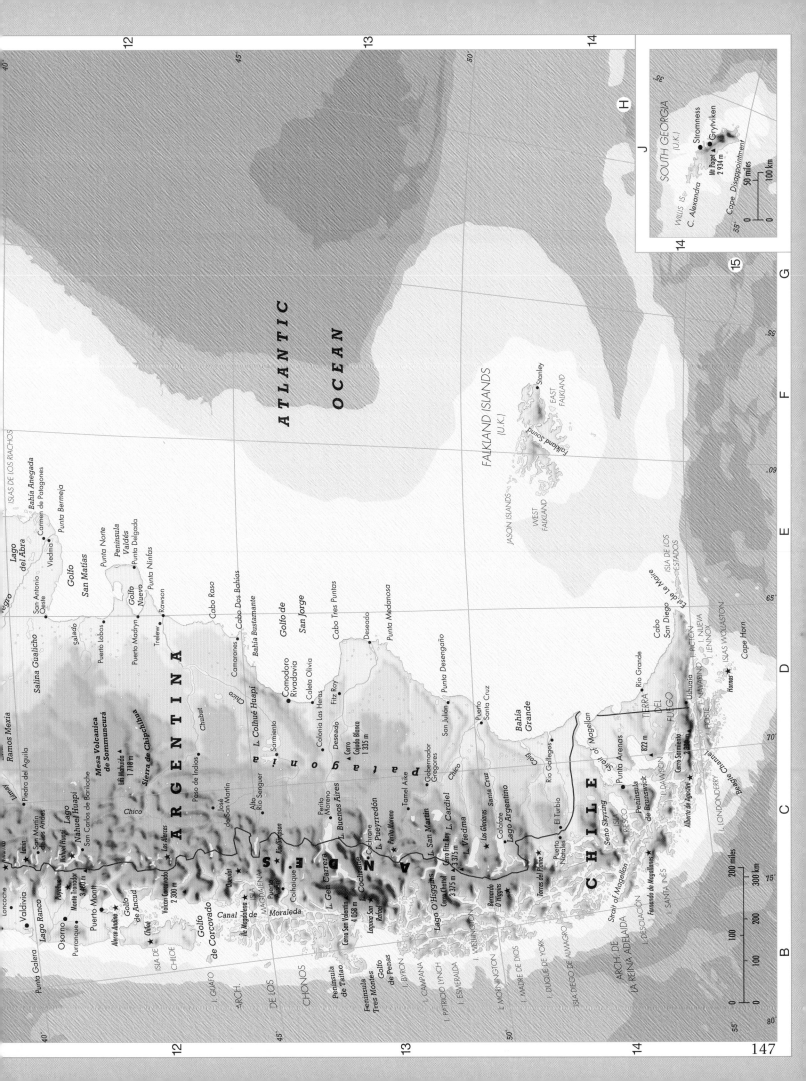

ATLANTIC

OCEAN

SOUTH GEORGIA
(U.K.)

WILLIS IS.
C. Alexandra
Stromness
Grytviken
Mt Paget ▲
2 934 m
Cape Disappointment

50 miles
100 km

55°

14

35°

15

FALKLAND ISLANDS
(U.K.)

Stanley
EAST
FALKLAND

Falkland Sound

JASON ISLANDS
WEST
FALKLAND

55°

60°

65°

70°

75°

80°

40°

45°

50°

55°

60°

G

F

E

D

C

B

ISLAS DE LOS RIACHOS
Bahía Anegada
Carmen de Patagones
Punta Bermeja
Lago
del Abra
Viedma
Punta Norte
Península
Valdés
San Antonio
Oeste
Golfo
San Matías
Punta Delgada
Golfo
Nuevo
Punta Ninfas
Rawson
Negro
Ramos Mexia
Salina Gualicho
Puerto Lobos
Puerto Madryn
Trelew
Cabo Raso
Cabo Dos Bahías
Piedra del Aguila
salado
ARGENTINA
Paso de Indios
Chubut
Camarones
Bahía Bustamante
Golfo de
San Jorge
Lanín
San Martín
de los Andes
Mesa Volcanica
de Sommuncurá
Lilú Mahuida ▲
1 718 m
José
de San Martín
Sarmiento
L. Colhué Huapí
Comodoro
Rivadavia
Coleta Olivia
Cabo Tres Puntas
Loncoche
Valdivia
Lago Ranco
San Martín
de los Andes
Lago
Nahuel Huapí
San Carlos de Bariloche
Sierra de Chipchihua
Alto
Río Senguer
Perito
Moreno
Chico
Deseado
Fitz Roy
Cerro
Cojudo Blanco
1 335 m
Deseado
Punta Medanosa
Punta Desengaño
Osorno
Purranque
Puerto Montt
Monte Tronador ▲
3 601 m
Volcán Corcovado ▲
2 300 m
Queulat
Los Alerces
Chico
L. Buenos Aires
L. Pueyrredón
Perito Moreno
Tamel Aike
Gobernador
Gregores
Chico
Punta Galera
Golfo
de Ancud
Golfo
de Corcovado
Piuchue
Coihaique
Río Simpson
Cochrane
L. San Martín
L. Viedma
L. Cardiel
San Julián
Puerto
Santa Cruz
Bahía
Grande
ISLA DE
CHILOE
ILE MAGDALENA
Canal
de
Moraleda
L. Gen Carrera
Cerro Chiltel
L. O'Higgins
Cerro Fitz Roy
3 375 m
3 375 m
Los Glaciares
Santa Cruz
Coig
Río Gallegos
I. GUAFO
ARCH.
DE LOS
CHONOS
Península
de Taitao
Laguna San
Rafael
Cerro San Valentín
4 058 m
Bernardo
O'Higgins
Calafate
Lago Argentino
El Turbio
Torres del Paine
Río
El Turbio
Magellan
TIERRA
DEL
FUEGO
ANDES
PATAGONIA
CHILE
Feninsula
Tres Montes
Golfo
de Penas
I. BYRON
I. CAMPANA
I. PATRICIO LYNCH
I. MORNINGTON
I. MADRE DE DIOS
I. DUQUE DE YORK
I. WELLINGTON
I. ESMERALDA
Puerto Natales
Seno Skyring
Seno Otway
Peninsula
de Brunswick
Punta Arenas
822 m
Cerro Sarmiento ▲
2 300 m
Río Grande
Ushuaia
I. DAWSON
I. RIESCO
Cabo
San Diego
Isla de los
ESTADOS
Estrecho Le Maire
Bahía San Sebastián
Cabo
San Pablo
Strait of Magellan
ARCH. DE
LA REINA ADELAIDA
ISLA DIEGO DE ALMAGRO
I. SANTA INÉS
Fernando de Magallanes
Bernardo de Magallanes
I. DESOLACIÓN
Alberto de Agostini
I. LONDONDERRY
I. NAVARINO
I. HOSTE
I. PICTON
I. NUEVA
I. LENNOX
Hornos
Cape Horn
ISLAS WOLLASTON
Beagle
Channel

200 miles
300 km
0
100
200
0

South America: the statistics

Twelve countries (thirteen if French Guiana is included), from the smallest (Surinam) to the largest (Brazil): a mosaic of peoples and cultures.

URUGUAY

Official name: The Eastern Republic of Uruguay
Capital: Montevideo
Area: 68 500 sq miles (177 500 km²)
Population: 3 360 000
Population density: 46 per sq mile (18 per km²)
Ethnic groups: white 86%, mestizo 8%, mulatto 6%
Religions: Catholic 79%, Protestant 3%, Jewish 0.9%, others or none 17.1%
Currency: Uruguayan peso
HDI**: 0.828
GDP per head: $3478
Language: Spanish*
Government: Republic with bicameral general assembly (Senate and Chamber of Representatives).

VENEZUELA

Official name: The Bolivarian Republic of Venezuela
Capital: Caracas
Area: 352 000 sq miles (912 000 km²)
Population: 24 630 000
Population density: 65 per sq mile (25 per km²)
Ethnic groups: mestizo 67%, white 21%, black 10%, Amerindian 2%
Religions: Catholic 92.4%, others or none 7.6%
Currency: Bolívar
HDI**: 0.765
GDP per head: $3370
Languages: Spanish*, Amerindian languages
Government: Federal republic with national assembly and executive presidency.

BOLIVIA

Official name: The Republic of Bolivia
Capital: Sucre/La Paz
Area: 424 600 sq miles (1 100 000 km²)
Population: 8 270 000
Population density: 18 per sq mile (7 per km²)
Ethnic groups: Amerindians 42%, mestizo 31%, whites 14%, creole 13%
Religion: Catholic 85%, Protestant 10%, others or none 5%
Currency: Boliviano
HDI**: 0.648
GDP per head: $897
Languages: Spanish*, Aymara, Quechua
Government: Democratic republic with Congress comprising two legislative assemblies (Senate and Chamber of Deputies).

FRENCH GUIANA

Status: French *département*
Chief town: Cayenne
Area: 34 700 sq miles (90 000 km²)
Population: 170 000
Population density: 4.4 per sq mile (1.7 per km²)
Languages: French*, Amerindian
Currency: Euro

ARGENTINA

Official name: The Argentine Republic
Capital: Buenos Aires
Area: 1 073 000 sq miles (2 780 000 km²)
Population: 36 120 000
Population density: 33 per sq mile (12.7 per km²)
Ethnic groups: European 85%, other 15%
Religions: Catholic 91%, Jewish 1%, other or none 8%
Currency: Argentine peso
HDI**: 0.842
GDF per head: $2767
Languages: Spanish*, Amerindian
Government: Federal republic with Congress comprising two legislative assemblies (Senate and Chamber of Deputies).

GUYANA

Official name: The Cooperative Republic of Guyana
Capital: Georgetown
Area: 83 000 sq miles (215 000 km²)
Population: 850 000
Population density: 9.3 per sq mile (3.6 per km)
Ethnic groups: Indian 51%, black 30.5%, mestizo 11%, Amerindian 5.2%, other 2.3%
Religions: Hindu 34%, Protestant 34%, Catholic 12.5%, Muslim 9%, others or none 10.5%
Currency: Guyana dollar
HDI**: 0.704
GDP per head: $983
Languages: English*, English Creole, Hindi, Urdu
Government: Republic with a legislative National Assembly and executive presidency.

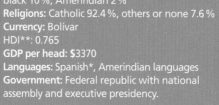

BRAZIL

Official name: The Federative Republic of Brazil
Capital: Brasília
Area: 3 286 000 sq miles (8 512 000 km²)
Population: 169 544 000
Population density: 4.8 per sq mile (1.9 per km²)
Ethnic groups: white 54%, mestiço 39%, black 5.9%, Amerindian 0.1%, others 1%
Religions: Catholic 70%, Protestant 19%, other or none 11%
Currency: Brazilian real
HDI**:** 0.750
GDP per head: $2447
Languages: Portuguese*
Government: Democratic republic with a Congress consisting of two legislative assemblies (Senate and Chamber of Deputies).

CHILE

Official name: The Republic of Chile
Capital: Santiago
Area: 290 000 sq miles (757 000 km²)
Population: 15 400 000
Population density: 50 per sq mile (19.3 per km²)
Ethnic groups: mestizo 91.6%, Amerindian 6.8%, other 1.6%
Religions: Catholic 76.7%, Protestant 13.2%, others or none 10.1%
Currency: Chilean peso
HDI**:** 0.825
GDP per head : $4119
Languages: Spanish*, Indian languages
Government: Democratic republic with two legislative chambers (Senate and Chamber of Deputies).

COLOMBIA

Official name: The Republic of Colombia
Capital: Bogotá
Area: 440 000 sq miles (1 140 000 km²)
Population: 43 070 000
Population density: 91.4 per sq mile (35.3 per km²)
Ethnic groups: mestizo 58%, white 20%, mulatto 14%, black 4%, Amerindian 1%, other 3%
Religions: Catholic 95%, other or none 5%
Currency: Colombian peso
HDI**:** 0.765
GDP per head: $1861
Languages: Spanish*, Indian languages, English, Creole
Government: Democratic republic with Congress comprising two legislative chambers (Senate and House of Representatives).

ECUADOR

Official name: The Republic of Ecuador
Capital: Quito
Area: 104 500 sq miles (270 670 km²)
Population: 12 880 000
Population density: 114 per sq mile (44.1 per km²)
Ethnic groups: mestizo 40%, Quechua 40%, white 15%, black 5%
Religions: Catholic 93%, others or none 7%
Currency: US dollar
HDI**:** 0.726
GDP per head: $1677
Languages: Spanish*, Quechua and other Amerindian languages
Government: Democratic republic with a single legislative assembly (National Congress).

PERU

Official name: The Republic of Peru
Capital: Lima
Area: 496 000 sq miles (1 285 000 km²)
Population: 26 350 000
Population density: 49 per sq mile (19 per km²)
Ethnic groups: Quechua 47.1%, mestizo 32%, creoles 12%, Aymaras 5.4%, other 3.5%
Religions: Catholic 92.4%, Protestant 5.5%, others or none 2.1%
Currency: Nuevo sol
HDI**:** 0.743
GDP per head: $2086
Languages: Quechua*, Spanish*, Aymara*
Government: Democratic republic with two legislative chambers (Senate and Chamber of Deputies).

PARAGUAY

Official name: The Republic of Paraguay
Capital: Asunción
Area: 157 000 sq miles (407 000 km²)
Population: 5 640 000
Population density: 32 per sq mile (12.5 per km²)
Ethnic groups: mestizo 90.8%, Amerindian 3%, other 6.2%
Religions: Catholic 93%, others or none 7%
Currency: Guaraní
HDI**:** 0.738
GDP per head: $953
Languages: Spanish*, Guaraní*
Government: Democratic republic with two legislative chambers (Senate and Chamber of Deputies).

SURINAM

Official name: The Republic of Suriname
Capital: Paramaribo
Area: 63 000 sq miles (163 265 km²)
Population: 420 000
Population density: 6.7 per sq mile (2.6 per km²)
Ethnic groups: Creole 35%, Indian 33%, Indonesian 16%, black 10%, Amerindian 3%, Chinese 1.7%, European 1%, other 0.3%
Religions: Hindu 27%, Catholic 21.6%, Muslim 20%, Protestants 18%, others or none 13.4%
Currency: Surinam guilder
HDI**:** 0.758
GDP per head: $1875
Languages: Dutch*, pidgin, Hindi, Sranan, Javanese
Government: Democratic republic with a single legislative chamber (National Assembly).

* *Official language*   ** *HDI: Human Development Index – an index prepared by the UN Development Programme, on a scale of 0 to 3, based on longevity, education and income.*

149

Climate, relief and vegetation

South America is a continent of violent contrasts. Its incredible range of climates – from the heat of the equator to the chilly plains of Patagonia and the ice floes of Antarctica – is matched by the dazzling variety of its landscapes and vegetation.

Dried out *The Atacama Desert in Chile, which has suffered the longest drought in history. No rain was recorded for 400 years, until 1971.*

Surrounded by seas

The continent of South America stretches 4500 miles (7300 km) from north to south and 3000 miles (4800 km) east to west at its widest point. Its surface area is 7 million sq miles (18 million km²). With the Pacific to the west, the Caribbean to the north and the Atlantic to the east, the climates of South America are strongly influenced by the surrounding seas and their prevailing winds.

A climate of extremes

Three main factors push the climates of South America to extremes: the enormous barrier of the Andes, which deprives much of the south of rain; the cold Humboldt Current that flows along the west coast, lowering both rainfall and temperatures; and low-pressure centres in the centre and extreme south that powerfully affect wind patterns inland. It is not surprising, therefore, to find world extremes of rainfall, cold and drought. Tutunendo in Colombia has registered the world's highest mean annual rainfall at 463 in (11 770 mm), while Antofagasta in Chile holds the global record for the lowest at 0.016 in (0.4 mm).

CLIMATIC REGIONS ▼

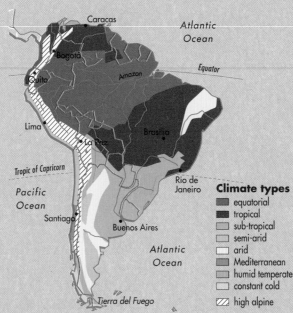

Climate types
- ▢ equatorial
- ▢ tropical
- ▢ sub-tropical
- ▢ semi-arid
- ▢ arid
- ▢ Mediterranean
- ▢ humid temperate
- ▢ constant cold
- ▨ high alpine

MEAN TEMPERATURES		
	January	July
Buenos Aires*	+ 30°C	+ 15°C
	(86°F)	(59°F)
Rio de Janeiro*	+ 30°C	+ 25°C
	(86°F)	(77°F)
Santiago*	+ 21°C	+ 8°C
	(69.8°F)	(46.4°F)
Quito	+ 14°C	+ 14°C
	(57.2°F)	(57.2°F)
Bogotá	+ 14°C	+ 14°C
	(57.2°F)	(57.2°F)
Asunción*	+ 27°C	+ 18°C
	(80.6°F)	(64.4°F)
Lima*	+ 22°C	+ 16°C
	(71.6°F)	(60.8°F)
Montevideo*	+ 23°C	+ 11°C
	(73.4°F)	(51.8°F)
Caracas	+ 15 °C	+ 26 °C
	(59°F)	(78.8°F)

* Southern Hemisphere: seasons reversed

RAINFALL ▼

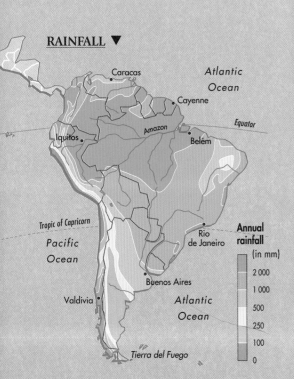

Annual rainfall
(in mm)
- 2 000
- 1 000
- 500
- 250
- 100
- 0

Antarctica and the South Pole

Antarctica is the fifth largest continent, 3700 miles (6000 km) across, with a surface area of 5.5 million sq miles (14.2 million km²) almost entirely covered in ice. The Transantarctic Mountains, a continuation of the same chain as the Andes, divide the continent in two: East and West Antarctica. The highest peak is Mt Vinson at 16 863 ft (5140 m). Most of East Antarctica is a high plateau, while the west is an archipelago of mountainous islands. The shape of the coast changes according to the seasons: in winter, the ice floes freeze together, and this increases the area of the solid ice to 7.7 million sq miles (20 million km²). Around the coast, ice shelves and glaciers are constantly 'calving' or releasing icebergs – some as big as 40 x 60 miles (60 x 100 km) – into the sea.

Antarctica has rich deposits of iron and coal, and may well have oil, platinum, copper and gold as well, but the ferocious climate and the Antarctic Treaty of 1961 have protected the continent from exploitation.

Winter temperatures vary from -30°C (-22°F) to -89.2°C (-128.6°F) – the world's lowest temperature, recorded at Vostok station on July 21, 1983. In summer, temperatures can reach a relatively warm 15°C (59°F). The extreme climate and two months of winter darkness mean that few plants can survive, but a rich animal life is based around the sea: whales, krill, plankton and seals, and 45 species of bird. There is also a year-round human population of about 1000 scientists.

Antarctica
- ▢ pack ice
- • research station

Mountains, plains and plateaus

The Andean cordillera passes through seven South American countries in a curling ribbon down the Pacific coast: Venezuela, Colombia, Ecuador, Peru, Bolivia, Argentina and Chile. At its centre it encloses high plateaus (*altiplanos*) at an average altitude of 13 000 ft (4000 m). Tropical forests and coastal deserts alternate along the coast, culminating in an impressive barrier of ice 500 miles (800 km) long in the south of Chile.

The Amazon Basin and its equatorial rain forest are limited to the south by the Brazilian Plateau, and to the north by the Guyana Highlands and the *llanos* or great plains of Colombia and Venezuela. The Mato Grosso and the Gran Chaco to the south are dry areas, unlike the Atlantic coast, which is tropical and humid from Guyana to Río, then temperate along the shores of southern Brazil and Uruguay.

In the south of Argentina the immense grassy plains of the pampa give way to Patagonia's spectacular landscapes of snow-capped granite massifs and desolate steppes scoured by unceasing winds.

▼ FOREST COVER AS A PERCENTAGE OF TERRITORY

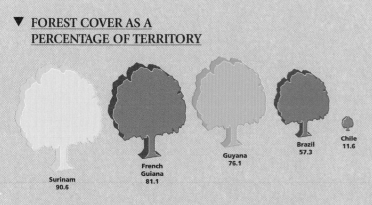

Surinam 90.6
French Guiana 81.1
Guyana 76.1
Brazil 57.3
Chile 11.6

▲ RELIEF MAP OF SOUTH AMERICA

Relief
Height in metres

4 000
2 000
1 000
500
200

Rivers and lakes

The rivers of South America form the largest hydrographic network in the world. The Amazon is the second longest river in the world after the Nile, 4000 miles (6400 km) from its westernmost source 16 500 ft (5000 m) up in the Andes to the Atlantic Ocean. Its width varies according to the seasons, with floods expanding the river bed by up to 60 miles (100 km). At its mouth the Amazon is 150 miles (240 km) wide, and discharges 170 billion gallons (770 billion litres) of water per hour into the sea, turning it brackish for 100 miles (160 km) from the shore. The river is navigable by ocean-going ships as far as Manaus, 1000 miles (1600 km) upstream, and by smaller ships up to Iquitos, more than 1250 miles (2000 km) further.

Lake Titicaca is 12 500 ft (3800 m) above sea level and 1000 ft (300 m) deep: this remnant of a lagoon from the Quaternary era is the highest navigable lake in the world. The Río de la Plata separates Argentina and Uruguay and forms the estuary of the River Paraná, which is 2600 miles (4200 km) long, as well as the rivers Paraguay and Uruguay. It provides access by waterway to the interiors of four countries and the two major international ports of Buenos Aires and Montevideo are found on its banks.

Majestic river The Orinoco River is 1330 miles (2140 km) long, with the third largest drainage basin in South America.

LAKES AND LAGOONS

Patos Lagoon (Brazil)	3860 sq miles (10 000 km²)
Lake Titicaca (Bolivia/Peru)	3200 sq miles (8300 km²)
Mirim Lagoon (Brazil/Uruguay)	1540 sq miles (4000 km²)
Lake Poopó (Bolivia)	1000 sq miles (2600 km²)

RIVERS

Amazon	4000 miles (6400 km)
Paraná	2600 miles (4200 km)
São Francisco	1926 miles (3100 km)
Paraguay	1553 miles (2500 km)
Purus	1553 miles (2500 km)
Tocantins	1500 miles (2415 km)
Orinoco	1330 miles (2140 km)
Japurá	1208 miles (1945 km)
Tapajós	1115 miles (1795 km)

HIGHEST MOUNTAINS

Aconcagua (Argentina)	22 831 ft (6959 m)
Ojos del Salado (Argentina/Chile)	22 571 ft (6880 m)
Bonete (Argentina)	22 545 ft (6872 m)
Tupungato (Argentina/Chile)	22 309 ft (6800 m)
Pisis (Argentina)	22 224 ft (6774 m)
Huascarán (Peru)	22 204 ft (6768 m)
Llullaillaco (Argentina/Chile)	22 056 ft (6723 m)
Incahuasi (Argentina/Chile)	22 010 ft (6709 m)
Mercedario (Argentina/Chile)	21 981 ft (6700 m)
Sajama (Bolivia)	21 390 ft (6520 m)
Illimani (Bolivia)	21 187 ft (6458 m)
Chimborazo (Ecuador)	20 702 ft (6310 m)
Misti (Peru)	19 100 ft (5822 m)
Vinson (Antarctica)	16 863 ft (5140 m)

Population, economy and society

South America's 350 million inhabitants are a lively cultural mix of peoples, religions and ways of life. There are, however, huge disparities in levels of income. In the overcrowded cities spectacular wealth and extreme poverty often exist side by side.

Shades of Brazil *Colours in the school yard.*

Strictly speaking there is no single 'population' in South America. While the Andean peoples are mainly indigenous, with local ancestry stretching back 20 000 to 35 000 years, most inhabitants of the continent are more recent immigrants from every imaginable corner of the world.

A young population

One-third of all South Americans are aged under 15; only 6 per cent are over 64. This youthful population has a much higher birth rate than that of most developed Western countries. In the poorer parts of the continent, large families are the norm. Bolivia has the highest birth rate, with an average of 4.8 children per woman. The richer countries come closer to the Western average of 2 children per woman. Uruguay has the lowest birth rate at 2.2 – roughly the same as Ireland – while Chile, Argentina and Brazil all report rates of around 2.4. High fertility rates are usually accompanied by high infant mortality. In Bolivia, 74 children per 1000 die in their first year of life. In Chile the rate is only 12 per 1000 – much closer to rates in the Western world.

An ethnic melting pot

Since the first nomadic Asian hunters crossed the Bering Strait land bridge between Siberia and Alaska around 30 000 years ago, the American continent has been a refuge, a home, a source of life and opportunity for people from other places. In the past 500 years they have come from all over the world, driven by ambition or hope, economic hardship, political or religious persecution; arriving as adventurers, conquistadores, exiles or labourers. Many had no choice, and were shipped as human cargo from Africa. In the 19th

and 20th centuries, thousands of Germans, French, Basques and English emigrated to Chile, while Italians, Poles, Greeks, Russians and even Syrians (such as the parents of ex-president Carlos Menem) moved to Argentina. In Brazil Africans, Europeans, Amerindians and Asians are all ingredients in an extraordinary racial and cultural brew that gives the country its unique character. Ecuador, Bolivia, Colombia, Peru and Paraguay have significant numbers of indigenous peoples including Quechuas, Guaranís and Aymaras, many of whom speak only their own language. Paraguay recognises this cultural fact by having two official languages: Spanish and Guaraní.

Unequal shares

Everywhere in South America the countryside is emptying as the rural poor flood into cities in search of work. Venezuela's population is 92.8 per cent urban – an extreme example of a trend that affects every country in the continent to a greater or lesser extent. This is not a healthy

situation. The cities are becoming dangerously overcrowded, ringed with shantytowns where the poor live in makeshift houses, often without water or sanitation, far from hospitals, public transport and schools. The shantytowns have become notorious for crime, drug abuse and child prostitution. Favela Rocinha in Rio de Janeiro, Villa el Salvador in Lima, La Cava in Buenos Aires: these are the places where the urban dream of work, wealth and glamour is cruelly shattered.

NATIONAL POPULATIONS ▼ (IN MILLIONS)

Brazil 170
Colombia 43
Argentina 36.2
Peru 26.3
Venezuela 24.6
Chile 15.4
Ecuador 12.8
Bolivia 8.2
Paraguay 5.6

Porteños

If Mexicans are descended from the Aztecs, and Peruvians from the Incas, who are we descended from? Our names are Binetti, Gomez, Jacquelin, Papaioannou, Grubstein. Our parents or grandparents were immigrants from Italy, Spain, France, Greece or Central Europe. We are Catholics, Jews, Orthodox or agnostic. We are proud, self-confident, dynamic, but also full of humour. We love cafés, bars, nightlife and sport. We have the highest number of psychiatrists of any city in the world. We are the people of Buenos Aires – South America's greatest port and most cosmopolitan city – the *Porteños*.

▼ **PERCENTAGE OF POPULATION LIVING IN CITIES**

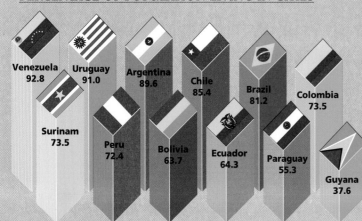

Venezuela 92.8
Uruguay 91.0
Argentina 89.6
Chile 85.4
Brazil 81.2
Colombia 73.5
Surinam 73.5
Peru 72.4
Bolivia 63.7
Ecuador 64.3
Paraguay 55.3
Guyana 37.6

MAJOR URBAN AREAS *(Number of inhabitants)*	
São Paulo	16 583 000
Buenos Aires	13 935 000
Rio de Janeiro	10 192 000
Lima	7 195 000
Bogotá	6 276 000
Santiago	5 440 000
Caracas	4 000 000
Montevideo	1 500 000
Quito	1 490 000
Asunción	1 224 000
La Paz	1 004 000
Paramaribo	294 000
Georgetown	275 000

LIFE EXPECTANCY *(Men and women)*		
	M	W
Argentina	70	77
Bolivia	61	64
Brazil	64	72
Chile	72	78
Colombia	68	75
Ecuador	67	73
Guyana	59	67
Paraguay	68	72
Peru	66	71
Surinam	68	73
Uruguay	71	78
Venezuela	70	76

Mercosur

Mercosur (*Mercado Común del Sur*, or Common Market of the South) is to Latin America what the European Union is to Europe. Founded in 1991 by the Treaty of Asunción, Mercosur comprises four member states – Argentina, Brazil, Paraguay and Uruguay – plus two associate members, Chile and Bolivia. They share a free trade area of 5.4 million sq miles (14 million km²), which has 239 million inhabitants.

In terms of combined gross national product, *Mercosur* is the fourth largest economy in the world. It aims to improve the economies of its member countries by making them more efficient and competitive, by enlarging their markets, by improving communications and by encouraging better use of available resources, while at the same time preserving the environment. A customs union has been established to make trade within the Mercosur area simpler and more efficient.

The creation of a free trade area this size is a significant step in a globalised world. Foreign investment in the group of member states increased by 50 per cent in the years from 1991 to 1999. In its quest to become a key player on the world's political and economic stage, Mercosur signed an outline agreement with the European Union in 1995. There are also plans to extend Mercosur's activities and influence with the creation of the FTAA (Free Trade Area of the Americas) in 2005.

Under licence *Brazil produces nearly 2 million vehicles per year for foreign manufacturers.*

Mineral resources

◇ silver
△ bauxite
● copper
▽ diamonds
☆ tin
▲ iron
◇ gold
▢ lead
▢ coal
△ gas
▢ oil

AIRPORTS ▼ *(Annual traffic in millions of passengers)*

- ■ **São Paulo (22.4)**
- ■ **Bogotá (13.63)**
- ■ **Rio de Janeiro (8.7)**
- ■ **Buenos Aires (13.6)**
- ■ **Caracas (6.8)**
- ■ **Santiago (5.9)**
- ■ **Lima (3.9)**
- ■ **Brasília (3.6)**

▼ GROSS DOMESTIC PROUCT PER INHABITANT (IN $US)

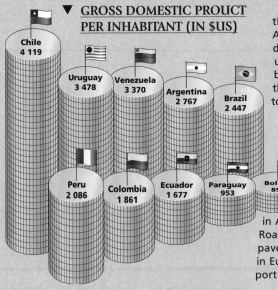

- Chile 4 119
- Uruguay 3 478
- Venezuela 3 370
- Argentina 2 767
- Brazil 2 447
- Peru 2 086
- Colombia 1 861
- Ecuador 1 677
- Paraguay 953
- Bolivia 897

the population benefited little. In 2002 Argentina became a bankrupt state – it defaulted on its loan, the currency was devalued and many people found themselves below the poverty line. By the end of the year, the economic collapse appeared to be bottoming out. Despite the technical know-how and potential wealth, both in land and mineral deposits, South American countries are still saddled with huge loan repayments on foreign debts.

Transport

There are few motorways in South America – around 400 miles (600 km) in Argentina, and 17 miles (27 km) in Bolivia. Roads are often mediocre, and many are not paved. Journey times are much longer than in Europe and the USA. Railways mainly transport goods. Air travel, which would suit the continent's long distances, is underdeveloped and under-used because ticket prices are so expensive. São Paulo airport has a quarter of the traffic volume of New York. Despite having three major airports, Brazil's annual air traffic is less than half that of Paris. Most South Americans use buses for long journeys.

Economies in chaos

For most of the 20th century, the economies of Latin America were largely state-controlled. In the 1980s and 1990s the situation changed as the free-market model and globalisation took hold, leaving governments with less say in the running of their economies. After years of hyperinflation (Argentina's was running at 4923 per cent in 1989), the International Monetary Fund imposed new policies – financial stabilisation, restricted public spending, low inflation and the sale of state industries to the private sector. Yet even though these policies attracted foreign capital,

MAIN PRODUCTS, BY COUNTRY, ▶ WITH WORLD RANKING

- **SURINAM** — 8th Bauxite, 20th Aluminium
- **PERU** — 2nd Fish, 2nd Silver
- **BRAZIL** — 2nd Iron, 1st Coffee, 1st Sugar cane, 1st Oranges
- **COLOMBIA** — 3rd Coffee, 1st Emeralds
- **ECUADOR** — 3rd Bananas, 7th Cocoa
- **GUYANA** — 9th Bauxite
- **URUGUAY** — 12th Cattle
- **PARAGUAY** — 6th Soya, 19th Cotton
- **BOLIVIA** — 2nd Coca, 5th Tin
- **ARGENTINA** — 5th Cattle, 5th Corn
- **CHILE** — 1st Copper, 3rd Fish
- **VENEZUELA** — 7th Bauxite, 8th Oil

MOST VISITED COUNTRIES
(Number of tourists per year)

Brazil	5 313 000	Chile	1 742 000
Argentina	2 991 000	Peru	1 027 000
Uruguay	1 968 000	Ecuador	615 000

ILLITERACY ▼
(Percentage of adult population)

16.4 16.0 11.3 9.3 9.1 4.8 3.5 7.6 1.9 2.5 7 8.0

- ■ Argentina
- ■ Bolivia
- ■ Brazil
- ■ Chile
- ■ Colombia
- ■ Ecuador
- ■ Guyana
- ■ Paraguay
- ■ Peru
- ■ Surinam
- ■ Uruguay
- ■ Venezuela

***Many faiths** Surinam has freedom of religious worship. Each of the ethnic groups has retained its way of life and its faith. Churches, temples and mosques can all be seen in Paramaribo.*

Divided societies

The gap between rich and poor is not a new problem in South America, but it has recently been growing at an ever more alarming rate. The middle classes who once partly filled the gap are now becoming noticeably poorer. In Brazil, 1 per cent of the population owns 17 per cent of the wealth; 10 per cent own another 50 per cent, leaving 89 per cent of the people to share the rest. Similar inequalities can be found in every other country of the continent.

Unemployment is at record levels: 19 per cent in Argentina, 13 per cent in Guyana and Surinam. Lower rates reported by other countries – Bolivia for example (11 per cent), Peru (8 per cent) or Brazil (7 per cent) – are not totally accurate fig-

ures because they include seasonal and short-term work as well as full-time employment. Unemployment is not the only problem facing these societies. There is also violence, crime and corruption.

Religion

Latin America is often thought to be the Roman Catholic continent. And yet a number of other religions have successfully taken root here, brought in by immigrants of various other faiths and cultures. In Surinam, with its rich mix of communities (Indian, African, Indonesian, Japanese, Chinese, Amerindian, Lebanese and Creole), 27 per cent of the population are Hindus and 20 per cent Muslims.

There are also significant Jewish minorities: 150 000 in Brazil, 44 000 in Uruguay, 21 000 in Venezuela and 228 000 in Argentina – the fourth largest Jewish community in the world.

PUBLISHING AND THE PRESS ▼

BOOKS
(Titles published per year)

NEWSPAPERS

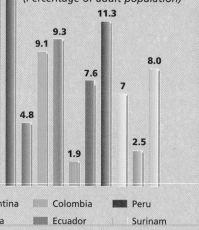

	BOOKS	NEWSPAPERS
Brazil	21 574	1882
Argentina	9 113	198
Venezuela	3 660	139
Chile	2 469	93
Colombia	1 484	28
Peru	1 294	69
Uruguay	1 143	32
Bolivia	447	11

Privatisation of education

School teachers' salaries in Argentina are about a quarter of those in most European countries, while the cost of living is more or less the same. Schools are very dilapidated, classes are overcrowded, and there is a chronic shortage of textbooks and educational equipment. Like other social benefits (such as pensions, health insurance and hospitals) education is being privatised, and many families have to sacrifice everything to pay for private schools for their children.

NUMBER OF INTERNET ADDRESSES ▼

(Per 1000 inhabitants)

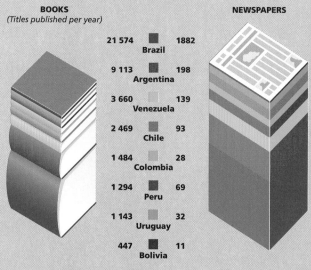

2.06 3.18 2.63 0.47 0.9 1.81 13.12 5.32 0.69 4.2

- ● Argentina
- ● Bolivia
- ● Brazil
- ● Chile
- ● Colombia
- ● Ecuador
- ● Paraguay
- ● Peru
- ● Uruguay
- ● Venezuela

HEALTH SERVICES
▶

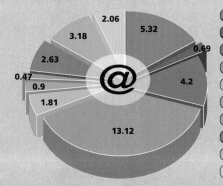

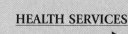

(Per 1000 inhabitants)

	DOCTORS	HOSPITAL BEDS
Argentina	3.05	3.3
Bolivia	1.31	0.99
Brazil	1.3	3.1
Chile	1.53	2.7
Colombia	1.2	1.5
Ecuador	1.88	1.6
Guyana	0.33	3.33
Paraguay	0.71	1.15
Peru	0.9	1.5
Surinam	0.81	4.71
Uruguay	3.54	4.65
Venezuela	2.27	1.5

Index

Page numbers in *italics* denote illustrations. The letter and number references in brackets are the co-ordinates for places in the map section, p. 140-147.

Acknowledgments

Abbreviations: t = top, m = middle, b = bottom, l = left, r = right.

FRONT COVER: *Corcovado, Rio de Janeiro:* HOA QUI/ ZEFA/Damm. BACK COVER: *Ecuadorian herdsmen beneath Chimborazo:* HOA QUI/ R. Manin.

Pages 4/5: ALTITUDE/Y.Arthus-Bertrand; 6/7: COSMOS/S.P.I./T.Van Sant; 8/9: ALTITUDE/Y.Arthus-Bertrand; 9b: BIOS/F.Suchel; 10t, 10/11: HOA QUI/F.Gohier; 11b: BIOS/J.J.Alcalay; 12/13: ALTITUDE/Y.Arthus-Bertrand; 13t: COSMOS/Steinmetz; 14t: ALTITUDE/Y.Arthus-Bertrand; 14/15: G.Ziesler; 15t, 16t: HOA QUI/P.de Wilde; 16b: GAMMA/G.Wemborne; 17: PHONE/J.P.Ferrero; 18bl: DIAF/P.Cheuva; 18mt: BRIDGEMAN ART LIBRARY/British Museum, London; 18tr: G.DAGLI ORTI/Private collection, Quito; 18br: G.DAGLI ORTI/Museum of the Central Bank, Quito; 19tr: DIAF/Pratt; 19m: BIOS/J.E.Molina; 19tl: G.DAGLI ORTI/National Archeological Museum, Lima; 19bl: DIAF/Pratt-Pries; 19br: ROGER-VIOLLET/Coll.Viollet; 20tr: HOA QUI/F.Gohier; 20ml: G.DAGLI ORTI/Château de Versailles; 20bl: ROGER-VIOLLET/Coll.Viollet; 20br: G.DAGLI ORTI/Museum Library, Lima; 21t: LAUROS-GIRAUDON/Américae Tertia Pars - Th.de Bry/Naval historical service, Vincennes; 21m: G.DAGLI ORTI/Museum Library, Lima; 21br: BRIDGEMAN ART LIBRARY/Private collection; 22tl: BRIDGEMAN ART LIBRARY/New Atlas, 1643/Private collection; 22tr: G.DAGLI ORTI/Painting by Félix Parra 1875/National Museum of Art, Mexico; 22br: G.DAGLI ORTI/watercolour by C.Juliao 1775/National Library, Rio de Janeiro; 22b: ROGER-VIOLLET/Coll.Viollet; 23t: KEYSTONE/*L'Illustration*; 23tr: J.L.CHARMET/Archives Académie des Sciences, Paris; 23b: BRIDGEMAN ART LIBRARY/British Library, London; 24tl: G.DAGLI ORTI/Museum of History, Lima; 24tr: G.DAGLI ORTI/watercolour by Guéricault 1821/Military Museum, Callao; 24m: M.Langrognet/Simon Bolivar - F.Léger, ADAGP, Paris 2000/Bibliothèque de l'Opéra, Paris; 24b: G.DAGLI ORTI/taken from Voyage pittoresque au Brésil - Engraving J.B.Debret 1834/BN, Rio de Janeiro; 25bl, br: ROGER-VIOLLET/Coll.Viollet; 26t: J.L.CHARMET/Bibliothèque Arts Décoratifs, Paris; 26bl: ROGER-VIOLLET; 27tl: KEYSTONE; 27tr: KEYSTONE/*L'Illustration*; 27m: CORBIS-SYGMA/Carlos-Carrion; 27b: ROGER-VIOLLET/Harlingue-Viollet; 28tl: AFP; 28tr: CORBIS-SYGMA/Perfil Editorial; 28bl: GAMMA/R.Wollmann; 28b: DIAF/J.M.Rodrigo; 29tr: ALTITUDE/Y.Arthus-Bertrand; 29tl: CORBIS-SYGMA/A.Balaguer; 29mb: BIOS/STILL PICTURES/M.Edwards; 29br: GAMMA/F.Savariau; 30/31: DIAF/SIME; 32/33: ALTITUDE/Y.Arthus-Bertrand; 34t: PHONE/R.Valter; 34b: BIOS/J.C.Munoz; 35t: ALTITUDE/Y.Arthus-Bertrand; 35b: DIAF/MARKA/S.Pitamitz; 36: DIAF/SIME; 37t: ALTITUDE/Y.Arthus-Bertrand; 37b: EXPLORER/C.Boisvieux; 38tl: PHONE/R.Valter; 38tr, bl: BIOS/D.Siméonidis; 38br: BIOS/Y.Tavernier; 39t: ALTITUDE/Y.Arthus-Bertrand; 39bl, br, 40tr: G.ZIESLER; 40b: DIAF/SIME; 41tl, mr: RAPHO/A.Balaguer; 41bl: G.ZIESLER; 41br: DIAF/P.Cheuva; 42tr, bl, b: RAPHO/A.Balaguer; 43t: BIOS/F.Suchel; 43m: ASK/J.P.Degas; 43b: PHONE/AUSCAPE/J.Plaza Van Roon; 44/45b: DIAF/SIME; 45hl, mr: DIAF/R.Mazin; 45mb: PHONE/AUSCAPE/J.Plaza Van Roon; 46b: HOA QUI/Ph.Bourseiller; 47t: G.ZIESLER; 47m: EXPLOR-ER/J.L.Etienne; 47br: RAPHO/A.Balaguer; 48bl: DIAF/P.Cheuva; 48/49b: DIAF/SIME; 48/49t: ALTITUDE/M.Gottschalk; 49tr: BIOS/J.C.Munoz; 49br: GAMMA/X. Rossi; 50/51: ALTITUDE/Y.Arthus-Bertrand; 50tr: HOA QUI/H.Collart; 50tl: ALTITUDE/Y.Arthus-Bertrand; 50mr: BIOS/Barischi; 50b: HOA QUI/P.de Wilde; 51tl: G.ZIESLER; 51m: BIOS/STILL PICTURES/E.Parker; 51mb: ALTITUDE/M.Gottschalk; 51bl: HOA QUI/H.Collart; 51br: ALTITUDE/H.Collart; 52tl: CORBIS-

SYGMA/H.Collart-Odinetz; 52ml: ALTITUDE/Y.Arthus-Bertrand; 52b: G.ZIESLER; 53tr: PHONE/F.Gohier; 53mr: G.ZIESLER; 53ml: BIOS/STILL PICTURES/H.Giradet; 53b: G.ZIESLER; 53br: ASK IMAGES/F.Goifman; 54tr: BIOS/L.C.Marigo-P.Arnold; 54mtl: HOA QUI/H.Collart; 54mtr: BIOS/STILL PICTURES/M.Edwards; 54m: BIOS/STILL PICTURES/N.Dickinson; 54b: BIOS/J.C.Munoz; 54br, 55tl, tr: HOA QUI/H.Collart; 55bl: HOA QUI/Ph.Bourseiller; 55br: CORBIS-SYGMA/H.Collart-Odinetz; 56t, bl: HOA QUI/Ph.Bourseiller; 56br, 57tr: G.ZIESLER; 57br: HOA QUI/Ph.Bourseiller; 58/59: CORBIS-SYGMA/El Universal; 60tr: CORBIS-SYGMA; 60b: AFP/G.Guevarra; 61bl: STUDIO B/BLACK STAR/C.Ledford; 61br: AFP/A.Smith; 61tr: AFP/P.de Gobierno; 62tr: AFP/El Comercio; 62m: AFP/E.Verdugo; 62b: AFP; 63t: HOA QUI/B.Espin; 63mb, br: GAMMA/Y.Husianycia; 64t: AFP/F.Carrillo; 64b, 65tl: AFP/M.Salinas; 65tr: AFP; 66ml: HOA QUI/Kraft; 66t: BIOS/F.Suchel; 66/67b: HOA QUI/R.Manin; 67tr: CORBIS-SYGMA/J.Langevin; 68/69: ALTITUDE/Ph.Bourseiller; 70tr: TOP/F.Ancellet; 70br: GAMMA/O.Vedrine; 71mt: COSMOS/S.Seitz; 71bl: CORBIS-SYGMA/Ph.Bourseiller; 71br: CORBIS-SYGMA/J.B.Russel; 72t: EXPLORER/C.Boisvieux; 72b: EXPLORER/S.Costa; 73tl: GAMMA/Wandrille; 73m: HOA QUI/H.Collart; 73b: ALTITUDE/Y.Arthus-Bertrand; 73bl: HOA QUI/H.Collart; 74t: G.ZIESLER; 74bm: BIOS/STILL PICTURE/Edwards; 74br: HOA QUI/H.Collart; 75t: EXPLORER/S.Gutierrez; 75ml: COSMOS/S.Clifford; 75mr: EXPLORER/S.Gutierrez; 75b: ALTITUDE/Y.Arthus-Bertrand; 76tr: CORBIS-SYGMA/N.Piwonka; 76m: ASK/J.P.Degas; 76b: G.ZIESLER; 77br: DIAF/SIME; 77tl: BIOS/Th. Petit; 78t: HOA QUI/F.Gohier; 78bl: ALTITUDE/F.Lechenet; 78br: HOA QUI/NF/P.Escudero; 79tr: CORBIS-SYGMA/A.Keler; 79ml: DIAF/MARKA/F.Staccone; 79mr: DIAF/IFA-BILDERTEAM; 79br: G.DAGLI ORTI/*The Coffee Worker* - C.Portinari (1903-1962) Museum of Art, São Paulo; 80/81: COSMOS/ASPECT/ G.Tompkinson; 82tr: HOA QUI/J.Horner; 82mt: ANA/M.Borchi; 82/83b: HOA QUI/ZEFA; 83t: HOA QUI/P.Escudero; 83m: COSMOS/ASPECT/G.Tompkinson; 84t: BIOS/STILL PICTURES/H.Girardet; 84m: BIOS/J.E.Molina; 84b: BIOS/R.Mittermeier; 84br: HOA QUI/H.Collart; 85tr: CORBIS-SYGMA/C.Carrion; 85m: CORBIS-SYGMA/P.Eranian; 85bl: BIOS/STILL PICTURE/M.Edwards; 85br: HOA QUI/M.Troncy; 86t: CORBIS-SYGMA/J.Van Hasselt; 86bl: HOA QUI/M.Troncy; 86br: GAMMA/Ch.Guerretsen; 87tl: Rede Globo; 87tr: CORBIS-SYGMA/P.Fridmann; 87m: Rede Globo; 87b: Rede Globo/N.Di Rago; 88tl: STUDIO B/BLACK STAR/E.Lansner/D.R Illustrateur; 88b: RAPHO/G.Sioen; 88tr: VANDYSTADT/Ch. Petit; 89tr: DIAF/SIME; 89ml: OASIS/G.Baralé; 89b: HOA QUI/J.Horner; 90t: COSMOS/P.Maître; 90ml: DIAF/C.Pinheira; 90bl: CORBIS-SYGMA/M.Pelletier; 90/91b: HOA QUI/F.Gohier; 91t: CORBIS-SYGMA/G.Giansanti; 91m: COSMOS/D.Laine; 92t: EXPLORER/C.Boisvieux; 92b: COSMOS/R.Freck; 93t: DIAF/P.Cheuva; 93m: COSMOS/R.Freck; 93br: HOA QUI/J.Horner; 94tr: ASK/TRIP/M.Mac Laren; 94bl: ABRIL IMAGENS/P.Jares; 94b: HOA QUI/ZEFA/V.Leal; 95tr: KEYSTONE; 95m: ROGER-VIOLLET/Coll.Viollet; 95bl: VANDYSTADT/ J.M.Loubat; 95b: VANDYSTADT/ALLSPORT/ P.Rondeau; 96tr: CORBIS-SYGMA/Ph.Caron; 97t: GAMMA/G.Van de Berg; 96bl: VANDYSTADT/ALLSPORT/D.Lean; 97bl: GAMMA/News; 97br: ALTITUDE/Y.Arthus-Bertrand/Architects Rafael Galvao, Pedro Paulo Bastos, Antonio Dias Carnevio, Orlando Azevedo; 98t: HOA QUI/J.Horner; 98/99b: DIAF/SIME; 99t, mr: ANA/M.Borchi; 99br: ANA/S.Gutierrez; 100/101: ALTITUDE/Y.Arthus-Bertrand; 102t, br: CORBIS-SYGMA/H.Van Hasselt; 102bl: GAMMA/SPOONER/B.Allistair; 103t: DIAF/MARKA/F.Giaccone; 103mb: G.DAGLI ORTI/Museum of Gold, Bogota; 103br: GAMMA/R.Gaillarde; 104t: HOA

QUI/J.D.Joubert; 104b: HOA QUI/M.Troncy; 105tr: HOA QUI/F.Gohier; 105mr: G.DAGLI ORTI; 105bl: COSMOS/VISUM/W.Staiger; 105br: G.DAGLI ORTI/Provincial Museum, Salamanca; 106t: ASK/TRIP/M.Barlow; 106b: ABRIL IMAGENS/P.Marcos; 107t: CORBIS-SYGMA/F.Fridman; 107m: ASK IMAGES/B.Martinez; 107b, 108t: ALTITUDE/Y.Arthus-Bertrand; 108b: COSMOS/COLORIFIC/G.Davis; 109tr: ABRIL/IMAGENS/R. de Freitas; 109ml: ALTITUDE/Y.Arthus-Bertrand; 109br: DIAF/J.P.Langeland; 110t: DIAF/SIME; 110b: ABRIL IMAGENS/R.Cepeda; 111t: HOA QUI/P. de Wilde; 111ml: HOA QUI/H.Collart; 111b: COSMOS/P.Maître; 112tl: DIAF/F. Le Divenah/Les Guerriers - B.Giorgi; 112mr: HOA QUI/P.de Wilde; 112b: ALTITUDE/Y.Arthus-Bertrand; 113tl: ANA/M.Vautier; 113tr, b: HOA QUI/P.de Wilde; 114m: ALTITUDE/Y.Arthus-Bertrand; 114b: HOA QUI/P.de Wilde; 114/115t: DIAFTh. Jullien; 115m: ALTITUDE/Y.Arthus-Bertrand; 115bl: G.ZIESLER; 115mb: HOA QUI/S.Grandadam; 116t, mr, bl: ANA/G.Cozzi; 117tr, br: FOCUS/C.Goldin; 117bl: FOCUS/A.Querol; 118t: HOA QUI/E.Simanor; 118ml: ANA/M.Borchi; 118bl: HOA QUI/P.Escudero; 118br: HOA QUI/F.Michele; 119t: CORBIS-SYGMA/A.Balaguer; 119bl: DIAF/F.Berthillier/Palacio Portales; 119br: CORBIS-SYGMA/J.B.Russel; 120t: DIAF/SIME; 120b: HOA QUI/Escudero; 120m: HOA QUI/C.Boisvieux; 121tr: SIPA/G.Piko; 121m: Festival Mar del Plata/D.R; 121b: DIAF/M.Vérin; 122tr: DIAF/SIME; 122ml: COSMOS/H.Horvath-Anzenberger; 122mr: ANA/G.Cozzi; 122b: G.ZIESLER; 123tr: GAMMA/Russel; 123m: FOCUS/J.A.Perez; 123bl: FOCUS/R.R.Cinto; 124/125: COSMOS/R.Freck; 126tr, m: TOP/M.Schilder; 126b: G.ZIESLER; 127t: ASK/Th. Nectoux; 127m: DIAF/L.Jacobs; 127b: TOP/D.Bourguignaud; 128t, b: I.GOMEZ-PULIDO; 128m: EXPLORER/DUNE/S.Fouillet; 129mr: DIAF/TPC/C.Bowman; 129b: DIAF/SIME; 130tr: HOA QUI/C.J.Lenars; 130b: ALTITUDE/Y.Arthus-Bertrand; 131tl, m, b: G.DAGLI ORTI; 132tr: G/DAGLI ORTI/Bruning Musuem, Lambayeque; 132m: RAPHO/A.Balaguer; 132b: BRIDGEMAN ART LIBRARY/Autoportrait, 1987 - F.Botero. Private collection; 132/133b: G.DAGLI ORTI; 133t: G.DAGLI ORTI, Archeological Museum, Lima; 133m: CORBIS-SYGMA/J.Van Hasselt/J.R.Soto, ADAGP, Paris 2000; 134tr: DIAF/M.Vérin/Casa Blanca, Buenos Aires; 134m: C.GASSIAN; 134/135b: HOA QUI/M.Renaudeau; 135tl: ASK IMAGES/Degas-Parra; 135bl: ENGUERAND/M. Cavalca/Folklore Ballet of Bahia; 135tr: ANA/M.Borchi; 135br: AFP/G.Riquelme; 136tr: CORBIS-SYGMA/S.Bassouls; 136ml: CORBIS-SYGMA/G.Arici; 136b: GAMMA/Guerrini; 136br: CORBIS-SYGMA/P.Fridman; 137t: AFP/*The Cloud*, F.Solanas/Film du Sud-Acacia Studio 2000; 137m: GAMMA/BUENA VISTA/Central do Brasil *(Central Station)*, W.Salles Junior/Bac Films-Mact Productions 1998; 138/139: ALTITUDE/Y.Arthus-Bertrand; 152: PHONE/AUSCAPE/J.Plaza van Roon; 153: ALTITUDE/Ph.Bourseiller; 154: HOA QUI/P.de Wilde; 155: CORBIS-SYGMA/P.Fridman; 156: HOA QUI/ZEFA/P.Jares.

Printed and boiund in the EEC by Arvato Iberia
Colour Separations: Station Graphique, Ivry-sur-Seine
Paper: Perigord-Condat, France